# THE FISCAL SYSTEM AND THE POLLUTER PAYS PRINCIPLE

# The Fiscal System and the Polluter Pays Principle

## A Case Study of Ireland

ALAN BARRETT
JOHN LAWLOR
SUE SCOTT

**Routledge**
Taylor & Francis Group

LONDON AND NEW YORK

First published 1997 by Ashgate Publishing

Reissued 2018 by Routledge
2 Park Square, Milton Park, Abingdon, Oxon, OX14 4RN
52 Vanderbilt Avenue, New York, NY 10017

*Routledge is an imprint of the Taylor & Francis Group, an informa business*

A Library of Congress record exists under LC control number:

ISBN 13: 978-0-367-02695-0 (hbk)
ISBN 13: 978-0-429-39834-6 (ebk)

# Contents

# Figures and tables

# Acknowledgements

The authors are grateful for the comments and support given by many individuals, most of whom have been referenced in the text. It should be said, however, that the references do not do justice to the extent of their contributions in numerous instances. In addition to these individuals, there are several others who had a material involvement in our work or provided documentation, whom we wish to thank. These include Garry Byrne, John Fitz Gerald, Deirdre Kearney, Denis McDonald and Finian Matthews in the Department of the Environment, Tom Arnold, Jim Flanagan and Frank Rath in the Department of Agriculture. The work benefited from constructive comments and explanations from Owen Carton in Teagasc, Noel Bourke, Jim Bowman, Marie Sherwood, Larry Stapleton and Paul Toner in the Environmental Protection Agency, Kingsley Tetteh of the Ghanaian EPA, Eugene Deegan in the Department of Tourism and Trade, Noel Kavanagh in Bord Failte, Bob Bradshaw, John Kelly and Vincent Palmer in the Department of Finance, Alex Wiedow of DG XXI in the European Commission, and Richard Foley and John Kilgallon in Forbairt.

People whose own research provided a valued feedback to ours include Peter Clinch, Frank Convery and Sheenagh Rooney in the Environmental Institute, Bernard Feeney of Goodbody James Capel, Michael Kennedy of the National Roads Authority, Jack Short of the European Conference of Ministers of Transport and Jean-Philippe Barde of OECD. A debt of gratitude is also owed to those who attended our workshops. The presentations of Alec Dubgaard of KVL in Denmark, Paul Herrington of the University of Leicester and David Maddison of CSERGE to the conference, *Economic Instruments Supporting Environmental Policy: The Polluter Pays Principle in Practice,* formed an important contribution.

We wish to thank our colleagues, Maura Rohan and Regina Costello who dealt with our requirements for books and documents, Pat Hopkins who managed the copies, Mary McElhone and Deirdre Whitaker for editing the text, and Phil Browne and Regina Moore who prepared the document for publication. Terry Baker, John Fitz Gerald, Patrick Honohan and Brendan Whelan generously gave their time to the editorial meeting and made valuable suggestions. All remaining errors are those of the authors, as are the opinions expressed.

Finally, we are especially grateful to Geraldine Tallon and Maureen Doyle of the Department of the Environment for their help and advice, and for the funding from the Department which has supported this work, undertaken by the Environment Policy Research Centre at the ESRI.

# 1 Introduction

*A. Barrett and S. Scott*

While much has been written in recent years about so-called 'environmental taxes', less attention has been paid to the environmental implications of the fiscal system in general. In this book, we go some way towards redressing this imbalance by systematically examining the Irish fiscal system in an effort to (a) identify the environmental effects of the system through the incentives it creates and (b) suggest ways of altering the system in an environmentally friendly way.

The issues we explore are of the following types. In many instances, if an activity is polluting, the activity should be taxed and if an activity leads to environmental enhancement it should be subsidised.[1] We consider a range of sectors and ask to what extent is this rule being applied. It will be seen that in some cases polluting activities are actually subsidised. This can arise directly, for example, through tax breaks or grants being given to certain activities. It can also arise indirectly, when agents are not charged for the full costs of their activities. This latter situation can occur when taxes or charges are in place, but when these taxes or charges do not cover the environmental costs about which we are concerned.

Having identified the environmental shortcomings of the fiscal system, we then go on to consider how the shortcomings can be removed and how environmental improvements to the system can be made. In doing this, however, we are mindful that not all environmental problems can be solved by the fiscal system and that regulation must be relied upon in certain circumstances.[2]

There are several inter-related reasons for undertaking this examination and it is appropriate that we set them out. Our primary concern is with the state of the Irish environment, or perhaps more correctly, possible future changes in state of the Irish environment. Relative to many other areas of the European Union, the environment in Ireland is generally good. However, to a certain extent this situation is the result not so much of conscious policy decisions but of the lower level of development in Ireland relative to other EU countries.

Along with Ireland's economic development in recent years have come some associated environmental pressures. Examples of these are as follows. According to a recent report on the Irish environment (Environmental Protection Agency, 1996) traffic is now the main source of air pollution in the country, especially in urban areas. With continuing rises in income levels, this situation could well become worse.[3]

Another source of development-related pollution has arisen in agriculture. While reforms to the EU's Common Agricultural Policy have lessened this problem, it has been the case that incentives existed for the intensification of agriculture. The implications of this have been seen in terms of pollution related to fertiliser use and also in terms of environmental degradation related to over-grazing. And while the CAP reforms may have reduced some of the environmental implications of agriculture, the reforms themselves may have generated further environmental problems. In particular, the incentives that have been created for diversification into forestry have lead to rapid afforestation and possible environmental difficulties.[4]

As a final example of environmental pressures we can note that tourist numbers have doubled since the late 1970s. This has led to congestion in certain parts of the country at certain times of year. In addition, proposals have been made regarding the development of facilities to cater for tourists, some of which may lead to construction in sensitive areas.[5]

Given these increasing environmental pressures, it is important that the fiscal system in no way contributes to the problem. But if certain polluting activities are seen as contributing to economic growth, and in particular to job creation, there will be a temptation to steer away from taxing such activities; what is more, there will also be a temptation to subsidise them. The principle of 'sustainable development' has become a guiding principle, at least in the rhetoric if not the reality, of policies aimed at generating economic growth. Therefore, it is important that policy-makers take due account of the environmental implications and costs of certain types of growth.

While concern for the environment is the important motivating factor in this study, the particular approach is motivated by another factor. It could be that whatever incentives are created by the fiscal system, the negative environmental effects could be offset by regulations. Our focus on the fiscal reform option is prompted by the growing international awareness of the advantages of the fiscal approach, that is the use of taxes, charges and subsidies to provide incentives for environmentally positive actions.

A more formal discussion of the advantages of the fiscal approach to environmental protection over the regulatory approach is given in Chapter 3. For now we can simply say that the use of fiscal incentives can generate the same amount of environmental protection at a lower cost to the economy than the use of regulations. The existence of such fiscal measures also generates an on-going incentive for pollution abatement, which is not the case with regulations. Finally, the taxation of polluting activities may generate revenue which in turn may be used to reduce other taxes.

2

The use of fiscal incentives for environmental protection is being advocated increasingly as part of a general move towards the use of 'economic instruments' in this area.[6] In documents such as *Agenda 21* (UNCED, 1992) and the EU's *Fifth Environment Action Programme*, calls are made for the greater use of economic instruments. Allied with these calls is the Polluter Pays Principle, a notion first given prominence by the OECD in its 1975 publication *The Polluter Pays Principle* and now an accepted cornerstone of environmental policy as seen, for example, in the EU Treaty (Commission of the European Community, 1992). In Ireland itself, this policy interest could be seen in the budget speech of the Minister for Finance in 1996 when he asked Departments and relevant agencies to 'examine the strategic impact of taxation on environmental policy and to bring forward specific tax measures for the 1997 Budget'.

As we noted above, this move towards the use of economic instruments for environmental protection has led to much attention being given to the development and implementation of environmental taxes. As part of this general movement, we believe it is important to take a step back and to consider the fiscal system as it currently operates and to assess its environmental implications. In this way the introduction of environmental taxation can be part of a much broader environmental reform of the fiscal system and therefore the environmental benefits can be that much greater.

The remainder of the book is structured as follows. In Chapter 2, we provide three elements of background information which are relevant to any proposals for fiscal change. These are (a) some notes on the Irish fiscal system, (b) a similar piece on the legal framework in which the Irish fiscal system is set and (c) some evidence on the attitudes of Irish people to the types of changes we propose.

In Chapter 3, we outline the arguments in favour of the use of economic instruments for environmental policy. We also show how economic theory can be used to set optimal levels of charges and taxes. Some additional remarks are made regarding when regulation may be preferred over the use of economic instruments. For those familiar with the theory of economic instruments for environmental protection, Chapter 3 can be skipped without any loss.

In Chapter 4, we begin our sector-by-sector analysis with agriculture. We first discuss the environmental effects of the sector; we then discuss the existing fiscal treatment of the sector and relate it to environmental effects; examples of fiscal approaches from elsewhere are considered; finally, some suggestions regarding reforms of the fiscal system, as they relate to the sector, which would be environmentally beneficial are made.

We should specify at this point that the objective implicit in our proposed fiscal reforms will be to ensure that polluters are made to pay the full cost of their actions. In the language of public economics, we suggest reforms whereby the external costs of pollution are internalised.[7] Taxes and charges can also be used for the achievement of specified targets, such as emission levels or waste volumes, and for raising revenue; these uses, however, are not the basis for our recommendations.

In Chapter 5 we follow this same approach with respect to the use of environmental services by industry and households. Similarly in Chapters 6 through 9, we apply this approach, in broad terms, to energy, transport, tourism and construction.

Finally, in Chapter 10 we draw together our conclusions and suggest priority areas for reform.

**Notes**

1   A more rigorous discussion of these taxing and subsidising arguments is presented in Chapter 3.
2   Again, this issue will be considered more fully in Chapter 3.
3   Chapter 7 is concerned with transport generally.
4   Both agriculture and forestry are examined in Chapter 4.
5   Tourism is the subject of Chapter 8.
6   Fiscal incentives are part of a set of policy tools that are referred to as market-based or economic instruments. Other tools in this group include tradeable permits and deposit-refund schemes, a discussion of which is contained in Chapter 3.
7   A more formal description of what we mean by the 'internalising of external costs' will be given in Chapter 3.

# References

Commission of the European Community (1992), 'Treaty on European Union', *Official Journal of the European Community*, C224, Vol. 35.

Environmental Protection Agency (1996), *State of the Environment in Ireland*, Environmental Protection Agency: Wexford.

OECD (1975), *The Polluter Pays Principle: Definition, Analysis, Implementation*, OECD: Paris.

UNCED (1992), *Agenda 21*, United Nations Conference on Environment and Development: Conches, Switzerland.

# 2 Background and scope for change

*S. Scott*

Before we discuss pollution taxes and other economic instruments in detail in the following chapter, it is important to consider the framework within which decisions on these instruments would be taken. Three aspects will be addressed, namely, (1) the fiscal framework, (2) the legal framework, and (3) attitudes of the public.

The fiscal framework determines the present scope for raising pollution taxes and for funding environmental protection, as well as the ability of the authorities to charge for damage. The legal framework includes, among other things, the powers and functions of local authorities, the Environmental Protection Agency and EU directives. The public's views on pollution taxes and charges for environmental services, and concern for the effects of these on low-income households and on competitiveness, need to be considered to ensure that policies are acceptable in the minds of the public. If they are not, there is little chance that politicians will feel able to advocate and adopt them. We will consider each of these aspects in turn.

## 2.1 The fiscal framework

### 2.1.1 Central government

What scope is there, at central government level, for introducing economic instruments, such as pollution taxes, into the existing tax system? There is no question but that there is a ready use for any revenue arising from pollution taxes. It has long been remarked that the present structure of the tax system relies heavily on labour taxes, that is on income taxes and social insurance contributions, and that this feature sits uncomfortably beside high unemployment and a rapidly growing labour force. Therefore any revenue accruing from pollution taxes could be used to replace labour taxes. However the introduction of new taxes, or the alteration of existing taxes will need to have regard for the long-term objective[1] of more neutral tax regimes, which involves making tax rates more uniform and reducing concessions.

There are indeed good arguments for streamlining the tax system, removing some allowances and for making subsidies explicit, arguments that are reinforced by the open borders policy of the EU. The introduction of special differentiated taxes for environmental reasons could run counter to this. The following constraints relate to the main taxes. For Corporation Tax, Ireland has a derogation from the EU to apply the low rate of 10% to manufacturing until 2010, and to certain financial services and activities in the Shannon Free Airport area until 2005. Some flexibility is permitted on the allowances against corporation tax, subject to compliance with the restrictions on state aids to industry. This will be touched on in several chapters, including the chapters on transport and on construction.

There is not much scope for differential VAT rates. The standard rate is stipulated by the EU VAT Directive to be applied at a rate of 15 per cent or more. One or two reduced rates are allowed for specified goods and services (environment-enhancing items are not listed), and zero or super-reduced rates in existence in January 1991 are allowed to remain until end-1996 at least. Ironically, the VAT Directive allows energy to be subject to a reduced rate of VAT. Deposit-refund schemes, in which the return of items is encouraged, might in some cases ideally be incorporated in the VAT system, since documentation on inputs and outputs is already a requirement of the system. It would be helpful if in some situations the VAT rebate could be made conditional on specified environmental behaviour, though the scope for doing so looks slim at present. However, it may be permissible, subject to the normal requirements of confidentiality, to use the information on inputs and outputs gathered in the VAT system. This will be seen to offer potential in the chapter on agriculture.

There is scope for excise taxes, which are at present applied to hydrocarbon fuels, tobacco and drink, to be used for environmental protection. Excise taxes may also be maintained or introduced on other goods, provided that countries do not introduce border checks, and that the freedom to purchase abroad is respected. The potential for extending excise taxes will be relevant in the chapter on energy.

In sum there is reasonable scope for the introduction of economic instruments by central government, though, given the aim of streamlining the fiscal system, the full potential may not be realised without more flexibility at EU level.

### 2.1.2    Local government

What flexibility and scope are there for the introduction of economic instruments at the local level? We find that a prominent feature in the fiscal framework is the arrangement whereby local authorities undertake the provision of many local environmental services while central government provides much of the finance. To be more specific, central government supplies nearly 40 per cent of total current receipts and nearly 80 per cent of the capital receipts of local authorities, as shown in Appendix Table 2.4.

The shortfall of revenue from charges to customers of the major environmental services which local authorities provide is illustrated in Table 2.1. It shows that current cost recovery from charges is just under 50 per cent. Furthermore, capital costs (not shown here) are barely covered, except for some contributions, mainly from industry, to the capital costs of waste water treatment (Scott and Lawlor 1994).

**Table 2.1**
**Cost recovery by charges for water, waste water and solid waste services (operating costs only) delivered by Local Authorities, 1994**

| Service | | Receipts from charges £m | Operating costs £m | Cost recovery % |
|---|---|---|---|---|
| **Water:** | Domestic | 39.8 | } 96 | } 75 |
| | Commercial | 32.0 | | |
| **Waste water:** | Domestic | 1.3 | } 41 | } 18 |
| | Commercial | 6.0 | | |
| **Refuse:** | Domestic | 5.1 | } 50 | } 23 |
| | Commercial | 6.5 | | |
| **Total services** | | 90.7 | 187 | 49 |

*Note:* Several local authorities which were represented at an Economic and Social Research Institute workshop on charges impose separate effluent charges on commercial enterprises, others combine water and effluent charges under the heading 'water' (Lawlor, 1996) .

*Sources:* Department of the Environment: *Returns of Local Taxation* (various issues), and Department of the Environment communication.

Local authorities' revenue base was eroded when domestic rates (a local property tax) were abolished in 1978. They were replaced by grants financed by taxes raised by central government, especially by income taxes. Reports[2] have highlighted the high degree of centralisation of government and on the subject of finance have advised that:

There must be a link between spending and raising money in order to promote responsibility and accountability.

9

Local authorities should raise a significant proportion of their revenue from non-central sources.

Specific purpose grants (from central funds) should, in so far as practicable, be confined to situations where the benefits flowing from the expenditure accrue substantially to people outside of the area of the local authority.

The striking feature is that there have been perhaps ten studies or committees investigating local government reform or finance, with little action taken. Recent work by KPMG points to a strong case for charges as they would 'promote efficiency on the part of both the provider and the consumer'. Because income taxes are still quite high, local authorities feel inhibited from raising more charges for environmental services, the costs of which are rising. Central government grants are considered inadequate, so that authorities have to rely heavily on rates on businesses for their income. Businesses resent additional charges because they claim that the rates that they already pay should cover their usage of services.

It is technically feasible and indeed sensible, in the case of business, for authorities to reorganise a part of their revenue to come from charges rather than rates. This is not an option in the case of households which, as we saw, pay no rates and feel strongly that the previous income tax hikes replaced rates. Consequently there has been strong resistance from some households to charges, including refusal to pay.[3]

Meanwhile, local authorities found that they had heavy environmental commitments to supply and improve water, refuse and sewerage services and they had no option but to raise charges for environmental services. Now all of them do so, except municipal Dublin and Limerick, though mainly via a flat-rate charge, which, as seen, barely covers half the operating costs. The government introduced an allowance against income tax to those who paid the charge in full and on time, in the 1996 budget.

It is clear that local authority finance requires rationalisation, and that charging for local environmental services would be a step in the right direction, as will be further explained in the chapter on environmental services. It would also allow a reduction (or obviate a rise) in tax-financed grants from central government.

## 2.2 The legal framework

We are interested to know whether there would be legal impediments to altering the fiscal and charging structure. In relation to local government, uncertainty has occasionally been expressed in the past as to the right of local authorities to raise charges for services. This right has now been established and clarified, however.

Where non-domestic users are concerned, the Local Government (Water Pollution) Act 1977, as amended by the 1990 Act (section 12 (a)) gives powers to the local authority to charge non-domestic polluters for 'the expenditure incurred or to be incurred by the local authority in monitoring, treating or disposing of' a discharge. The 1977 Act also permits the Minister to make regulations allowing local authorities to charge for discharges to waters, even if no treatment has been carried out by the authorities on such discharges. Where domestic users are concerned, the Local Government (Financial Provisions) (No 2) Act 1983 empowers local authorities to levy charges for the services they provide, that is water, refuse and sewerage services, as they 'consider appropriate'.

Furthermore, section 93 (1) of the Environmental Protection Agency Act 1992 paves the way for the EPA to raise emissions charges:

> The Agency may, in accordance with regulations made by the Minister of the Environment, subject to the consent of the Minister for Finance and the Minister for Industry and Commerce, under this section, make charges in relation to such emissions to the environment from such activities as may be specified in the regulations.

Some points to note are as follows. Regulations allowing local authorities to charge in some cases have not been made as yet. However, if desired, there is scope for introducing them. Also the ability to charge for expenditure 'to be incurred' is an important facility if one is concerned to implement incentive pricing correctly (i.e., marginal cost pricing).

An important development is that the *ultra vires* clause in local government law (which stipulated that local authorities can do only that which the law states they can do) has been relaxed. They have more freedom to act, provided that the action is not forbidden in law. Now local authorities have a general competence to act in the interests of their local community in a much broader way than heretofore.

### 2.3 Attitudes

Attitudes are an important factor in determining policy. In addition, while the reforms might be neutral in the sense that the environmental taxes that are being raised can be given back in some neutral or even beneficial manner, there could be some losers.

The losers would be those who cannot benefit from the new situation, perhaps being in low-income groups, and those who are big polluters. The latter group, in theory, should not be a cause for concern - up to this point they have received external benefits at other people's expense by not being charged. Long lead-times in introducing charges might however be needed, otherwise the effects could be harsh if polluters' adjustment times were necessarily long and if disruption would otherwise occur.

Losers would frequently be businesses which, say, use a lot of energy, or farmers who cause eutrophication of waterways. Vulnerable or vociferous groups within sectors may object strongly, at the risk of denying the greater overall benefit to society. This behaviour is not surprising - there are many examples of pressure

11

groups exerting influence beyond the strength of their representation. In some Scandinavian countries where pollution taxes are more widespread, heavy polluters have received exemptions. Rather than grant exemptions which leave the wrong incentives in place, it might be preferable in extreme cases to devise temporary compensation which does not distort correct incentives.

At the root of the problem is the fear of loss of competitiveness. Studies at national level, such as those described by OECD (1993), state that environmental compliance costs constitute but 1 to 2 per cent of total costs in most sectors. Consequently environmental policies and compliance costs are not a significant factor affecting competitiveness or trade at the *macro-level*.

However at the level of the firm, environmental compliance costs can have a more significant effect, especially for pollution-intensive and resource sectors such as chemicals, mining, oil refining, pulp and paper. Compliance costs might have an especially harsh effect on firms which already have competitive weaknesses in other areas relating to labour, capital or technology. It has been claimed[4] alternatively that environmental regulations or charges can be good for competitiveness by spurring firms to develop more resource-efficient methods of production and to reduce costs, possibly yielding front-runner and spin-off advantages to the firms that respond to the challenge. It is likely that large multi-national firms are able to benefit from other technological improvements which are part of any environmental upgrade, and can market differentiated or green image products. Firms which compete on the basis of relative prices, however, such as primary producers of agricultural and resource commodities, could be unfavourably affected. In sum competitiveness effects will vary, but harm can be mitigated by reasonable lead-times to facilitate adaptation, and by aiming for international application of the Polluter Pays Principle.

We now consider the other potential losers, low-income households. These households are in a bad position to pay pollution taxes and environmental charges because the scope for compensating them via reduced labour taxes is limited, by virtue of their low or zero tax bill. Also the reform can be regressive, affecting the poor proportionately more: the poor would spend a higher proportion of their incomes on the items which are candidates for the tax: water services, fuel and other resource-intensive or polluting goods and services. Compensation via the social welfare system needs careful consideration and costing. There is already experience with compensation for the requirement that only relatively expensive smokeless fuel be sold in Dublin. After some initial problems, this compensation has performed satisfactorily.

We have described two likely objections to environmental tax reform, namely distributional effects and impacts on competitiveness, both of which need to be addressed but which should not be insuperable. The third perceived objection is the belief that the proposals will be only half-delivered. People may reject proposals because they do not believe that the whole package will materialise: that the reduction in other taxes will not occur or that administrators will absorb too large a share of the revenue. Perhaps all the above objections apply, alongside inadequate clarification of the arguments in favour of the reform.

Finally, how and when attitudes are formed, and indeed, the extent to which they can be summarised, are issues for debate. In Ireland in the 1970s, a combination of events such as the oil crises, media attention to documents with an environmental message, and an official statement of the need for a nuclear power station, raised environmental consciousness. Towards the end of the eighties, after a decade of preoccupation with high levels of government debt and unemployment, global environmental issues gained people's attention, foreign influences playing a large part. A recent opinion survey[5] revealed that 49 per cent felt that the quality of the environment 'is deteriorating', while 19 per cent thought that it was improving and the remainder felt that it was staying about the same. Without prompting, first-mentioned environmental problems of concern were, in descending order of citation: water pollution, air pollution, rubbish on streets, waste management, global pollution, loss of nature and other problems, including build-up of chemicals and pesticides and over-use of resources.

On the use of economic instruments per se, the popular perception may be that subsidies are required to achieve environmental aims, though this view will be tempered by the general realisation that subsidies are not feasible until the demands on public funds of other priorities had been satisfied. What information do we have on the general attitude[6] to charges? The aforementioned survey asked the following question:

> To meet EC obligations regarding the protection of the environment, it will be necessary to improve our methods of waste disposal and other services. These improvements will have to be paid for, one way or another. This may be through *higher taxes* such as income tax, VAT etc., or through *fixed service charges* on households or by *charges based on the amount of the service* a household or firm uses (for instance, by metering water and charging per gallon used). In relation to each of the following services, how do you feel it should be paid for ?

Respondents were asked to consider four services: drinking water, sewage treatment and disposal, household rubbish disposal and industrial waste disposal. Replies for each service are shown in Tables 2.2a, b, c and d.

A point to emerge from the replies shown is the extent to which people are apparently abandoning the idea that 'the government should pay'. Payment through general taxation would be logically preferred by those people who reckon that in this way others will pay, or if they think that the tax system is progressive and they perceive themselves as poor. However, we see from looking at the replies for 'increase in taxes' in the four tables, that less than ten per cent of people would favour improvements to environmental services being paid for out of higher general taxation. Leaving aside the last table, on industrial waste, the majority of respondents choose fixed service charges. However the suggestion that people

13

should pay according to their *use* is in fact quite well supported. Over 40 per cent think that drinking water and household rubbish disposal should be paid for by amount used.

Males are more inclined than females to favour charging by amount used, 51 per cent favouring metered water charging. The proportions favouring volume-based charges can perhaps be explained - roughly half of households should consider their consumption to be below average, so that they would gain in a situation of volume-based charges. Perhaps many people prefer explicit charges given the choice, and realise that they will be paying for the service one way or another, anyway. If one looks at the age breakdown (not given here), the younger age groups are relatively more in favour of charging by the amount of service used in the cases of drinking water and rubbish removal.

### Table 2.2a
### Preferred method of paying for drinking water

|                        | Male | Female |
| ---------------------- | ---- | ------ |
| Increases in Taxes     | 2%   | 3%     |
| Fixed Service Charge   | 48%  | 55%    |
| Charge for Amount Used | 51%  | 42%    |
| Total                  | 100% | 100%   |

### Table 2.2b
### Preferred method of paying for sewage treatment
### and disposal

|                        | Male | Female |
| ---------------------- | ---- | ------ |
| Increases in Taxes     | 5%   | 5%     |
| Fixed Service Charge   | 64%  | 67%    |
| Charge for Amount Used | 31%  | 29%    |
| Total                  | 100% | 100%   |

### Table 2.2c
### Preferred method of paying for household
### rubbish disposal

|                         | Male  | Female |
| ----------------------- | ----- | ------ |
| Increases in Taxes      | 3%    | 3%     |
| Fixed Service Charge    | 52%   | 55%    |
| Charge for Amount Used  | 45%   | 42%    |
| Total                   | 100%  | 100%   |

### Table 2.2d
### Preferred method of paying for
### industrial waste disposal

|                         | Male  | Female |
| ----------------------- | ----- | ------ |
| Increases in Taxes      | 8%    | 9%     |
| Fixed Service Charge    | 31%   | 34%    |
| Charge for Amount Used  | 60%   | 56%    |
| Total                   | 100%  | 100%   |

*Source:* Murphy, Scott and Whelan (1994).

Between 56 and 60 per cent of respondents think that industry should pay for waste disposal according to the amount disposed of. Only about a quarter of households include a person employed in industry, or would associate themselves with industry, so that for the other three quarters of respondents, it is like saying that 'someone else' (i.e., industry) should pay. So, when asked about a sector which is not in the main their own, respondents side firmly with payment according to the amount discharged.

In any event, the results as a whole show consistency between public responses on how to pay for environmental services and what economic theory would advise. The furore in Ireland in recent years over the rise in Residential Property Tax and over the rebalancing of telephone charges, indicates how carefully any simultaneous imposition of charges with reduction in central taxes, and attention to the problems of low-income families and other losers, would have to be addressed.

Finally in this discussion of public attitudes, having looked at people's preferred method of payment, we should look at what people think in general about paying to protect the environment. The aforementioned survey also asked 'How willing would *you* be to pay *much higher prices* in order to protect the environment?' In addition to 'pay much higher prices', they were asked the same question in respect of 'much higher taxes' and 'accept cuts in your standard of living'. Table 2.3 summarises their replies.

**Table 2.3**
**How willing would you be to protect the environment?**

|  | Pay much higher prices | Pay much higher taxes | Accept cuts in standard of living |
|---|---|---|---|
| Very willing | 8% | 3% | 4% |
| Fairly willing | **41%** | 20% | **25%** |
| Neither willing nor unwilling | 10% | 8% | 11% |
| Fairly unwilling | 19% | 24% | 23% |
| Very unwilling | 20% | **43%** | **36%** |
| Can't choose | 1% | 1% | 1% |
| No answer | 0% | 0% | 0% |
| Total | 100% | 100% | 100% |
| Number replying | 957 | 957 | 957 |

*Note:* Percentages over 25 per cent are highlighted.
*Source:* Murphy, Scott and Whelan (1994).

The replies in the first column show that only a half (49 per cent) of the population would be willing to pay much higher prices to protect the environment, though outnumbering those who are unwilling. However subsequent columns make it clear that they are rather more unwilling to entertain alternative methods to higher prices. Less than a quarter would be willing to pay more if it entailed much higher taxes; cuts in standards of living are not much more attractive either. This lends support to the suspicion that accountable and explicit taxes or charges are actually preferred.

These general attitudes are broadly in line with those revealed in a later survey undertaken in the context of the Eurobarometer (European Commission 1995). Results for the fifteen member states of the EU indicate that nearly three quarters of respondents strongly agree or agree somewhat with the idea of switching taxes from income taxes or social security contributions, to goods and processes which damage the environment, such as wastes, carbon dioxide and pesticides. Furthermore the attitudes in Ireland in particular were not atypical of those in the fifteen member states combined.

## 2.4 Summary

The fiscal and legal framework can accommodate the adoption of economic instruments for environmental protection fairly well, having regard, however, to the requirements of EU harmonisation, which could be a constraint. In the case of environmental services provided by local authorities, the user or 'polluter' is barely paying half the current costs at the point of use. Therefore there is scope, and the legal facility exists, to raise charges to improve coverage of costs.

Attitudes could be a constraint. Service charges are widely perceived as taxes and not as prices, indeed as double taxation, and they have become a focus of grievance. This has to be borne in mind in future rationalisation. Careful presentation of reforms would be needed, not only in addressing the concerns mentioned, but also having regard to other changes which might be underway, such as restructuring in the energy supply industry. Such restructuring, to meet competition in a more open market, might in itself entail price changes. Earmarking the revenue from pay for pollution taxes to environmental improvements is sometimes advised in order to promote acceptance of the tax. In this way people know that they are getting something in return, and might be better disposed to the reform. However, they might actually prefer that the pollution tax fund a reduction of other taxes. In this way there is no net increase in taxes.

Media reports lead one to believe that economic instruments, other than subsidies, would be badly received. However there is a degree of realism in public opinion when people are actually faced with the issues. This is what survey replies suggest, when people are reminded that they are paying for the services anyway, or that environmental quality has to be financed one way or another. However, bearing in mind that there has been wide support for an anti-water charges electoral candidate, a difference could emerge between what people say and what they do.

In fact economic instruments are already quite widespread, as the summary table in Appendix Table 2.5 shows, and several of them will be discussed in the relevant chapters below. Many operate so smoothly that people are not conscious of them. Nevertheless there are still some real constraints to be confronted. These are that new charges for pollution and environmental services are more easily implemented if imposed *at the same time* as a reduction in central government taxes, alongside compensation by means of raised social welfare payments and carefully considered introduction to vulnerable sectors. The time to phase in environmental taxes and charges is now, before environmental protection costs rise to meet the higher standards required in EU directives.

# Notes

1.   E.g., Ruding (1992).
2.   E.g., Stationery Office, 1991 and the Commission on Taxation (Stationery Office, 1984).
3.   In addition, the calculation of the Rates Support Grants from central government to local authorities requires rationalisation. Large differential shifts between authorities, in terms of their needs and resources have occurred as numbers of inhabitants and conditions changed over the years. The recommendations of an analysis by Ridge (1992), commissioned to establish objective criteria for deciding the size of grants to each authority, were not adopted as they would have entailed sizeable shifts between authorities and possibly over time. This made the recommendations hard to implement, whatever about the lack of rationale in continuing with the present pattern of grants.
4.   Notably by Porter and van der Linde (1995).
5.   With replies from nearly one thousand respondents, by Murphy, Scott and Whelan (1994). An ordinary random sample was chosen, households being picked from the Electoral Register using the RANSAM procedure developed by Whelan (1979).
6.   On the subject of charges and volume-based charges in particular, it is interesting that a report of the National Economic and Social Council written in 1985 stated that it would be worth considering phasing in water metering for domestic consumers, which might reduce consumption, result in lower current and capital expenditure and facilitate charging for sewerage too. It added that assistance would be required for households which cannot afford the charge. However the report's recommendations for domestic solid waste were different. Refuse disposal was considered to have a strong public good element, and 'we think it would be impractical to devise a form of charge which was directly related to the "volume" of service consumed'. Yet, within a decade, some fourteen local authorities were actually implementing volume-based charges for solid waste, from households as well as industry. Furthermore some private solid waste collectors may be using volume-based charges also. This shows the extent to which attitudes, technology and administrative methods can change over a decade.

# References

Department of the Environment (1990, 1995), *Returns of Local Taxation*, Dublin.

Department of the Environment (1995), *Local Authority Estimates*, Dublin.

Department of Finance, *Public Capital Programme*, various issues. Dublin.

European Commission (1995), *Europeans and the Environment in 1995, Survey conducted in the context of the Eurobarometer 32.1 bis*. Report for DG XI, Unit XI/A/3 by INRA (Europe) - E.C.O. November.

KPMG (1996), *The Financing of Local Government in Ireland*. Paper read by O'Brien, T. of KPMG Management Consulting to the Economic Policy Conference of the Dublin Economic Workshop, Kenmare, 18-21 October.

Lawlor, J. (1996), 'The Use of Economic Instruments for Environmental Services in Irish Local Authorities', in *Administration*, Vol. 44(1), Spring.

Murphy, M., Scott, S. and Whelan, B.J. (1994), *Report on Attitudes to the Environment - A Survey undertaken for the Department of the Environment*, Economic and Social Research Institute, Dublin. (Survey appended to the International Survey of Attitudes to the Environment.)

National Economic and Social Council (1985), *The Financing of Local Authorities.* No. 80. Dublin.

OECD (1993), *Environmental Policies and Industrial Competitiveness*, Paris.

Porter, M.E. and Van Der Linde, C. (1995) 'Towards a New Conception of the Environmental-Competitiveness Relationship', *The Journal of Economic Perspectives*, Vol. 9, no. 4, Fall 1995, American Economic Association.

Ridge, M. (1992) 'Local Government Finance and Equalisation: The Case of Ireland', *Fiscal Studies*, Vol. 13, No. 3, London.

Ruding, (1992) *Report of the Committee of Independent Experts on Company Taxation*, Office for Official Publications of the European Communities, Luxembourg.

Scott, S., Lawlor, J. (1994), *Waste Water Services: Charging Industry the Capital Cost*, Dublin: The Economic and Social Research Institute, Policy Research Series No. 22.

Stationery Office (1984), *Third Report of the Commission on Taxation: Indirect Taxation*, June, Dublin.

Stationery Office (1991), *Local Government Reorganisation and Reform, 'The Barrington Report'*, Pl. 7918, Dublin.

Whelan, B.J. (1979), 'RANSAM: A Random Sample Design for Ireland' in *The Economic and Social Review*, vol. 10, no. 2. January, Dublin.

## Table 2.4
### Local Authorities' current receipts and capital receipts, from central government, rates, rents, charges, etc., 1990 and 1994

| Receipts | 1990 £m | 1990 % | 1994 £m | 1994 % |
|---|---|---|---|---|
| Current Receipts: | | | | |
| Government grants/subsidies | 470 | 44 | 451 | 39 |
| Commercial rates | 239 | 22 | 302 | 26 |
| Other incl. rent, charges etc. | 366 | 34 | 400 | 35 |
| Total current receipts | 1,075 | 100 | 1,153 | 100 |
| Capital receipts: | | | | |
| Government grants | 300 | 82 | 509 | 79 |
| Internal sources + borrowing | 64 | 18 | 137 | 21 |
| Total capital receipts | 364 | 100 | 646 | 100 |

*Source:* Department of the Environment, *Returns of Local Taxation 1990, 1994, Local Authority Estimates 1995* and Department of Finance, *Public Capital Programmes.*

## Table 2.5
### Summary of economic instruments in use in Ireland

| Economic Instruments | Details | Comments |
|---|---|---|
| **Charges/fines:** | | |
| Derelict sites levy: | 3 per cent annually of an urban property's market value. | Low coverage. Revenue in 1994 was £21 000, on property worth £0.7 million. |
| Litter fines : | Not applied very thoroughly. | No information on revenue. |
| **User charges:** | | |
| Domestic water, refuse and sewerage: | Mainly fixed charge. Some volume-based refuse charges. | Costs only partially covered. |
| Non-domestic water, solid waste and waste water: | Volume-based charges wide- spread for water and solid waste, less so for waste water. (Charges at domestic level are mainly flat-rate). | About half of all solid waste disposal costs covered, fraction of waste water treatment costs. |
| Urban parking: | Meters and fines (but much free business parking). | Meters and fines revenue was £9.28 million in 1995. |
| **Product charges:** | | |
| | High hydrocarbon taxes. $CO_2$ tax studied, not applied. | Mainly to raise revenue. Net benefits could ensue. |
| **Admin./monitoring fees:** | | Monitoring costs not covered. |
| Trade effluent: | Small fee. | |
| Integrated Pollution: | Licence fee to firms. | To recover EPA costs. |
| **Tax differentiation:** | | |
| Leaded/unleaded petrol: | 7 per cent price difference. | Unleaded sales rose from 7% in 1989, to over 60% by 1996. |

| | | |
|---|---|---|
| Vehicle Registration Tax: | % of vehicle value, higher for vehicles > 2500 cc. | VRT revenue was £271 million in 1994. |
| Annual road tax: | Graded by engine cc. | Revenue was £249 million in 1994. |
| Tax relief if scrapping 10-year-old car: | £1000 Vehicle Registration Tax relief. | Ran from 1.7.1995 for 1 year, then renewed for another year. Cost is 20 % of VRT revenue. |
| Exemption of VAT on public transport. | Ticket sales are not charged VAT. | To reduce the price of public transport. |
| Excise tax on fuel used by public transport is rebated. | To reduce costs of public transport providers. | Discourages fuel efficiency in public transport. |
| Exemption from excise duty: waste oil: | On processors of waste oil. | To encourage recycling. |
| Urban renewal special tax rates: | 10 year Rates relief, double rent allowance and other reliefs. | Effective relief is high. |
| **Subsidies:** Food industry: | Pollution control grants from EAGGF. | 8 to 10% of investment. |
| Industry and commerce energy audit grant and efficiency grant: | 40% up to £3000 for audit. Up to 40% to a value of £156 000 for investment. | £2 million expenditure in first year, 1995. |
| Rural Environment Protection Scheme REPS: | Premium to farmers of £122/ha up to max 40 ha. Extra for Natural Heritage Areas (NHAs), Environmentally Sensitive Areas (ESAs) and organic farming. | Part of CAP reform: budget of £230 m over several years. To influence farming practice on small farms in its totality. |

| | | |
|---|---|---|
| Control of Farmyard Pollution Scheme: (suspended) | Grants up to 60% to a value of £22 500 to small farms for slurry storage etc. | Under Operational Programme (OP) for Agriculture, Rural Development & Forestry. |
| Afforestation grant. | £1300 to £3000 per ha plus 20 year premium of £130 to £300 per ha. | Part of CAP reform. Also OP grants for forestry improvement and amenity, of £500 to £3000. |
| Explicit subsidy to public transport. | Mainly to rail transport. | To reduce the price of public transport. |
| **Deposit refund schemes:** | Cans and plastic bags. | Isolated and very smallscale. |
| **Market creation:** | Government departments and agencies use recycled paper. | |
| **Allowance for insurance bonds:** | Payments of insurance bonds for rehabilitation of mines is allowable against tax. | Cost to Exchequer is £1 million per year. |

# 3 Theory of economic instruments

*A. Barrett*

In this chapter, we will present the economic arguments in favour of the use of economic instruments for environmental protection. For those familiar with this material, the chapter can be skipped without any loss. For those who wish to read a very brief outline of the arguments, such an outline is presented in the concluding section of the chapter.

## 3.1 The problem that economic instruments seek to address[1]

Environmental policy is concerned with reducing the amount of environmental degradation that arises due to a range of human activities. Typically, production and consumption lead to the generation of waste in the forms of solid or liquid waste and air-borne particles. When the assimilative capacity of the environment is unable to fully absorb this waste, environmental degradation occurs. Similarly, when human activities put demands on resources at rates that exceed their re-generative capacity, a negative environmental outcome emerges. And finally, when human activities intrude on either natural environments, or built environments of cultural and social value, the quality of the environment is reduced and hence the wealth of the nation is reduced also. In Chapter 1 we mentioned examples of the environmental pressures being faced in Ireland and more examples will be provided in the chapters that follow.

The use of policy to reduce the type of environmental degradation just described presupposes that the degradation is in some sense excessive. In addition, policies that seek to reduce levels of pollution implicitly assume that there is something desirable about the target levels. In an extreme case, a policy that would reduce pollution to zero says that zero-level pollution is optimal.

In opening our discussion of the theory of economic instruments supporting environmental protection, it is helpful to consider first the economist's view of why the level of pollution in the absence of government intervention might be greater than society would want. We also consider what the optimal level of pollution might be and demonstrate the circumstances in which this level is greater than zero. We show how it is possible that this level of pollution may be reached without government intervention, through negotiation between private parties. As this 'no-government' solution is unlikely to emerge in reality, we go on to look at the possibilities for government intervention through the use of economic instruments. In an ideal situation, such economic instruments could be used to achieve the optimal level of pollution. However, in reality economic instruments are more likely to be used to achieve what we can describe as acceptable levels of pollution.

Even in achieving this more limited objective, it will be shown that economic instruments have important advantages over the more traditional and widely used regulatory approaches to environmental protection. First, economic instruments allow the same amount of pollution abatement to be achieved at a lower cost. Second, economic instruments in the form of taxes and charges allow for the possibility of reducing other taxes which have negatively distorting effects, in addition to aiding environmental protection; this is the so-called 'double dividend'. Third, economic instruments provide an on-going incentive for pollution abatement; this dynamic incentive is not present under regulatory measures.

## 3.2 Sub-optimal and optimal levels of pollution

To see why economists believe that the level of pollution may be above that which is optimal in the absence of government intervention consider Figure 3.1.

In this figure we are depicting an enterprise (be it an industrial plant as in Chapter 5 or a farm as in Chapter 4) whose production gives rise to pollution. The vertical axis measures monetary values while the horizontal axis measures output. For now we will assume that there is a one for one link between output and pollution but this assumption will be relaxed later in the chapter and its implications discussed. As output increases, its associated pollution also increases and this is represented in the diagram by the marginal external cost (MEC) line. 'External cost' refers to the cost that pollution imposes on people other than the firm responsible and for which these others are not compensated. 'Marginal' means we are describing the cost associated with each additional unit of output. Although this is a cost of production from society's point of view, the firm does not take it into account in making its production decision. It is only interested in the net benefits it derives from production, and this is represented by the marginal net private benefit (MNPB) line. This line is derived by subtracting the private marginal cost of each unit of output from the price received, that is, for each unit of output we subtract the cost to the firm from the price received by the firm. With a given price and a rising marginal cost[2], MNPB decreases as output (and pollution) rises. MEC rises as output rises on the assumption that the external costs of additional pollution rises as the level of pollution rises.

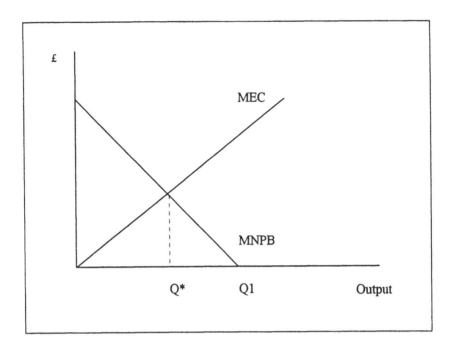

**Figure 3.1    The optimal level of pollution**

Without government intervention the firm will maximise its net private benefits. In terms of the diagram, it will produce additional units of output as long as MNPB is positive and so production will be at the level Q1. At this level of output the MEC of the associated pollution is greater than MNPB so although the firm is better off at this level of output than at a lower level of output, society at large is worse off. By reducing output, the benefits to society from a lower external cost of the pollution is greater than the loss of net benefits to the producer and so the welfare of society at large would be higher at lower levels of output.

It is for this reason that economists view the level of pollution when output is at level Q1 as being sub-optimal, i.e. the welfare of society at large is not maximised when output and pollution are at this level. In essence, the reason for the sub-optimal outcome is that the pollution costs are external to the market mechanism and so this mechanism, which under normal circumstances produces socially optimal allocations of resources, produces a sub-optimal outcome in this case. By extending the logic, we can establish the level of output that is consistent with the optimal level of pollution. By reducing output from level Q1 the external costs of pollution are reduced by a greater amount than the net private benefits of that pollution, at least up to output level Q*. Reducing output below level Q* reduces net benefits more than external costs. As such output level Q* is consistent with a level of pollution that maximises social welfare.

### 3.3 Achieving optimal pollution levels without government intervention (The Coase Theorem)

The externality just described would lead one to believe instinctively that government intervention was required for the social optimum to be arrived at. This was accepted without question until 1960 when Coase produced his famous theorem.[3] Coase's idea is as follows. Suppose residents in an area have a property right such that they are entitled to an environment with no pollution. Initially this will mean that the firm in Figure 3.1 will not operate. However, as the net benefits of production to the firm exceed the costs to residents at lower levels of production the firm could bargain with the residents and offer to compensate them for the cost of the pollution. In order for this to happen, we must assume that the costs involved in arriving at such a deal, i.e. the transactions costs, are zero or at least relatively low. In this way, the residents can be made as well off as they were before while the firm is better off. Such compensation will continue up to output $Q^*$. After that level of output, the compensation required by residents is greater than the net benefits earned by the firm so that output level will not be exceeded and the social optimum is achieved.

Such an outcome can also be attained if the firm has the property right and is allowed to pollute. In this case output will initially be at level Q1. Those suffering the pollution now have an incentive to bargain with the firm and to compensate the firm for reducing its output. At higher levels of output this is possible because the gains to the residents exceed the losses to the firm. Such compensation will continue up to output level $Q^*$, after which the compensation required by the firm would exceed that which the residents would be prepared to pay and so again, the social optimum is arrived at without government intervention. It should also be pointed out that the final production/pollution outcome does not depend on who is given the rights to the environment. The only result that differs between the two rights allocations is the distribution of costs between the firms and residents, in that the polluters pay in one case and the victims of pollution pay in the other case.

While the Coase Theorem is certainly an enormously clever theoretical argument, it is based on assumptions violated in the real world, so that the type of bargaining and compensation envisaged rarely occurs. We need only point out the main real world difficulty for this to be seen. Transactions are not costless and so there is no guarantee that they will occur. In the example we are discussing, the transactions costs would likely be prohibitive, such as the costs of organising the residents in such a way that their compensation requirements could be measured and voiced. It may even be difficult to establish who are the victims of pollution, especially when the effects of pollution manifest themselves over a long time. For these reasons, the Coase Theorem has not convinced many economists that government intervention is unnecessary in the face of externalities. Instead, economists have sought to work out how intervention can be most efficiently conducted. It is the output of these efforts that informs the discussions in the following chapters so we will now discuss the insights which have been derived.

## 3.4 Using economic instruments to achieve the optimal level of pollution

The use of economic instruments, in the form of taxes, to produce optimal environmental outcomes was first proposed by Pigou.[4] In order to see how the Pigovian tax works we reproduce the essence of Figure 3.1 in Figure 3.2.

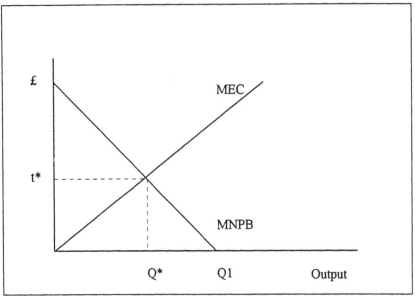

**Figure 3.2    The Pigovian Tax**

Once again, the firm faces the MNPB curve as shown while society at large faces MEC arising from the firm's production decisions. In the absence of government intervention or a Coasian-type bargain, the firm will produce output level Q1. The imposition of a tax on output, equal to t*, alters the firm's production decision. At output levels above Q* the marginal net private benefit is less than the tax which the firm faces if it produces the additional output. For this reason, it is no longer optimal for the firm to produce Q1; its optimal level of output is instead Q*. The tax has 'internalised' the external cost that the firm imposes on society and so the socially optimal level of output now corresponds with the firm's optimum. In order for the tax to bring the level of output to the social optimum it must equal the marginal external cost of the pollution at its optimal level. This can be seen in the diagram or shown mathematically.

The ideal Pigovian tax is clearly a powerful economic instrument but it has practical limitations. In order to set the tax, it is necessary to know the marginal cost of pollution, not just at its current level, but at its optimal level. This is a task which, though possible, would be costly and time-consuming as it involves undertaking contingent valuation studies or estimating values using hedonic pricing analysis. For this reason the setting of ideal Pigovian taxes in all instances is not possible. However, this does not mean that there is no benefit to be derived from the use of environmental taxes or other economic instruments. As we demonstrated above, the level of pollution in the absence of government intervention is likely to be above the optimum so some amount of pollution reduction is likely to be an improvement. Where economic instruments can be most beneficial is through achieving such reductions at lower costs than the alternative regulatory approach. We will now move on to show how this can be under the headings: (i) taxes, charges and subsidies, (ii) tradeable permits and (iii) deposit-refund schemes.

### 3.4.1 Taxes, charges and subsidies

In this section, we move away from thinking in terms of the optimal level of pollution as defined by the equality of marginal external costs and marginal net private benefits. Instead we will work with a situation in which an acceptable level of environmental quality is chosen; it could be argued that this level represents a socially derived proxy for the optimum. We continue to maintain that the choice should be informed by an effort to put a value on the environmental quality being pursued but once a level is chosen, the task for policy makers is to achieve this level at the lowest possible cost. In Figure 3.3 we show how taxes can achieve such a level at a lower cost than regulations.

Figure 3.3 differs from Figures 3.1 and 3.2 in that the horizontal axis now represents pollution. The new lines show marginal abatement costs (MAC) for two enterprises. These are the costs to enterprises of taking action to reduce pollution, which could mean reducing output or installing pollution control processes and technology. An example might be a pharmaceutical company which could install a waste water treatment plant instead of emitting waste water into a nearby stream. The MAC lines slope upwards from right to left for the following reason: pollution will be eliminated initially using the cheapest route but as the cheaper routes are exhausted the more expensive ones must be taken. Alternatively, one can think in terms of initial reductions being easier and hence cheaper but that further reductions are more difficult and hence more expensive.

Suppose the government decides that pollution should be reduced and issues a regulation saying that each firm must control its pollution to a level Pg. Since the government will not have detailed information on each firm's cost structure it cannot identify the relative abatement costs of the two firms. It can be seen from the diagram that for one firm the marginal cost of pollution abatement at Pg is greater than for the other. Specifically, the marginal abatement cost schedule of firm 1 is MAC1 and that of firm 2 is MAC2. Starting from Pg, if firm 1 increased its pollution by one unit while firm 2 reduced its pollution by one unit, the additional cost incurred by firm 2 would be less than the cost saving achieved by firm 1. In this way, the same level of pollution is achieved but at a lower cost to the economy. As long as MAC1 is greater than MAC2 such cost savings are possible. Once the

MACs are equal, the chosen level of pollution abatement is achieved at the lowest cost.

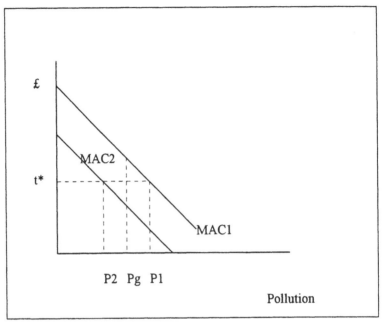

**Figure 3.3   The least-cost property of taxes**

Now suppose that instead of imposing a regulation the government imposes a tax on pollution equal to t*. Each firm will produce output, with its corresponding pollution, as long as the MAC is greater than the tax since the firm would prefer to pay the tax than incur the higher abatement cost. For firm 1 this means that pollution will occur up to level P1 while firm 2, for whom pollution abatement is cheaper, will only pollute up to level P2. The tax can be set in such a way that P1+P2 is equal[5] to 2Pg. In this way the same level of pollution is achieved under the two policy regimes but under the tax situation MACs are equalised across the two firms, i.e. they are both equal to t, and by the logic of the previous paragraph this implies that pollution abatement is cheaper under the tax situation.[6]

In much of the following chapters, this approach of taxing polluters will form the basis of our analysis. Our focus will be on providing polluters with an incentive to reduce their pollution by taxing them in such a way that the external costs of their activities become internal to their decision-making process. And where possible, the level of the taxes we suggest attempt to follow the Pigovian requirement of reflecting the value of the external cost.

The taxation of pollution has been described as the stick approach to environmental management. An alternative approach in the manner of a carrot has been proposed, that of subsidies. Not only were subsidies proposed as an alternative to taxes but it was argued that essentially symmetric results could be achieved with either approach. Referring again to Figure 3.3 we can develop the logic underlying the subsidy proposal. Suppose that instead of taxing pollution at tax rate t*, firms are paid a subsidy equal to t* for each unit of pollution reduction. Starting at higher levels of production, firms see that the amount of the subsidy is greater than the MAC and so pollution reductions yield net benefits, to the firms and society. However, for each firm, once MAC exceeds t* there is no longer a net benefit to pollution reduction and so such reductions cease. As in the tax situation, firm 1 reduces its pollution to P1 while firm 2 reduces its pollution to P2. As MACs are equalised we would appear to have the same low-cost solution as we did under the tax regime. The only difference between the tax and subsidy approaches would appear to be that the costs of pollution abatement are borne by the firms on the one hand and by the taxpayer, via the government, on the other.

While the two firm, static approach yields insights that are still valid in a more expanded model for the case of taxes, this is not the case with subsidies. When we take account of other firms and the dynamic character of decision making, we see that the apparent symmetry between the tax and subsidy approaches no longer holds.

While taxes increase the average costs for firms, subsidies reduce average costs. Now consider a marginal firm in an industry that causes pollution.[7] Under the tax approach, the increase in average cost will push the firm into a loss making position and so it will exit the industry. This will lead to a reduction in pollution. But in the case of a subsidy, average costs are lower and so the marginal firm is moved into a more profitable position. In addition, the reduction in average costs may allow a firm that previously would have been in a loss making position to enter the industry, thereby adding to pollution. In this way, although the subsidy may reduce pollution at the level of the individual firm, it can increase pollution by attracting more firms into the industry.[8] In addition, the availability of subsidies may create the expectation of further subsidies and so reduce incentives for firms to undertake pollution abatement themselves. In an extreme situation, pollution could be encouraged as firms attempt to gain from subsidies.

An additional point should be made regarding subsidies. For the government to pay a subsidy, it must raise revenue through taxes. However, as taxes distort the allocation of resources and hence move the economy away from the most efficient allocation, the cost of the subsidy should not be taken to be simply the same as its value in pounds. It has been estimated in Ireland that an adjustment factor of 1.5 should be used to establish the true cost of providing a subsidy with public money (Honohan, 1996).

From this we can conclude that taxing pollution leads to the achievement of a given level of pollution at a lower cost to society than a regulatory approach which imposes equal pollution reduction requirements on firms. Subsidies do not share this efficiency property. And on a more philosophical point, subsidies, by requiring the victims of pollution to pay for the clean-up imply an allocation of property rights that is in contradiction of the Polluter Pays Principle.

*3.4.1.1 Differential taxes* The tax/charge tool just described aims to raise the price of a good or input relative to all others and so to generate a substitution away from the good or input in question and towards any others. It is also possible, however, to use taxes and charges in an effort to generate a more targeted substitution effect.

If two goods[9] are close substitutes and one is a clean good while the other is a dirty good, it will be possible to generate a substitution between the two by altering the rates of tax between them. An example of this would be the differential rate of excise duty on leaded and unleaded petrol. The question arises though of what size the differential should be. In the case of the Pigovian tax above, we were looking for an absolute tax level; in the differential tax case, it is relative tax rates that matter. As such, it is necessary to establish what level of substitution between the two goods is optimal and then to establish what tax differential will establish this.

*3.4.1.2 Fines* Fines for polluting will have similar incentive effects to charges and taxes although the philosophy underlying them is quite different. While taxes and charges allow emissions, fines reflect an underlying view that emissions above and beyond a certain level are 'wrong' and so punishment should be imposed on those who violate the predetermined standard. In this way, fines blend elements of the regulatory approach (requiring standards to be set) with the economic instrument approach (providing economic incentives not to pollute).

As in the case of differential taxes, the question arises of what level the fines should be. Before answering that question, however, it firstly has to be determined what the probability of detection will be. In deciding how to react to the existence of fines potential polluters will balance the level of the fines and the probability of having to pay them with the economic benefits of polluting. If either the fines or the probability of detection (or prosecution) is low, the potential polluter may decide that the risk is worth taking and so will pollute. Hence, the size of the incentive not to pollute will depend on two parameters and decisions on the level of fines cannot be taken in isolation from decisions regarding the extent of monitoring. In the extreme, if monitoring was perfect the fine would essentially act as a charge on pollution beyond the standard, and would have similar effects to a tax if it was structured in such a way that bigger violations of the standard implied higher fines.

*3.4.2 Tradeable permits*

An alternative way of achieving specified levels of pollution at a lower cost than regulation is that of tradeable permits. We develop the theory behind tradeable permits using Figure 3.4. We begin by assuming that the government decides that it will allow P* units of pollution. It tells firms that they must buy permits which will allow them to emit units of pollution and that these permits[10] are priced at Pr. From the diagram we can see that firm 1 will buy more permits than firm 2 and that MACs are equalised. Hence, we have our least-cost condition satisfied and so we can see how permits share the tax efficiency property.

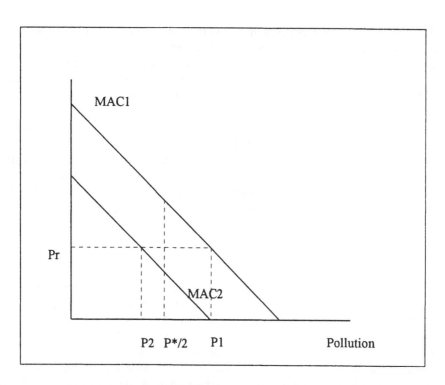

**Figure 3.4   A tradeable permit scheme**

Permits as economic instruments work differently from this in practice so we will
now show how they work and how again MACs are equalised. The government
gives permits to each firm, allowing them to emit P*/2 units of pollution each,
assuming that each permit allows for the generation of one unit of pollution. In this
way the government constrains the level of pollution to be P*. So far this is the same
as the regulatory approach described above in which each firm is told how much it
can emit. Tradeable permits move a step further, however, and as the name
suggests, firms are allowed to trade their pollution allocation. In the case of the two
firms shown, firm 2 will be prepared to sell permits as long as the price it can
charge is greater than its MAC. By selling a permit it will have to reduce pollution
by one unit. But as long as the selling price is greater than its MAC, there is a net
benefit to selling the permit. By a similar reasoning firm 1 will find it optimal to
buy permits as long as the price is lower than its MAC. These trades will continue
as long as MAC1 is greater than MAC2 and cease once they are equal, at which
point the permit price will be Pr. The equality of MACs implies, as before, that the
least cost approach to pollution abatement has been achieved. Once again, we see
that the firm for which pollution abatement is cheaper does more abatement so our
intuitive expectation is confirmed.

The United States has pioneered the use of tradeable permits. The 1977 Clean Air Act set up a scheme whereby companies that had restricted emissions more than was required were given credits for the excess reduction. These credits could then be traded in a number of ways. One such way was to sell these credits to firms that were setting up. In this way, emissions in an area could be capped without unduly restricting industrial entries.[11] Such schemes are not used in Europe to the same degree; this may reflect a greater acceptance of taxation measures in Europe relative to the United States. In the case of Ireland, the use of such schemes will generally be constrained by the lack of sufficiently large markets in emission permits. For this reason, we will not, in general, be suggesting the setting up of such schemes. However, it is possible that an analysis of industry at a level below our sectoral focus could point to a viable scheme so we do not wish to suggest that the issue be ignored.

*3.4.3 Deposit-refund schemes*

Deposit-refund schemes are a more narrowly based economic instrument. They operate through the imposition of a surcharge on a product at its point of purchase, and the subsequent refund of this surcharge once the product or its packaging are returned to a defined point. Typically they are concerned that the disposal of the product or its packaging (or their re-use or recycling) is done in a way that generates the minimum amount of pollution. For example, when applied to beverage containers the aim would be to reduce littering and to increase re-use and recycling. In the case of batteries, the aim would be to avoid dumping which could lead to groundwater pollution and instead ensure safe disposal.

Deposit-refund schemes, rather than being judged relative to regulation in terms of cost effectiveness, are seen to have an advantage in terms of bringing about levels of return that could not be achieved using regulation. For example, in the case of beverage containers deposit-refund schemes have achieved return rates of over 90 per cent.[12] A regulation requiring each household to return 90 per cent of their beverage containers would obviously be unworkable due to monitoring problems.[13] The difficulty in designing and implementing these schemes is in determining whether the costs involved in generating these rates of return, such as storage and transport, exceed the benefits. But if an evaluation of the benefits of, for example, the recycling of beverage containers indicates that a scheme that can achieve high rates of return is desirable, then a deposit-refund scheme will likely achieve this at lowest cost.

## 3.5 Relaxing the assumption that equal amounts of emissions create equal amounts of pollution

In Section 3.2, we made an assumption that there was a one to one relationship between emissions and pollution. In reality, this assumption is often violated. For example, a firm emitting untreated waste-water into a large river with a heavy current will cause much less pollution than a firm emitting the same volume of the same effluent into a stream. In circumstances such as these setting taxes or charges on the basis of emissions, or issuing permits on the same basis, will not lead to the least cost approach to pollution abatement. In the case of the two firms, it is clear that the firm whose emissions are more polluting should face a higher tax or a higher cost for emission permits in order for the least cost properties of the economic instruments to be restored.

In the case of taxes and charges, two proposals have been made to overcome the breakdown in the simple relationship between emissions and pollution.[14] The first proposal is to tax on the basis of two or more parameters instead of the single parameter, emissions. The two parameters could be emissions and the existing level of pollution of the receiving medium, whereby for given levels of emissions the tax would be higher, the more polluted was the receiving medium. Alternatively, if the emissions of firms in a particular zone have similar impacts, but impacts differ across zones, the taxes or charges could be varied across those zones.

In the case of either the two-parameter tax or the zone-based approach, there is an implicit trade-off between designing the tax to achieve the least cost properties and the administrative complexity that could emerge. Clearly, a balance should be achieved but in designing the tax it is instructive to be mindful of this complication introduced when the simple emission/pollution relationship is violated.

This issue has also been addressed in the case of tradeable permits. To see how the difficulty might be overcome, we will consider the design of three alternative tradeable permit schemes. These are (i) emissions-permit system (EPS), (ii) ambient-permit system (APS) and (iii) pollution-offset system (PO).

(i) Emissions-permit system[15]: Were there a one to one correspondence between emissions and pollution, this system would be the appropriate one. Permits are defined in terms of emissions and emission entitlements are traded on a one for one basis. The result of such a system is that all firms face the same cost of emissions. However, as was the case with taxes, if emissions differ in terms of their polluting impact across firms, this will not produce the least cost approach to pollution abatement. Again like the tax system, if emissions from firms within a zone have similar polluting impacts, restricting permit trades to within that zone may substantially overcome this problem. The ambient-permit and pollution-offset systems are more sophisticated ways of overcoming this deficiency, so let us consider each.

(ii) Ambient-permit system: Under this system, permits are issued for a number of receptor points and each permit allows some contribution to pollution at that point. Firms must then buy permits for a range of receptor points and emit only to a level where the resulting pollution is within their limit for each receptor point. Given that the permits are defined in terms of pollution and not emissions, the emission entitlements will not be traded on a one for one basis. A firm whose emissions are relatively more polluting will have to acquire relatively more permits if it is to increase emissions by the same amount as a firm whose emissions are less polluting. Hence, emissions will be more expensive for such a firm, which is desirable.

A difficulty with this system can be seen when one considers the receptor points more closely. A network of points that was spread too thinly might 'miss' pollution that was arising due to the changing location of production. To overcome this, a large number of receptor points would be needed. However, as firms have to buy permits for each receptor point, a large number of such points could put quite a burden on producers.

As the EPS may not provide the least cost approach to pollution abatement and the APS entails cumbersome requirements, an alternative system combining the advantages of both is required. This exists in the form of the pollution offset system (PO).

(iii) Pollution-offset system: Under this system, permits are defined in terms of emissions (as with EPS). However, trades in permits are subject to the constraint that the trade should not result in pollution at a receptor point exceeding some standard (as with APS). In this way, trades at the boundary of the pollution constraint will occur on the basis of pollution and not on the basis of emissions.

## 3.6 The 'double dividend'

We noted in the introduction that it has been argued that environmental taxes possess a positive feature in addition to their role in protecting the environment. The argument is as follows. Given that revenue is generated through the imposition of these taxes, this revenue can be used to reduce other taxes. If the revenue is then used to reduce what are known as distortionary taxes, then the cost of the tax system, in terms of the distortions it creates, is reduced. Hence one benefit of environmental taxes is environmental improvements and the other is the welfare increases, above and beyond the welfare benefits associated with the environmental improvements, that are associated with a switch away from the distortionary tax.[16] It was Pearce who first coined the phrase 'the double dividend' to sum up the argument (Pearce, 1991).

Since the idea of the double dividend was originally advanced, it has undergone a large amount of theoretical investigation, much of which has called into question its existence. Given the highly theoretical nature of much of this work, we will not review the literature on the topic.[17] We simply want to point out that there is a controversy over the existence of the double dividend and so there is a difficulty in using it as an extra argument for the introduction of economic instruments.

We can, however, describe one piece of research that has been undertaken on the issue in Ireland. In their 1992 paper, Fitz Gerald and McCoy use the ESRI HERMES-Ireland macroeconomic model to estimate the effects on the Irish economy of a carbon/energy tax of US$10 per barrel of oil. They investigated two scenarios, one in which the revenue was used to reduce the national debt and one in which it was used to reduce the social insurance tax on employment. Turning specifically to their estimates of the employment and unemployment effects under the tax reduction scenario, they find that employment would increase by between .5 and .8 per cent although reduced emigration would essentially neutralise the effect on unemployment. As such, we can take this as providing some evidence of a double dividend, if we take the second dividend to mean increased employment. The carbon tax will be discussed again in Chapter 6.

## 3.7 Other issues

### 3.7.1 When to regulate

It would be incorrect to leave the impression that all environmental threats can be, and should be, dealt with using economic instruments. There are certain circumstances in which regulation is the preferred policy tool and so we must set out what these circumstances are.

Regulations such as standards, permits and quotas possess an important feature: they provide greater certainty as to their environmental outcome than many economic instruments. It is when this greater certainty is of particular importance that regulation should be relied upon. There are two broad circumstances in which this will apply. First, where the consequences of the environmental threat are sufficiently dangerous, it would be wrong to leave control of the threat to fiscal instruments. For example, emissions which may threaten human life should be subject to regulations. Second, when the environmental threat is such that its consequences are both important and irreversible, it would again be incorrect to rely on fiscal instruments. An example of this would be the protection of endangered species; if a species was to be lost because hunting charges turned out to be too low, the cost of the mistake could be enormous. A combination of regulation and economic instruments may often be the best policy.

### 3.7.2 Employment, competitiveness and who should pay for environmental protection

It will be argued that economic instruments for environmental protection, other than subsidies, should not be introduced in Ireland because this will put businesses here at a competitive disadvantage and hence job losses would occur. There are a number of elements to this discussion so let us deal with each in turn.

The first issue relates to the costs of environmental protection policy in general and in particular, who should bear those costs. As we discussed in the section on the Coase Theorem above, one can think about who should pay in terms of property rights. If the population in general is granted the right to clean air and clean water, those who intrude upon that right must pay to do so. Alternatively, if the right to pollute is given, for example to industry, those wanting clean air and clean water must pay.

As Ireland accepts the Polluter Pays Principle, there is an implicit recognition that the property right belongs to the nation at large and that polluters must pay if they are to use the environment for extractive or sink-hole purposes. If we take this as given, it is in the interests of polluters and the economy that the cost of environmental protection is as low as possible. As we have demonstrated, economic instruments will generally provide the lowest cost approach and it is for this reason that we believe economic instruments to be in the interests of polluters as well as society in general.

While this least cost property of economic instruments may hold in general, there will be sectors, enterprises and households which may have to pay more under the proposals which will be made in the following chapters and the argument may be made that this extra cost could lead to job losses. Our response would be the following. By allowing firms to use the environment at a cost that does not reflect the burden of environmental degradation which they impose, these firms are being implicitly subsidised. If a subsidy is required to keep these firms in business, as is implied by the competitiveness argument, it would be preferable to subsidise another input, such as labour, that does not lead to the environmental damage which we are concerned about. By allowing firms to use the environment at less than full cost, we are essentially giving a resource away and giving enterprises the right to use the resource as they wish. This is in direct contradiction of the polluters pays principle and creates a situation in which environmental degradation is guaranteed.

## 3.8 Summary

In this section, we will briefly outline again the advantages of economic instruments and in particular the taxing and charging approaches to environmental management which informs much of the discussion in the following chapters.

Economic instruments for environmental protection are seen as having three advantages over the traditional regulatory approach. First, they can generate the same level of pollution abatement at a lower cost than regulations. In essence, the reason for this is that when each enterprise is faced with a tax or a charge on, for example, emissions, it can decide for itself how to react. Firms for which pollution abatement is cheaper will undertake more abatement relative to other firms. Under regulations, where all firms are required to undertake a given level of abatement or to install a particular technology, the information advantage which each enterprise has regarding the ease with which it can reduce waste or emissions is left unused. Just as a decentralised approach to production and consumption in general leads to economically efficient outcomes, so too can the efficient use of the environment be generated by bringing the advantages of the market mechanism to bear.

The second main advantage of economic instruments is that their use creates an on-going incentive for pollution abatement, a feature not generally shared by regulations. If a charge is in place, there will always be a potential advantage to reducing emissions because liabilities under the charge will be reduced.

Finally, the use of economic instruments such as taxes and charges can lead to the generation of revenue which can in turn be used to reduce other taxes. While this advantage is true at a basic level of analysis, more complex analyses have questioned the broader economic implications of such tax changes. As such, we will not put too much emphasis on this advantage and will instead concentrate on the role of economic instruments in environmental protection.

The economic instruments which can be used are: taxes (including differential tax rates), charges, subsidies, tradeable permit schemes, fines and deposit-refund schemes. As our primary goal is to ensure that the Polluter Pays Principle is adhered to, we will place most stress on instruments that facilitate this, notably taxes and charges and tradeable permits.

**Notes**

1     Much of the discussion is taken from Pearce and Turner (1990).

2     We are assuming that the firm is in a perfectly competitive market and so it faces the same price regardless of its level of output. The assumption of a rising marginal cost is a standard assumption regardless of market structure and is based on the notion of diminishing marginal returns.

3     Coase, Ronald (1960) 'The Problem of Social Cost', *Journal of Law and Economics* Vol. 3 pp. 1-44. It should be noted that this paper was partly responsible for Coase winning the Nobel prize in Economics.

4     Pigou, Arthur (1920) *The Economics of Welfare* (First Edition) London: Macmillan.

5     Even if the tax rates which will induce the firms to pollute at levels P1 and P2 are not known initially, the rates can be adjusted over time so as to bring about the desired level of pollution. Having said that, it is an advantage of regulation over economic instruments that a greater degree of certainty over outcomes can be attributed to the former relative to the latter.

6     The simple two firm model can be generalised to a model of n firms. Baumol and Oates (1988) present a mathematical proof of the proposition that:'A tax rate set at a level that achieves the desired reduction in the total emission of pollutants will satisfy the necessary conditions for the minimisation of the program's cost to society'.

7     By marginal we mean price is equal to average cost and so the firm is just breaking even.

8     On this point Baumol and Oates (1988) demonstrate the following proposition: 'In a competitive industry, where polluting emissions are a fixed and rising function of the level of industrial output, equal tax and subsidy rates will normally *not* lead to the same output levels or to the same reductions in total industry emissions. Other things being equal, the subsidy will yield an output and emission level not only greater than those that would occur under the tax, but greater even than they would be in the absence of either tax or subsidy.'

9     Anything we say with regard to goods in this section applies also to inputs.

10    As with the tax on pollution, the government may not know initially how many permits will be bought at the price Pr and hence how much pollution will result. But again like the tax, the price can be adjusted in each period. However, in practice the quantity as opposed to the price of the permit will be set and so this uncertainty does not arise.

11    This point is taken from Pearce and Turner (1990).

12    Porter (1983) found that Michigan's scheme for beverage containers achieved a return rate of 95 per cent.

13     One could make the argument that the enforcement costs of a regulation requiring households to return a given percentage of their beverage containers would be large relative to the costs involved in achieving the same return percentage using a deposit-refund scheme.

14     Baumol and Oates (1988).

15     This is the type of system described in Section 3.4.2.

16     It should be noted that the notion of a welfare increase is not the same as an increase in GNP or employment. Its precise meaning will be discussed later in the text.

17     Readers interested in a fuller review of the theoretical, and the empirical, work on the double dividend should consult Goulder (1995).

# References

Baumol, W. and Oates, W. (1988), *The Theory of Environmental Policy* (2nd Edition), Cambridge: Cambridge.

Coase, R. (1960), 'The Problem of Social Cost', *Journal of Law and Economics* Vol. 3 pp. 1-44.

Goulder, L. H. (1995), 'Environmental Taxation and the Double Dividend: A Readers Guide', *International Tax and Public Finance* Vol. 2, No. 2, pp. 157-184.

Fitz Gerald, J. and McCoy, D. (1992), 'The Macroeconomic Implications for Ireland' in Fitz Gerald, J. and McCoy, D. (eds.) *The Economic Effects of Carbon Taxes*, ESRI: Dublin.

Honohan, P. (1996), 'Methodological Issues in Evaluation of Irish Industrial Policy' Working Paper No. 69, ESRI: Dublin.

Pearce, D. (1991), 'The Role of Carbon Taxes in Adjusting to Global Warming', *Economic Journal*, Vol. 101, pp. 938-948.

Pearce, D. and Turner, K. (1990), *Economics of Natural Resources and the Environment*, Harvester Wheatsheaf: London.

Pigou, A. (1920), *The Economics of Welfare* (First Edition) Macmillan: London.

Porter, R.C. (1983), 'Michigan's Experience with Mandatory Deposits on Beverage Containers', *Land Economics*, Vol. 59, No. 2.

# 4 Agriculture and forestry

*S. Scott*

This chapter begins by surveying the environmental effects of the sector and any evaluations of them. A rundown follows of the existing fiscal treatment of the sector and its environmental impacts. We will see that in the case of agriculture, what can broadly be termed fiscal policy in the last couple of decades has had profound environmental effects, especially through its encouragement of intensive agriculture, though, farming and forestry can provide many environmental benefits to society, such as maintenance of bio-diversity. Options for addressing the problems, based on information from Ireland and abroad, will be assessed, leading to suggestions as to which economic instruments should be adopted. The underlying aim is neither to raise revenue, nor, necessarily, to achieve a stated environmental objective; the aim is to raise well-being by reducing pollution, so long as the benefits of so doing outweigh the costs, with external effects taken into account. This is an ideal approach, because external benefits and harms are not easily valued. Though the ideal is likely only to be approximated, the general direction of the use of economic instruments will be indicated, as well as the immediate steps which can be taken.

## 4.A Agriculture

### 4.A.1 Environmental impact of agriculture and the costs of damage

Climate change, acidification, impacts on air quality, damage to nature and biodiversity and to the quality and quantity of water - these are the harmful effects attributed to agriculture. By contrast, it is sometimes less widely realised that agriculture, in its role as major occupier of land, can be a force for good in the countryside, providing stewardship of the rural landscape and maintaining habitation in rural areas and villages. We will discuss these effects in turn; they are summarised in Table 4.1 below. The table indicates, in general terms for any region, which elements are released or affected by agricultural activity, their importance and, in the final column, the potential for improvement.

Agriculture's effect on climate change arises through the sector's use of energy and burning of straw, which release carbon dioxide, through methane emissions from livestock, which is a prominent effect in Ireland, and through release of nitrous oxide from fertilisers.

**Table 4.1**
**Effects of agriculture on the environment**

| Theme | Element | Importance of Agriculture | Potential for Change |
|---|---|---|---|
| Climate change | Carbon dioxide $CO_2$ | ** | ** |
| | Methane $CH_4$ | *** | ** |
| | Nitrous oxide $N_2O$ | *** | *** |
| | Overall | * | * |
| Acidification and air quality | Ammonia $NH_3$ and Nitrogen | ** | *** |
| | Volatile organic compounds VOCs | * | - |
| | Overall | * | * |
| Nature and biodiversity | Soil loss | **** | *** |
| | Habitat loss | **** | **** |
| | Overconcentration of species, genetic engineering | ** | ** |
| | Overall | **** | *** |
| Water quality/management | Water shortage | *** | *** |
| | Nitrates $NO_3$ and Phosphates $PO_4$ | **** | **** |
| | Pesticide residues | **** | *** |
| | Overall | *** | *** |

*Note:* More asterisks means more importance or potential for change.
*Source:* Adapted from DRI et al. (1994) (Travers Morgan Environment).

Agriculture's effect on air pollution and acid rain arises through the release of ammonia by slurry spreading, of nitrogen from fertilisers, and of volatile organic compounds by a variety of activities. In addition to the effect on climate change from methane emissions from cattle, the main impact of agriculture in Ireland is on the last two themes in the table. Its impact on nature and biodiversity arises from many causes, including soil loss due to overgrazing or spread of contaminated wastes, and habitat loss brought about by use of pesticides, fertilisers, monoculture, removal of hedges and ditches and other land developments. The other major impact of agriculture in Ireland is the deterioration of water quality - impact on water *quantity* not being the problem that it is in several mainland European countries - through release of nitrogen and phosphorus from manure and fertiliser application, and through pesticide residues.

Agricultural activity, undertaken on a small scale and non-intensively, does not in general impose serious adverse effects. It is large changes and heavy concentrations which, depending on the characteristics of the surroundings, can cause degradation. During the 1980s much land was converted from arable uses to pasture for an increasing number of beef cattle, and for a dramatic increase in sheep, which more than doubled.[1] Poultry and pigs also rose in numbers, with heavy concentrations in counties Monaghan, Cork and Cavan. Ireland has the highest concentration in Europe for sows; over 80 per cent are in units of more than 100 sows, compared to Germany where only 16 per cent of sows are in units of over 100. Relative to European standards the numbers and herd size in Ireland are small: it is the extent of localised concentrations, and the sensitivity of the surroundings, which makes them significant. Another important change with environmental implications is the strong swing away from hay-making to silage. The pollution potential from silage effluent (in terms of $BOD_5$) is some 20 times greater than that for untreated domestic sewage.[2]

Thirty million tonnes of manure must be managed by farmers each year. Though the nutrient value of this is put at some £117 million, disposal as a waste is more frequent than use as a nutrient. Total BOD and phosphorus content of animal wastes (excluding that from grazing animals) is put at 663,000 tonnes and 32,000 tonnes respectively, which is six times the levels from sewage and industrial wastes combined. Some 85 per cent of dairy and beef cattle manure is in the form of slurry from slatted sheds, most of the remainder being in farmyards. The pollution potential can be controlled by careful timing and manner of spreading, but this tends to cause extra work and inconvenience to farmers.

Meanwhile fertiliser is relatively cheap and easy to use and it is not surprising to find that fertiliser use has increased significantly. Annual phosphorus (P) fertiliser use quadrupled between 1950 and the early eighties, since when it has been static at about 60,000 tonnes. Nitrogen (N) fertiliser use shows a similar pattern, having levelled off at about 380,000 tonnes. The other important source of phosphorus is animal feed, which amounts to 9,000 tonnes of phosphorus in concentrate fed to cattle and sheep, and 5,850 tonnes in concentrate fed to pigs and poultry. Where there are heavy concentrations of manure there would be high levels of phosphorus.

The upshot of these developments is the increased risk of pollution from manure concentrations requiring disposal, from fertiliser application and from silage effluent. Are these features having an effect on the environment, can we put a value on the effect or, at any rate, can we say whether or not it is serious?

*4.A.1.1 Effects on water quality* Despite the relatively good quality of most Irish surface waters, a continuing decline is noted by the Environmental Protection Agency (1996). This is of particular concern because of the salmonid status of Irish rivers. The trends are best understood by looking at Table 4.2 which shows the evolution of the quality status of 2,900 km of river length from 1971, in the first two columns. Since 1987-90, 96 per cent of total river length has been monitored, amounting to 12,700 km, and the trend in their quality status is shown in the last two columns.

**Table 4.2**
**Trends in quality of water in selected rivers**

| Quality status | 2,900 km of river | | 12,700 km of river | |
|---|---|---|---|---|
| | 1971 | 1994 | 1987-90 | 1991-94 |
| Generally unpolluted | 84.3 | 57.5 | 77.3 | 72.2 |
| Slight to moderate pollution at times | 9.7 | 41.4 | 21.7 | 27.2 |
| Serious pollution at times | 6.0 | 1.1 | 0.9 | 0.6 |
| TOTAL | 100.0 | 100.0 | 100.0 | 100.0 |

*Source:* Data used for *Water Quality in Ireland 1991-1994*, Environmental Protection Agency, (1996b).

The table shows the decline of the two extreme categorisations, that is, unpolluted river length and river length which is seriously polluted at times. Meanwhile the length with 'slight to moderate pollution at times' has increased. The increase since 1971 for these categories is from 9.7 per cent of length to 41.4 per cent in 1994, for the shorter stretch of monitored rivers. Results of the wider coverage in the last two columns show a firm increase in slight to moderate pollution, to over a quarter of river length. This leaves no room for complacency. Agricultural runoff, industrial waste and sewage are all involved. However, the fact that in many cases known 'point' sources are not implicated suggests that agriculture is the major cause: farms are very dispersed, and pollution off the land flows from 'non-point' sources. These features in fact make it difficult to monitor and control, and will constrain policy as we will see.

The nutrients which are implicated are phosphorus and nitrogen. Levels of phosphorus in water above 20mg per cubic metre (or 0.02 mg per litre) in slow-moving waters can lead to eutrophication, a situation where excessive supply of phosphorus and nitrogen leads to growth of algae, thus disturbing the oxygen balance, with loss of fish, diminished aesthetic quality, reduced amenity value and a deterioration in the quality of drinking water.[3] Even small quantities of phosphorus can be harmful. The problem is apparent in certain lakes, since in these waters phosphorus levels can build up. In rivers, particularly those that are fast flowing, the nutrients are ultimately flushed out to sea, though, more recently, nutrient excess has been identified as the main cause of deterioration in river water quality.

Average phosphorus levels in soil samples have increased ninefold since 1950 to 9 mg per kg. A balance sheet study undertaken for 1988, detailing the inputs of phosphorus (P) to farms and the amount embodied in outputs of farms, expressed in tonnes, is summarised in Table 4.3 below:

**Table 4.3**
**Phosphorus inputs to farms, outputs from farms and remainder (tonnes P)**

| | | |
|---|---|---|
| **P inputs to farms** | | **77,296** |
| of which: | Chemical P fertiliser | 62,446 |
| | Concentrates fed to cattle and sheep | 9,000 |
| | Concentrates fed to pigs and poultry | 5,850 |
| **P outputs from farms** | | **27,810** |
| of which: | Tillage crops | 12,177 |
| | Cattle and sheep production | 8,717 |
| | Milk | 5,170 |
| | Pig and poultry production | 1,746 |
| **Remainder** | | **49,486** |
| of which: | Soluble P loss to water | 3,445 |
| | Build-up of soil P | 46,041 |

*Source:* Tunney (1990).

The table shows that inputs are over double the amount accounted for in output from farms. The problem then is that the remainder can find its way to inland waters. The ideal is to have a balance so that soils have adequate fertility for production, and that losses to water are low enough not to cause pollution. One study showed that farmers could get 6 years growth with no phosphorus application, if they had proper manure control (McGarrigle 1996). This represents an unnecessary cost to farmers, and some £25 million is wasted annually in unnecessary application of inorganic phosphate fertilisers (EPA 1996). By contrast it should also be said that 25 per cent of soil samples have been found to be deficient in P, which is an indication of the diversity of conditions and also has implications for policy.

Phosphorus losses from agriculture have been identified as a significant cause of water quality decline in Lough Conn, Lough Derg, the Lee catchment and county Monaghan. Large surpluses to agriculture's requirements of phosphorus were found, at 7 kilograms per hectare per year for the Lough Derg catchment, and at 28 kilograms in county Monaghan. This was attributable to animal wastes and chemical fertilisers. Concern about eutrophication in Inniscarra reservoir during the summer months, the annual build-up of phosphorus and the threat posed to domestic and industrial users of water, led to a detailed study of the river Dripsey catchment by Reynolds (1996). Results suggest that more than half the excess P comes direct from farmyards and overland flow from fields is probably still excessive. Slurry spreading after the first silage cut is recommended rather than in October and November. Even with no application of chemical P fertiliser it will take many years to reduce the P level in soils from their present figure, of over 10 mg per kg, to a recommended 6 mg per kg. These recommendations indicate that policy should encourage specific behavioural changes.

Turning now to nitrogen, a nitrogen balance sheet by Sherwood and Tunney (1991) shows that 72 per cent of N inputs are not recovered in the soil or in animal product, and must therefore be lost to water and the atmosphere. However, a study of the vulnerability of soils and groundwater to nitrate leaching showed that only 4 per cent of Irish soils are at high risk. Recent measurements show that effects on surface waters are generally low, and well within the limits set for abstraction and drinking waters. However, contamination affects a considerable number of rivers and streams at times, particularly in the south-east where there is a greater than average proportion of land under tillage. In addition, the south-east displays a continued upward trend in nitrate levels.

A further warning against complacency arises from the fact that pollutants carried in overland or subsurface flows may not reach groundwater supplies of lakes and streams for years after their generation, according to Shortle and Abler (1996). Contemporary problems can reflect decisions and events that occurred many years in the past. Time lags of 30 to 60 years have been reported in Southern California and, similarly, the benefits of current control actions may not be fully realised for many years. While Irish geology is different, it is important to be on guard.

*4.A.1.2 Value of harm to water*   What is the harm done by excess nutrients and eutrophication? What is the value of the ensuing damage? As is frequently the case with environmental damage, many aspects are uncertain or controversial. For example, nitrate pollution of drinking water has been linked to methaemo-globinaemia in babies (blue baby syndrome) and stomach cancer. A measure of the value of harm is the cost of treating water for abstraction and drinking, where this is considered necessary.

There is also evidence of the harm of eutrophication, other than to health, though no studies have been undertaken for Ireland. Barde and Pearce (1991) describe a number of evaluation studies. One study estimates the willingness-to-pay of around a thousand river-corridor users for water quality improvements. Results, based on interview surveys by WRC/FHRC (1989), indicated that the average household would be willing to pay an additional £6 per year in water rates for further water quality improvements. These studies, called contingent valuation studies, aim to elicit people's valuations contingent on an option being available.

Another study, undertaken in the Netherlands by Baan (1983) is quoted, which aimed to give an overview of potential benefits of improvements in the quality of Dutch surface waters. Benefits were calculated relating to recreation, fishing, commercial fisheries, navigation, reduction in public water supply costs, agricultural productivity gains and better drinking water. Many benefits were not estimated, such as aesthetics, effects on eco-systems, or option value. The once-off total monetary benefits were estimated to be between £76 and £210 million (Dfl 200 and 550 million).

A further study aimed to elicit how much Norwegians would be willing to pay for a halving of nutrient leaching to the North Sea (Magnussen 1992). People stated that they would be willing to pay between £50 and £200 annually in increased sewage taxes, which also indirectly gives a measure of the value of the damage.

While not implying that results from foreign studies are a substitute for a proper evaluation of the harm done by eutrophication caused by agriculture in Ireland, they demonstrate that people can place a high value on the quality of surface waters, and that this is without even taking account of the benefits of tourism angling, image abroad, restoration of habitat and the like. Indeed we note that, without prompting, concern for water quality is ranked as issue number one by Irish respondents to a recent survey of attitudes to the environment (Murphy et al. 1994).

*4.A.1.3 Effects on nature and biodiversity* Agriculture is central to the shaping of the rural landscape. Farming activities take place on more than 80 per cent of the land area in Ireland and continuation of habitat is vital to nature and biodiversity. There is little truly natural habitat remaining in Western Europe so that the wildlife resource is concentrated largely on agricultural land. In general, the systems most compatible with wildlife are the more traditional farming systems, which are characterised by low intensity, low nutrient input, low or zero use of pesticides and herbicides, relatively large areas of semi-natural vegetation and hedgerows, less drainage and irrigation and more continuity (Baldock 1995) - in effect, the opposite of the trend in agricultural development of the past few decades. Chemical contamination and introduction of exotic species may also be harmful.

Grassland being the dominant type of land use, Ireland is a low user of pesticides, annual sales being about one half the EU average, and measured concentrations in the soil are correspondingly low. However DDT and its breakdown products are still present at significant levels in some agricultural soils (especially fruit growing) and in town garden soils. Assessment of the effects on soils and habitats of increased hill grazing by sheep is under way. Grazing sheep have additionally led to erosion of peat soils, which enter rivers and lakes and cause harm to fish. Not being a straightforward case of pollution where clearly defined administrative procedures and legislation exist, extensive damage has occurred before any serious attempt at control.[4]

In Ireland, hedgerows are a part of the traditional landscape and form semi-natural habitats for farm wildlife. Since 1938 a loss of 16 per cent of hedgerow has been reported, equivalent to two kilometres squared. While this is not a huge loss, it is a loss which should not continue indefinitely. This is not to advance the idea that all change is harmful or that farming cannot evolve. However, there are benefits which farmers themselves may be forgoing if they do not conserve semi-natural habitats, by measures such as[5] reduction of pesticide use by exploiting pest predators and parasitoids, enhancement of crop pollinator populations, reduced soil erosion, maintenance of landscape diversity, promotion of game species and the like. As this list indicates, from the farmer's point of view, existence of habitats does not purely entail costs and, for the farmer's family, the preservation of landscape diversity would tend to be a benefit.

Some wildlife species have seen improvements in their numbers in the last decade, such as pine martens, Greenland white-fronted geese and buzzards, to name a few. However there is also a significant number of endangered, vulnerable and extinct species. For example, in relation to plants and ferns in Ireland, 10 species are probably extinct, 6 endangered and 44 are vulnerable (Curtis and McGough 1988). In relation to birds, Table 4.4 gives some examples. Internationally important species include the Irish hare which is under threat from agricultural intensification, the Greenland White-fronted goose from afforestation and peat extraction, and the otter from afforestation, water quality changes and recreational pressure, and so on.

Experience in Ireland echoes some of the problems encountered in the UK where, for example, there has been contraction of 24 out of 28 species of farmland birds between 1970 and 1990, the populations of seven species falling by more than half. Loss of habitats is a prominent cause. Ireland has some features which make it special in world terms and which will probably become more special as they become rarer world-wide and better known. For example, Ireland's waters and estuaries are strategically positioned on the migratory routes of many birds; and the extent and richness of its peatlands are only rivalled in Europe by those of Finland. While indeed extinction, as well as evolution of new species, are natural features of life, extinction of species is now taking place at an unprecedented rate, possibly 1000 times greater than the background or natural rate (Pearce 1993). OECD (1996) puts the rate of extinction of species at a possible 100 per day, probably the fastest rate since the natural catastrophes of 65 million years ago, which rendered the dinosaurs extinct. This is a loss to present generations and, owing to probable irreversibility, to future generations also.

### Table 4.4
### Some examples of birds under threat and nature of threat

*Species* — *Threat*

| | Resource-use changes | | | | | | | | Pollution | | | Killing/disturbance | | | | | | 'Natural' | | | |
|---|---|---|---|---|---|---|---|---|---|---|---|---|---|---|---|---|---|---|---|---|---|
| | 1 | 2 | 3 | 4 | 5 | 6 | 7 | 8 | 9 | 10 | 11 | 12 | 13 | 14 | 15 | 16 | 17 | 18 | 19 | 20 | 21 |
| Merlin | ● | | ● | · | | | | | | | | | | | | | | | | | |
| Grey partridge | ● | | | | | | | | | ● | | ● | | | | | | | | | ● |
| Corncrake | ● | ● | | | | | | | | | | | | | ● | | | | | | · |
| Golden plover | ● | | ● | ● | | | | | | | | | | | | | | | | | · |
| Dunlin | ● | | ● | | | ● | | | | | | | | | | ● | | | | | · |
| Roseate tern | | | | | | | · | | | · | | | | | | | | | ● | ● | ● |
| Little tern | | | | | | ● | · | | | · | | | | | | ● | | | | | ● |
| Barn owl | ● | | | | | | | | | ● | | | | · | ● | | · | · | | | |
| Wood warbler | | | | | · | | | | | | | | | | | | | | | | |

*Source:* Whilde (1993).

**Key to threats:**

*Resource-use changes*

1. Agricultural intensification
2. Agricultural abandonment
3. Afforestation
4. Peat extraction
5. Felling or destruction of woodland
6. Land reclamation and coastal development
7. Fishing intensification
8. Other changes in fishery management
   practices

*Pollution*

9. Water quality changes
10. Chemical and pesticide contamination
11. Oil pollution

*Killing or disturbance by humans*

12. Hunting/fishing
13. Legal (licensed) killing
14. Illegal persecution
15. Accidental killing
16. Recreational pressure and disturbance
17. Loss of roost sites

*'Natural' threats*

18. Climatic change
19. Interspecific competition
20. Natural ecological change
21. Predation, parasitism and disease

**Grades of threat**

● Major or principal threat

· Secondary or less important threat

Several studies have been undertaken which aim to place a value on the conservation of species, eco-systems or habitats. There is much overlap between countryside and habitat. Generally speaking there is a high demand for leisure in the countryside and a sizeable portion of this demand would be for the continuation of habitats. In Great Britain, for example, it is estimated that people spend one-fifth of their free time in the countryside, and 85 per cent make at least one excursion to the countryside per year, of which nearly 30 per cent visit the countryside regularly. For Germany, an informal estimate puts the value of a countryside visit at the equivalent of a cinema ticket, giving a value of some £4 billion per year (DM 10 billion, (Leser 1995)). Even on such a crude basis, the magnitude of values involved is an indication of the significance of the countryside.

However the value of visits to the countryside might be a poor guide to the valuation of some rare and possibly little known species. A study specifically aimed at estimating people's valuation of threatened species in Norway, namely brown bears and wolves (by Dahle et al., described by Navrud (1992)), involved a contingent valuation survey of about 2,000 persons. The mean annual willingness-to-pay per household for preservation as well as for extinction was calculated. As the animals are predators, respondents were given the choice of preservation or extinction. Willingness-to-pay for conservation was eight times that for extinction and the net annual willingness-to-pay per household worked out at £20.60 (210 NOK). While disposable income is a good deal higher in Norwegian households, the scale suggests that there would still be significant demand for bio-diversity in Ireland. This again omits other interests such as tourism and benefits to future generations.

*4.A.1.4 Other effects*   Other aspects of agriculture's impact on the environment will merely be itemised. Climate change was already mentioned above, however it is less well-known that grassland is believed to serve as a sink for carbon dioxide and nitrous oxide, and thus to help reduce climate change. However, ruminants which feed off grassland emit 200 grammes of methane gases per head daily. Ploughing and removal of grassland releases large amounts of carbon dioxide through decay of soil organic matter.

We have not considered the important effect of pollution on agriculture, but this will be indirectly covered by other chapters. Except in a few spots, pollution of soil by heavy metals is low, though there is concern at the effect of increased loading of sewage sludge on land, arising from the Council Directive Concerning Urban Waste Water Treatment.[6]

*4.A.2   Existing fiscal treatment and environmental effects*

The European Community's Common Agricultural Policy (CAP), the introduction of milk quotas in 1984 and the MacSharry reforms of 1992, are major influences on agricultural activity and its effects on the environment. A summary of the relevant aspects of European policy needs to be given here. The CAP it must be said has been highly effective as an economic instrument in terms of support for farm incomes in aggregate, levels of agricultural output, the yields that it promoted and the deceleration of urbanisation. It had manifest drawbacks however in the size of the surpluses generated, and the lopsided distribution[7] of benefits (Fitz Gerald and O'Connor 1991). The main original aims of providing stable affordable supplies of food and a fair standard of living for the agricultural community (EC Treaty article 39) seem to have been lost sight of. As predicted, the mismatch of using output price support, when it was incomes that required support, has become clear. With output prices held high, the cost of inputs appeared relatively low, causing a tendency for farmers to apply excessive amounts of inputs such as fertilisers (Delpeuch 1994). Profit-maximising farmers could raise net revenues by increasing output, but with land being a fixed factor, methods had to become more intensive.

Of course, even without the CAP, external effects arising from agricultural activity, as with any other activity, would require to be rectified, but the operation of the CAP exacerbated the problems. The damage that ensued was effectively subsidised by the taxpayer who, while evidently willing to support agricultural incomes, has become increasingly dissatisfied with paying for an undesired outcome. In addition to the environmental toll, the cost to the European taxpayer and consumer[8] (at well above Ireland's GNP), the surpluses and the likely admission to the EU of large agricultural producers such as Poland and Hungary, have recently caused much concern and added to pressure for reform.

*4.A.2.1 CAP reforms in 1992, environmental implications and other grant schemes* The most far-reaching reforms were those introduced by MacSharry in 1992, and they have environmental implications. The main features for the two items, cereals and animal products, are as follows. Support prices for cereals were to decrease by 29 per cent (from 155 ECUs to 110 ECUs per tonne). Income loss was compensated by subsidies in fixed amounts per hectare, distinguishing between small-scale and large-scale farmers. Large-scale farmers, operating more than 15 hectares, are only eligible to hectare compensations if they set aside at least 10 per cent (previously 15 per cent) of their average acreage which was allocated to crops during 1989 to 1991. Compensation per hectare is computed as the compensation per tonne (a figure between 25 and 45 ECUs) multiplied by 6.08 (which is Ireland's reference yield in tonnes per hectare). Small farms receive compensation without any set-aside obligation. The compensation is paid regardless of actual output and is determined purely on an area basis and producers whose yields had been above the reference yield would face an effective reduction in total revenue (Boyle 1995).

The reform measures for animal products are not quite so strong, with the intervention price for butter and dairy products reduced by 9 and 7.5 per cent respectively and intervention prices for beef lowered by 15 per cent. Premia for bulls and cows are subject to stocking limits, and stocking densities which do not exceed 1.4 livestock units per hectare receive an additional extensification premium. Farmers are still able to stock more but they do not then receive the premium. This is the first time that stocking limits have been specified. Given that

Ireland is more active in livestock farming than in growing cereals, this structure of reforms is perhaps to Ireland's advantage. There are accompanying measures for forestry, conservation and amenity (the agri-environment programme[9]) and early retirement. Import tariffs at the Community border are maintained but under the General Agreement on Tariffs and Trade, (now the World Trade Organisation) it is intended that they be further reduced.

The agri-environment programme in the McSharry reforms includes aid to farmers who reduce applications of fertilisers and pesticides, adopt organic farming, move to extensive production, rear rare breeds, set aside farmland for 20 years for purposes connected with the environment and manage land for public access and leisure activities. To qualify, member countries have to prepare implementation programmes, which will reflect their priorities. Farmers' participation is voluntary. In Ireland, the Rural Environment Protection Scheme (or REPS, described below) was prepared by the Department of Agriculture in 1992. Co-financing by the EU was put at 75 per cent in Objective 1 regions like Ireland.

Reservations have been expressed that the reforms were dominated by concern for farmers' incomes with lesser concern for the environment, which features rather modestly. Funding within the package dedicated to environmental subsidies is forecast at a mere 2.5 per cent of CAP spending (Dixon 1995). Other reservations arise concerning the adequacy of resources of staff to evaluate the proposals, which is a perennial problem with subsidies. Further worries focus on the relatively high subsidies to afforestation (which, for instance, under the Spanish forestry plan submitted to the Commission, could threaten a rare species of bustard, and which need to be carefully applied in Ireland's case, as we will see below). There is also a feeling that the most harmful farming practices will not be reined in.

These criticisms may stem from an underestimation of the benign incentive effects of the price changes in the McSharry reforms to the CAP. The study by Boyle, which investigates the likely response in Ireland to the cereal reforms, indicates that cereal production could fall by 9 to 14 per cent and consequently use of fertiliser in this sector could fall by 9 to 19 per cent. This is the result of disassociating revenue somewhat from output. It would be interesting to see if the impact on the environment were stronger as a result of the curtailment of these underlying incentives to production, rather than as a result of new subsidies for environmental activities. External events however may alter Boyle's results, in that world agricultural prices have recently risen, giving farmers a renewed production incentive. Then, more recently still, turmoil in the beef market could alter the outcome again.

So much for the all-important background. One must however question what lies in store for the future - will European taxpayers be able or willing to continue to pay similar supports to farmers in the EU, given that farmers' numbers will increase with entrants from Eastern Europe? This question is beyond the scope of this chapter, though it is probable that European taxpayers will prefer to pay for a system which is compatible with a healthy countryside.

The following is a list of the main agricultural grant schemes affecting the environment, which are specified in more detail in Appendix 4.1. Given their likely transitory nature, it is important that the best possible use be made of the EU monies.

*List of grant schemes to agriculture which have environmental impacts*:

- Control of Farm Pollution Scheme (currently suspended)

- Livestock Headage Schemes in Disadvantaged Areas (for cattle, equines, sheep and goats in Disadvantaged Areas)

- Livestock Premium Schemes

- Nutrient Management Planning via the Advisory Service

- Rural Environment Protection Scheme (REPS)

- Early Retirement from Farming

- Organic Farming

These grant schemes are recent and no evaluation has been undertaken. However the fact that the main scheme, REPS, is aimed at the smaller farmer means that the big polluters will be less influenced. On the other hand, the regions where take-up is likely to be strong are the more remote areas. These are indeed the areas which have most to offer in terms of biodiversity, and may be the more vulnerable, but again perhaps have less to offer in terms of pollution abated. The grants are not directly differentiated according to the existing levels of pollution.


**EU nitrates directive**

Though the Nitrates Directive is not an economic instrument, it requires a mention because implementation of the Directive abroad will be of interest, and the issue of nitrogen has some parallels with the phosphorus issue here. Recognising the problems caused by application of chemical fertiliser and manure, the Directive aims to achieve a groundwater standard of not more than 50 mg N per litre and the reduction of nitrate pollution of surfacewaters and marinewaters. Member states are required to identify vulnerable zones. No areas have been designated as vulnerable in Ireland. Member states must adhere to an action programme within these zones, as to timing and manner of fertiliser and manure application. Codes of good practice, including conditions such as the manner of application near watercourses, also have to be drawn up, and an Irish Code of Practice has recently been issued by the Departments of the Environment and of Agriculture (1996). Some farms in the UK which are located in Nitrate Vulnerable Zones are claiming that the restrictions are reducing the value of their land, by up to £200 per acre in some cases, and that nitrogen leaving their farms is in fact deposited from the atmosphere. Some 72 areas have been zoned. Conditions are imposed on them without compensation, and there are apparently 87 appeals to the UK Department of the Environment. How the situation evolves will inform the debate on when and how economic instruments versus regulations should be used.

**Fiscal treatment of chemical fertilisers, feed and pesticides**

Unlike other EU member states, Ireland has a concessionary zero rate of VAT on chemical fertilisers as shown in the Table 4.5.

**Table 4.5**
**Rates of VAT applied to fertilisers in member states**

| (Country | Rate of VAT) |
|---|---|
| Ireland | 0 |
| Luxembourg | 3 |
| Italy | 4 |
| Other EU member states | Standard rate |

*Source:* European Commission DG XXI (1995).

In addition to fertiliser, animal feed is also zero-rated for VAT. These are two inputs to farms which contribute to the nutrient levels on the land. Pesticides, on the other hand, are charged VAT at the standard rate of 21 per cent.

While on the subject of VAT, another current anachronism should be mentioned. A manure additive was introduced on the market recently, which has the environmentally benign effect of helping the spreading of manure on land. However its rate of VAT is 21 per cent, meaning that its use is at a disadvantage vis-à-vis the application of zero-rated fertiliser.

*4.A.3 Options based on information from Ireland and abroad*

In addition to the efforts made by the European Commission to rationalise the CAP, a Ministerial Meeting at OECD (1991) stated that there was a need to 'introduce low-energy, low polluting systems based on new technologies; and prices for agricultural inputs that reflect more fully their environmental costs'. A major difficulty, as we shall see, is that agriculture is characterised by highly variable and frequently unpredictable environmental conditions, and by the fact that its pollution tends to be 'non-point', that is, diffuse, rather than emerging from an identifiable pipe or smokestack. The communiqué underlined the need for governments to identify and eliminate those subsidies, taxes or other market interventions that distort the use of environmental resources. 'Getting the price right' for raw materials, goods and services was seen as critical, to enable them better to reflect their full environmental and social costs. A recent meeting of the OECD policy committee at ministerial level OECD (1996) stated the need for cost internalisation to be part of environmental policies to enable trade liberalisation to contribute to sustainable development, and welcomed the attention focused on the environmental implications of subsidies and tax disincentives. In similar vein, the first recommendation relating to agriculture in the report prepared for DG XI of the European Commission (DRI 1994) was that all subsidies on fertilisers be removed.

Before making practical suggestions for agriculture, we will briefly examine the scope for removing concessions, and for the imposition of pollution taxes, quotas and deposit-refund schemes, to see what each has to offer to deal with excess use of fertiliser. We will also look at competitive tendering to see what that might offer to the protection of biodiversity.

*4.A.3.1 Removing concessions*  One option is to remove the concessionary zero rate of VAT on fertilisers and feed. Some 98 per cent of farmers (out of a total of 108,600 farmers who come within Revenue Commissioners' remit) in Ireland are not registered for VAT and so they are not reimbursed their VAT payments in the usual manner by reclaiming them in VAT returns. Instead they receive a flat-rate rebate when they sell their output to a registered person. The rebate received is 2.8 per cent of the value of their sales and represents the amount of VAT paid in the *average* farmer's output. As the average farm spends £1,659 annually on fertiliser (Teagasc 1995), the absence of VAT on fertiliser inputs is worth £348 at the standard rate, or £208 at the reduced rate. If VAT were imposed on fertilisers, the flat-rate rebate would be correspondingly raised so that the agricultural sector as a whole, and average fertiliser users, would be overall financially unaffected, but would face higher fertiliser prices than at present. On the other hand, intensive users of fertiliser would be worse off and low intensity users better off. Average expenditure on feed is £3,597, the absence of VAT is worth £755 and £450 at the standard and reduced rates, respectively.

The 2,000 farmers who are registered for VAT would also be no worse off, except that they would face the costs of financing the VAT paid on inputs, until they received the credit or rebate due on their VAT returns. These farmers would tend to work the larger farms which in some cases may be doing the more environmental damage. The problem of how to correct the incentives facing VAT-registered farmers will be addressed below. Some non-registered farmers may in fact decide to become registered after the imposition of VAT, if they use more than the average amount of fertiliser per unit of output, in order to get the rebate. These might be dairy farmers, who use nearly double the average farm's input of fertiliser. As organic produce is grown without fertiliser, it would enjoy a relative advantage from the removal of the VAT concession on fertiliser. Organic farmers would receive the rebate on output, without having used and paid VAT on fertiliser as an input, leaving them better off.

In sum, given that expenditure on fertilisers in 1994 was £248 million (CSO, 1996), VAT on fertiliser would amount to something above £50 million at the standard rate, and about £30 million at the reduced rate. All farmers would be compensated in the rebate, but for 98 per cent of them the rebate would be according to a flat rate. As stated this would overcompensate relatively low fertiliser users, and vice versa. In other respects it is a non-specific compensation. It is an economic instrument with two good features: provided that fertiliser prices are stable it would operate like a tax per unit of volume of fertiliser. Secondly compensation is assured. This is in marked contrast with many proposed environmental incentives, where the problems of compensation to alleviate hardship and shortage of funds are serious stumbling blocks to their introduction. It is an ideal route for rectifying the current anachronistic incentive structure. The same could be applied to animal feed.

### 4.A.3.2 Pollution taxes

As opposed to merely removing concessions, a further step which is already implemented in a few countries, and being considered in others, is the introduction of specific taxes on fertilisers. This is in order to pay for the damage that they do. If this damage is not charged for there is a distortion to relative attractiveness of use of fertiliser versus use of manure, and the development of technology for spreading manure is at a disadvantage. The same relative price distortions apply to biomass. 'If biomass production is less fertiliser intensive than agricultural production, the effects of underpricing fertilisers through a failure to take account of environmental externalities is probably to raise agricultural production above its socially optimal level. The corollary is that the production of biomass may be reduced below its socially optimal level.'[10]

The story is somewhat similar when we consider pesticides. Agricultural chemicals are again just one of several factors of production which the farmer combines in order to yield output. The use of pesticides has been likened to the purchase of insurance against a possible attack of pests. In determining what level of chemicals to apply, the farmer weighs the costs of additional chemical usage against the prospective benefits from its use. There are exceptions of course but, in general, the farmer's private calculations will systematically result in over-application of pesticide, because the farmer does not include as a cost the potential health risks to other persons and the danger to wildlife, according to Swanson and Lloyd (1994). Without government regulation or tax there will be excessive application, in the sense that total costs (including environmental damage) outweigh benefits. Regulation, including bans, is the correct instrument for highly toxic or persistent substances. For example organochlorines were banned in the 1960s by many western countries, though paradoxically still produced for sale (e.g. DDT) in less developed countries. In tropical countries it was estimated that DDT had saved 10 million lives in a campaign to eradicate malaria: an example of the weighing of costs and benefits of chemical usage.

Chemicals of lesser toxicity can be taxed. In Denmark it was found that regulatory measures, such as stricter pesticide registration standards, mandatory education programmes and pesticide application book-keeping, have failed to attain the targeted reduction in pesticide use, according to Dubgaard (1996). That said, the essential role of regulations is not in question. Advising farmers and providing them with information on agri-chemicals are also necessary tasks, requiring funding.

We saw above that pesticide usage in Ireland is about half the EU rate. However it appears that for Ireland to comply with the EU Pesticides Directive, the level of monitoring will need to be strengthened. This will require extra funds, for which the Department of Agriculture has apparently been calling for five years. In the UK, the costs of monitoring of foods and the environment (e.g. water and wildlife) are now borne by the UK pesticide industry through a levy on the annual turnover. At the minimum in Ireland there should be sufficient funds to monitor pesticides. The annual costs of registration and monitoring would be at least £0.5 million and extra equipment could add more. Given that expenditure on crop protection is £36 million (or £50 million if one includes total pesticides) then we are talking of imposing a levy in Ireland of very roughly 2 per cent. This would still not cover the cost of surveys, such as the survey of pesticides in drinking water by the Environmental Protection Agency (1996a).

Other considerations of pollution taxes are worth examining. In Denmark there has been some concern about the nitrate 'front' gradually percolating towards many aquifers in certain regions. Farming organisations have wanted to solve this problem through voluntary measures and have understandably opposed statutory control or taxation of nitrogen. Complicated legislation was introduced in 1988 on manure storage capacity, but it soon became clear that there was no political willingness to furnish environmental control agencies with the resources needed to enforce this legislation. However, the non-point nature of nutrient runoff makes it difficult to devise a tax which discriminates according to the actual amount of pollution in the waters. The more indirect and crude measure of taxation of the nutrient input is therefore resorted to. Rude and Dubgaard undertook a study (described in Dubgaard 1991) of levying a hefty 150 to 200 per cent tax on the nitrogen in chemical fertiliser to achieve a targeted 30 to 35 per cent reduction in the use of nitrogen, alongside a flat-rate refund per hectare. As such a high level of tax would be required, they would prefer it to be levied on marginal quantities only. Such a scheme could be implemented by allocating a tax-free quota of nitrogen per hectare to farmers, and taxing additional nitrogen purchased. A levy on nitrogen in chemical fertiliser is currently being discussed by policy makers in Denmark. Meanwhile a pesticide levy has increased pesticide prices by about 50 per cent on average - with some differentiation between the various products. It is still too early to tell what the impact of this levy will be in terms of reduced pesticide utilisation. In any event some of the strongest effects might occur in the longer term.

Turning to analysis undertaken in Germany, most studies, according to Nutzinger (1994), agree that significant reductions in fertiliser application could only be achieved by large fertiliser taxes. However a gradual introduction would enable adaptation. Farmers' incomes could be compensated on the basis of hectares. More economical use of manure would be encouraged and more re-integration of animal breeding and plant cultivation would occur, the latter at present having no manure to substitute for fertiliser.

A survey by OECD in 1994 shows that five countries impose levies[11] of some sort on fertilisers as shown in Table 4.6. The four European countries charge on the basis of the N, P and K content whereas in the USA the charge (raised at sub-federal level only) is based on tonnage. Charges based on P, which is of interest in Ireland, range from 0.14 ECU per kg P in Sweden, which amounts to 10 per cent of the price, to 0.27 ECU per kg P in Finland, which is 20 per cent of the price. In Finland there was a decrease in the use of phosphorus per hectare which may be due to other policy instruments as well, some revenue from the charge being used for agricultural subsidies. The tax has recently been discontinued. In Norway, phosphorus usage per hectare decreased by around 40 per cent between 1980 and 1988, remaining constant thereafter. In Sweden there has been a small fall in the use of nitrogen.

The table also shows charges on pesticides, which are levied in Norway and Sweden. In Denmark an eco-tax was imposed on pesticides in January 1996, increasing pesticide prices by 15.35 per cent, depending on the type of pesticide. The model simulations indicate that the tax-induced reduction in pesticide use will probably be less than 10 per cent. It appears that rather than strengthening bureaucratic control, politicians may be becoming more willing to use economic incentives (Dubgaard op.cit.). In Sweden at the beginning of the 1980s it was decided to reduce usage of pesticides by 50 per cent. The Swedish Board of Agriculture has analysed the responsiveness of pesticide use to its price. They estimate that a 10 per cent price rise results in a decline in use of 2 to 5 per cent. In a study by Gren (1994), also for Sweden, the decline in use after a 10 per cent price rise would be 9.3 per cent for herbicides, 5.2 per cent for insecticides and 3.9 per cent for fungicides. In the Netherlands a levy on pesticides is planned which will aim to raise over £10 million for use in pesticide reduction action programmes.

Monitoring costs for enforcing legislation in general, and who should bear them, are also sources of debate. In Denmark, for example, a national monitoring programme, measuring nitrogen, phosphorus and organic matter in the aquatic environment was started in 1988. This is based on 255 monitoring stations on streams and rivers, 68 groundwater monitoring points and measurement of concentrations at 37 selected lakes. Some coastal waters are monitored also, as are a number of sources of pollutants. The programme costs Dkr 100 million, or over £11 million, per year. Turning to another country, Norway has a 6 per cent control charge on pesticides, in addition to the 23 per cent tax. In other countries, apparently, the high costs of monitoring have inhibited the monitoring programmes or restricted them to small areas, as in Finland. Ensuring adherence to

**Table 4.6**

**Levies imposed abroad on fertilisers and pesticides**

| Country | Charge base, rate and percentage of price | Incentive Int | Act | Revenue spending |
|---|---|---|---|---|
| *Fertilisers* | | | | |
| Austria | N-, P- and K- content: ECU 0.31, ECU 0.18 and ECU 0.09 per kg | - | - | Subsidies, environmental expenditure |
| Finland | N- and P- content: ECU 0.41 and ECU 0.27 per kg (5-20% of the price) | + | # | Agricultural subsidies, general budget |
| Norway | N- and P- content: ECU 0.13 (19% of the price) and ECU 0.24 per kg (11% of the price) | + | # | General budget |
| Sweden | N- and P- content: ECU 0.07 and ECU 0.14 per kg (10% of the price) | + | + | Subsidies, environmental expenditure |
| USA (certain regions) | ECU 0.07-1.11 per ton (<=2.5% of the price) | ¨ | ¨ | Environmental expenditure |
| *Pesticides* | | | | |
| Norway | 13% on wholesale price | + | ¨ | General budget |
| Sweden | ECU 0.9 per kg active ingredient ECU 3.6 per treated hectare | + | # | Environmental expenditure |

*Source:* OECD (1994), p.75.

*Notes:* Int = intended as an incentive instrument.
Act = actual incentive instrument.
+ = yes;   - = no;   ¨ = no data available;   # = unclear.
ECU exchange rate applies to 1 January 1992.

environmental legislation can be complicated, requiring individual assessment as in Denmark. Some prescriptions are hard to control effectively at realistic cost, such as the upper limit on the amount of nutrients that may be applied per hectare, or the 12 hour time limit after spreading for working manure into the soil. At any rate, with control so difficult and monitoring so expensive, the argument for the removal of concessions which are incentives to over-application is strengthened.

*4.A.3.3 Tradeable input quotas, pollution quotas or deposit-refund schemes*
Tradeable quotas are worth investigating because they are well-suited to situations where technical or agricultural conditions vary. Pollution taxes, on the other hand, are suited to situations where there is a measurable level of pollution. Will there come a time when measurement of water quality, and hence of pollution, becomes exceedingly cheap and automated? Even if one could overcome the measurement problems there might still be great variation as to an area's vulnerability. Each catchment area could be a special case, such that a uniform tax (not a mere removal of a concession) would be inappropriate, though possibly better than a blanket regulation. Quotas can have advantages over both.

In the option of imposing the standard rate of VAT on fertiliser, mentioned above, we saw that some 2,000 farmers in Ireland are registered for VAT and that removal of the concessionary rate would have virtually no effect on them, because they can reclaim the VAT that they paid. Yet it is these large farmers which probably release a large share of the excess nutrients and require an incentive to farm in an environmentally conscious manner. Several ideas are being discussed, such as tradeable pollution quotas, within catchment areas that are vulnerable.

The advantage of the tradeable quota regime is that the authorities can be more sure that a limit on use will be met. Another advantage is that the authorities do not need to have information on the abatement costs. One possibility is for a fertiliser quota to be imposed in vulnerable areas, such as a quota of 90 or 80 per cent of present application. Quotas would be based on the advice of experts such as soil scientists and chemists. Selected localities would be reasonably small such that the quota of fertiliser permits could be allocated on the basis of a uniform rate of application per hectare. Fertiliser permits would then be tradeable within the area. Those farmers who decided to use less fertiliser per hectare, by managing manure more carefully or altering their product, would be able to sell their excess permits. They would want to sell if the price offered were higher than the value of output forgone. If the output forgone is as minimal as the agronomists imply, then the trade price might be quite low, adding to the scheme's acceptability. However some funds will be required for monitoring and administration.

There are several difficulties with a tradeable quota scheme however, including the fact that there are other sources of nutrients such as feed, and adherence to the quota on inputs would need to be verified somehow. One suggestion is that the quota of fertiliser be coloured and that only coloured fertiliser be allowed within the region (like agricultural diesel being coloured to differentiate it from motoring diesel for tax purposes). No examples of such a scheme have come to light and there is a worry that the set-up costs for trading fertiliser permits might be a disadvantage.

On a theoretical level, tradeable permits are advised when the cost of damage from an extra unit of pollution is rising steeply relative to the abatement costs. By contrast, taxes are recommended when the marginal damage cost curve is relatively flat. Even if we suspect that cost of damage is rising steeply in some areas, theory may have to give way to practicality for now, though an experiment with tradeable quotas in a certain area would be worthwhile.[12]

*4.A.3.4 A practical solution* We can now draw the threads together to devise a practical solution. It is noted that nutrient management calculations are and will have to be increasingly undertaken. The calculations might cost a farm in the region of £200 to £300 per year to undertake. They entail the sampling of soil and the recording of inputs to, and outputs from, the farm. REPS participants undertake abbreviated nutrient management plans. Some other regions of the world, Pennsylvania for example, have mandatory nutrient management plans. Local authorities in Ireland now have legal powers to require farmers to submit nutrient management plans where they consider this to be necessary.[13]

We should further remember that ideally it is not that the P input needs to be discouraged, but rather the P excess, or remainder, when the soil type, inputs and outputs have been taken into account. In this context it may be better to think more in terms of a deposit-refund scheme, where a tax on nutrient inputs is refunded on nutrients in the recorded outputs. Unaccounted nutrients would then actually bear the tax. The items in the recorded calculations, like in Tunney's nutrient balance in Table 4.3 above, bear a marked similarity to the information required in calculating one's VAT rebate. If VAT were charged on fertilisers and feed, but the rebate were related to some adjusted P content of the output, VAT-registered farmers would have an incentive to minimise their inputs and maximise their outputs of P, or 'to return the bottles' drawing on the returnable bottles deposit-refund analogy.

Rather than set up a new procedure to deal with the phosphorus problem it would be worth considering how the VAT system might be exploited. Information required to calculate nutrient remainder would also need to cover changes in stocks on farms. This is not required in the VAT returns. Further information required would also include the timing of manure spreading, adherence to good practice in silage storage and the like. It is not just 'how much' nutrients are applied that matters, but also 'how' they are applied. The proposal, then, is that VAT-registered farmers would be charged VAT on inputs of fertiliser and feed, but the rebate would be made conditional on a satisfactory nutrient balance being demonstrated by the farmer. The rebate might be only a proportion of the VAT originally paid, the proportion being guided by the ratio of nutrient outputs to nutrient inputs. The higher the proportion of outputs to inputs the higher the rebate. The higher the nutrient excess or remainder, the higher the effective tax.

To overcome the mis-match in timing, that VAT is calculated 2-monthly and that the nutrient remainder should probably be calculated annually, cumulation of the intra-annual figures would be needed. To counter the variability problem, that nutrient excess in some regions may be doing a lot of harm and doing none in other regions, local authorities, which are the bodies with direct responsibility for Water Quality Management Planning,[14] would have the authority to stipulate adjustments to the calculated proportion. For example there might be, say, three types of region:

(1) non-vulnerable, (2) potentially vulnerable and (3) vulnerable regions. In non-vulnerable areas, the full rebate could be paid in the usual manner, perhaps.

If the system were not operated via the VAT mechanism, that is if the VAT procedures are not amenable to extensions of this sort, then this deposit-refund suggestion might at least be operated alongside the VAT procedures, so that there is some economy of administration. It would remove the need for setting up a completely new structure for gathering the same information again from the 2000 farmers. Possibly the most practical solution is the appointment of not much more than one or two extra persons to administer it, who would have to be situated inside the Revenue Commissioners Office - since the information cannot be released outside the Office.

Impediments to making the VAT rebate conditional on a satisfactory nutrient balance arise because under present legislation the right of VAT deduction may not be limited. In the meantime, however, a complete overhaul of the common system of VAT in the EU is underway and has been set out in a work programme[15] for 1996-1999. The overhaul will include the need to modernise the existing provisions relating to the *right to deduct*, which in fact is the rebate which we are discussing. In order to incorporate the condition which we are proposing here, approval of all EU member states would be needed. Failing this, as mentioned, the proposed method can operate alongside VAT procedures.

So much for the 2,000 or so farmers who are registered for VAT. What of the 98 per cent of farmers who are not registered? These tend to have small farms, though some might be intensive fertiliser users and have a large amount of manure for disposal. If VAT were imposed on fertiliser and feed, as described, they would automatically be compensated on a crude averaging basis, by a higher flat-rate compensation on their output. There may be an initial time-lag, while the flat-rate is adjusted and introduced. Farmers who use relatively less nutrients would gain, above average users would lose, and the incentives to use of manure relative to fertiliser will be improved - all of which are good features. Farmers employing organic methods would gain, and in theory subsidies awarded to them could be reduced. Fertiliser-intensive farmers may opt to become VAT-registered, in order to receive the full rebate, which is perhaps another good feature.

In sum, using the VAT mechanism with the credit or rebate conditional on good nutrient management is worth considering because:

- it tackles the real problem, namely the nutrient excess.

- only the excess is taxed, benign behaviour will not incur a net tax.

- the documentation on inputs and outputs is already obtained by the system.

- the tax authorities are better placed to take on such a task, as they can withhold the deduction from VAT.

- the number of extra personnel required is relatively small, though this depends on how much 'compliance' is incorporated in the conditions.

- it could be applied in a manner which is sensitive to different regional conditions.

- it requires large farmers in vulnerable areas to calculate nutrient balances, which they should be doing anyway.

- the VAT system is ideal because it is somewhat similar to a deposit-refund system.

Many difficulties with such an approach can be foreseen, but these should be looked at in the context of the scale of the problem, and of the objections raised to every other proposal for remedying excess nutrient application.

*4.A.3.5 Competitive tendering*    Competitive tendering is worth considering when the issue of nature and biodiversity is being discussed. To date, subsidies have been used and there are many areas in the reformed CAP where 'cross-compliance' is required. That is, for example, grants are only payable if the farmer complies with stocking density levels and the like. It is important that these methods be adequately monitored and sufficiently sensitive and flexible to deal with specific problems as they arise, such as the over-grazing of hill sides, as an example given earlier. We need to be mindful of the ease with which perverse incentives are introduced, and the difficulty of considering beforehand all the things that might go wrong.

A more targeted approach is for society to view farmers as potential providers of environmental services, which society wants to buy. DRI et al., in their report to DGXI, conclude that governments should ask farmers to tender for biodiversity projects which the government would list. In this way, rather than pay a fixed amount to all farmers who undertake to carry out a specific activity - maintaining meadows or historic breeds for example - farmers would be able to bid to undertake this activity.

The logic behind this proposal is that some farmers will be especially well disposed to this activity or have good conditions, as well as being knowledgeable and able to carry it out more cheaply and effectively than others. In this manner, society will have achieved its objectives at a lower cost. A list derived from DRI of the sort of activities which governments might put up to tender is given in Box 4.1. In effect the Countryside Stewardship Scheme in England, and a like scheme in Wales, use a similar approach: they will accept proposals from farmers which bring greatest environmental and public benefits.

The success of such policies is often more dependent on how it is undertaken rather than on what is done. The advantage of competitive tendering is that it could be well-focused but, as with REPS (the Rural Environment Protection Scheme, see

65

appendix for details), its success would depend largely on correct definition of objectives and monitoring of results. Cross-departmental and, indeed, cross-agency co-operation could be helpful. Non-governmental organisations, which have knowledge of local conditions and can assess results cheaply, could participate to good effect, as with recent efforts to revive the population of corncrakes.

---

Box 4.1: *Biodiversity activities which governments might put out to tender*

**Example 1: Biodiversity and Habitat Protection**
The authorities might invite farmers with land in specified areas, such as Environmentally Sensitive Areas, to submit bids for the minimum subsidy which they would demand in order to provide some type of habitat, or to encourage the expansion of a species. Care would be needed in defining success or failure, be it, for example, density of species or area of groundcover. A limited budget could then be spent in such a way as to obtain the best value for money in an area.

**Example 2: Landscape Enhancement**
Farmers in an area of natural beauty might be asked to submit bids for the minimum subsidy, based on length or area perhaps, which they would require in order to manage their hedges, ponds, turloughs, et cetera. A pre-determined density of these features could thus be assured at the lowest available cost.

**Example 3: Crop Diversity**
The authorities might determine that a certain share of crop should be of a specific variety. Bids could be invited from farmers for the minimum subsidy per hectare that they would require in order to grow the variety, enabling the target share to be reached at lowest cost.

**Example 4: Sustaining species**
The authorities could invite bids from farmers prepared to rear endangered breeds of animal or species of plant. This should allow a guarantee of survival of a set number of each particular breed or plant at the least cost, enabling more conservation to be achieved, given limited budgets.

*Source:* Derived from DRI et al.

---

*4.A.4    Suggested use of economic instruments*

Before summarising the proposals for agriculture, the question must be addressed as to whether one should tax the harm being done or subsidise those avoiding doing harm. A slightly different question arises in the case of past damage. How does one treat farmers who have caused degradation in the past relative to those farmers who genuinely, and at personal cost perhaps, operated in a careful manner, preserving turloughs and thickets and maintaining soil balance and water quality? Should not society pay its debt to them, rather than reward those who did the opposite by awarding them contracts to undo the damage? Moral hazard lies at the core of this issue: encouragement to future damage may be given if polluters are 'rewarded'. This is a basic criticism of many subsidy schemes. Furthermore, the award of a subsidy implies that the polluter had the right to pollute, which is now being bought. The fact that certain people have been polluting ought not to mean that they then have the right to do so. For practical purposes however, they may have the right. Apart from these reservations concerning moral hazard and uncertain rights, we have to start from the present and aim to get best environmental quality at cheapest cost to society, in the short and longer term.

There is a related issue, which is perhaps a question of definition. It is sometimes difficult to determine where the actual boundary lies between doing good and not doing harm. For example, is habitat conservation a good which should be rewarded, or simply the absence of a bad which, if the bad occurred, would need to be penalised? One is looking at a variable definition and, again, rights lie at the root of the question.

As for the context for framing proposals, there is continuing pressure from the World Trade Organisation to reform the system of price supports under the CAP and the prospect that all EU supports, at over 50 per cent of farmers' incomes, will no longer be affordable within an enlarged EU. Such supports are a clear example of an effective but misdirected subsidy. In sum, there is double downward pressure on farmers' future incomes. European consumers however would presumably be more willing to support agricultural incomes in return for better environmental quality. While the major CAP reforms may lie in the (not so distant) future, they require realistic consideration and preparation now. Meanwhile there are practical economic instruments for protecting the environment which can be readily adopted as follows.

1    Concessions on fertiliser and animal feed should be removed. VAT should be levied, in the knowledge that farmers are automatically compensated. For 98 per cent of farmers the compensation will materialise as an increase in the flat-rate credit or rebate on their outputs (at present 2.8 per cent), but the important point is that the relative price of fertiliser will have risen. This situation of no net financial effect on average and relative price change is ideal. The remaining 2 per cent of farmers, consisting of some 2,000 farmers with high turnover who are registered for VAT, would be individually unaffected financially by this measure, unless the next proposal is adopted.

2    The 2,000 farmers who are registered for VAT should be required to supply a satisfactory nutrient management balance in order to receive the VAT credit on their nutrient inputs of fertiliser and feed. Alternatively, given that

information on inputs and outputs is to hand in the VAT procedure, the tax could be effectively imposed on nutrients unaccounted for or 'lost'. The VAT system is in fact a good procedure to link into, because it resembles a deposit-refund system. Ideally the overhaul of the VAT system which is underway would reform the rules on deductibility to facilitate the introduction of conditional credits. Even if unanimity is required among EU states, this may not be a greater obstacle than the objections raised to every other proposal made to date for remedying the problem of excess nutrient use in agriculture.

An alternative, is to operate a similar scheme, consisting of a fertiliser tax with a rebate conditional on satisfactory nutrient balance, alongside newly-introduced VAT charges in the usual system, which exploits the same data. Less satisfactory suggestions include the imposition of a tax on the phosphorus content of fertiliser. Introduced at the lowest rate applied abroad, specifically at the rate 0.14 ECU per kg P (or £0.112 per kg) used in Sweden, this tax would raise some £6.7 million annually. Alternatively, the tax could be raised in vulnerable areas where only coloured fertiliser would be allowed, or else a fertiliser tradeable quota scheme might be used. These last two suggestions are untried, however.

3   A realistic monitoring charge should be levied on inputs which oblige authorities to undertake monitoring. These would include pesticides and possibly fertilisers. Present monitoring for pesticides is apparently under-resourced, and more knowledge of current pesticide levels is needed (Dollard 1994).

4   As long as CAP benefits are related to output, it is worth requiring cross-compliance, with set-aside, stocking limits and the like.

5   In addition to removing the perverse incentives to intensification, some landscaping and bio-diversity enhancing projects should be put out to tender. For example farmers could be invited to tender for maintaining barn owls or habitats, or lichens, once a satisfactory means of verifying the existence of the items has been developed. Environmental benefits will then be achieved at minimum cost to society by the farmers most disposed to providing them.

These proposals amount to a two-sided approach to agriculture and the environment. On the one hand the polluter pays, for damage to water mainly. On the other hand the farmer as steward is paid an efficient price, where the farmer acts as guardian of nature and guarantor of bio-diversity.

## 4.B Forestry

### 4.B.1 Environmental impact of forestry

After clearance of the indigenous deciduous woodland over many centuries, Ireland was left with less than 1.5 per cent of the country under forest at the turn of this century. Some of the forest has recently been restored, not with deciduous species but with conifers, and forests now cover 8 per cent of the land area (Department of Agriculture, Food and Forestry, 1996). It is in this context, of quite rapid afforestation predominantly by conifers, that we discuss the interaction between forestry and the environment. This contrasts with the situation in many other parts of the world where there is rapid deforestation, or forest decline mainly from airborne pollution.

As with agriculture, forestry has positive and negative external environmental impacts. On the positive side, trees take carbon dioxide from the atmosphere and store it. Therefore planting trees, or increasing their growth rates, can delay the build-up of greenhouse gases in the atmosphere and delay global warming. Lowland forests store more carbon than upland forests and fast growing trees, such as poplar, will take a shorter time to fix (or sequester) a given quantity of carbon than, say, oak trees. The carbon sequestered is eventually, but only gradually, released from the timber and paper, the final products, as a result of decay (Cannell and Cape 1991). The release time might range from hundreds of years for timber incorporated in construction, to less than a decade for pulpwood, pallet and packaging.

Also on the positive side, soil erosion can be reduced by the existence of established forest, once the planting stage is well over. Extremes of water levels can be smoothed. Furthermore forests have amenity value, in providing forest walks and adventure areas, as well as enhancing views and providing windbreaks, and habitats once the forest is established. An estimate of external benefits of forests of £21 million is quoted by the Department of Agriculture, Food and Forestry (op. cit.). Most of these benefits bestowed on society are not rewarded, and in this sense, without state intervention, forest planting will be lower than its ideal level.

On the negative side, the preparation of ground prior to planting causes erosion. Forestry can have a detrimental and intrusive effect on scenery, at least if planting has been insensitive to the existing landscape. This could become a disadvantage for tourism, as visitors do not come to Ireland with its forests in mind. Another negative environmental impact is soil and water acidification, occurring particularly at the mature stage when the plantation has been carried out on acid-sensitive soils, with detrimental effects on surface waters and fish. This occurs on sites such as over granite, which are said to be 'poorly buffered', that is they cannot absorb the deposition which occurs when clouds and fog droplets impact on the rough surface of a forest, causing polluting gases to deposit on the trees and drop to the ground. So the presence of the forest increases acid deposition, resulting

69

in increased acidity and heavy metals, particularly aluminium concentrations as a result of the sulphur and nitrogen pollution in sensitive upland freshwaters.

In fact these problems should apply to a minority of water catchments, that is where calcium-poor bedrock is overlain with peat or acid mineral soil, but it is important because the affected catchments are frequently salmonid fisheries. Vulnerable areas would include upland catchments in Wicklow, west and south county Galway, and parts of counties Mayo, Donegal, Clare, Kerry and Cork which have the largest acid-sensitive areas in the country.[16] In such areas, afforested streams tend to be more acid than unafforested counterparts. Acidified streams in Britain, as in numerous other places, are characterised by impoverished invertebrates and they may be fishless (Alott and Brennan, 1993). In Ireland all aquatic forms of life, water weeds, invertebrates and fish, are severely impaired by acidification as a result of afforestation according to Bowman (1991). If planting occurs up to the edge of the watercourse, this too will increase the risk of acidification, and cause shading of the waters at the mature forest stage, which leads to reduced growth rates of fish. The resulting more even temperature of the water may however be beneficial to fish.

Over 40 per cent of existing plantations in Ireland are on acid-sensitive peatland and there is some uncertainty as to whether the carbon sequestration by the forest compensates for the carbon losses resulting from oxidation of the peat during the development phase (Farrell, 1996).

Mature forests also absorb water, potentially reducing water availability in an area. This occurs because the interception of water passing overhead is more than offset by the high rate of evapotranspiration through the large leaf-surface area. Forested catchments can yield between 10 and 30 per cent less water than unafforested counterparts. Decreased water yield can be of concern generally, and especially in catchments that are used for public water supply.

Other negative effects of afforestation include the increase in sediment exports from the area at the development stage, causing habitat destruction to invertebrates, plant life and salmonid fish. Suspended sediment in water can also have harmful effects (Whelan, 1996). There are of course several courses of action which can restrain the damage, such as careful timing of ploughing and draining, the manner of ground preparation, et cetera. The impact declines as the terrain settles though even after several years, sediment yield can be several-fold higher than pre-drainage levels in some cases.

Finally the effects on wildlife and species diversity can be quite marked, though it depends on what was there before afforestation and again on how the forestry is managed and its type. Afforestation of wetlands, or replacement of broad-leaved trees by conifers, would have a negative effect on species diversity, as would fast maturing crops which are then clear-felled, that is, felled in one go. Bio-diversity grows with time in forests, so that longer rotations are more benign than short rotations. Also staggered felling is more benign though more costly than clear-felling. Wildlife populations need habitats with continuity. In addition to destroying habitat, clear felling can cause soil erosion and run-off and leave an unattractive scenery.

In sum, most concern about forestry would centre on acidification of water, on the effect on scenery and on wildlife, possibly in that order. No value has been put on these external costs though work is in train (Clinch and Convery, 1996). Only some of these problems can be avoided if precautions are taken and the new guidelines discussed below adhered to (Forest Service 1995/6). The EPA meanwhile is examining how to deal with acidification in particular. The major environmental benefits probably lie in carbon sequestration, and provision of habitat in some instances.

### 4.B.2   Existing fiscal treatment and environmental effects

An enhanced programme of planting is now underway, for farmers to counter the declines in support for traditional farming, and for the non-farming private sector. Private afforestation, of which farmers account for some two-thirds, is now nearly three-quarters of all afforestation. Conditions for forestry in Ireland are ideal with high growth rates at 12 m³/hectare per year, compared to 4.3 m³/hectare per year in the rest of Europe (McLoughlin 1996). It is expected that the Irish timber industry will become a net exporter of wood products.

The EU has supported forestry development in Ireland since 1981 through the Western package Scheme and the Operational Programme for Forestry 1989-93. Meanwhile the CAP gives higher returns to agriculture, such that mainly non-agricultural land tended to be used under these forestry schemes. The trend in CAP reform to move away from agricultural output support to direct income support is tilting the balance somewhat towards forestry. The present programme of support introduced in 1994 comes under the Operational Programme 1994-1999 and under the CAP Forestry Accompanying Measure (part of the McSharry CAP reforms). The grant differentials favour the afforestation of diversified species and broadleaves in particular. An additional premium is payable to farmers to help reduce agricultural output. A slightly lower premium is paid to non-farmers. Private afforestation has grown rapidly since 1985. Present subsidisation comes under two schemes: (1) the Afforestation Grant Scheme at a total cost of £87 million over the five years and (2) the Forest Premium Scheme at a total cost of £125 million, also over the five years (Department of Agriculture, Food and Forestry, 1994). In addition, (3) there are tax incentives applying to forestry development in the areas of income tax et cetera, and subsidies to the timber industry. These are now described in more detail.

(1) The Afforestation Grant Scheme awards an afforestation grant in two stages. At the development stage three-quarters is awarded, subject to approval conditions, and four years later as a maintenance grant the remaining quarter is awarded. The total amount per hectare ranges from £1,500 for non-diverse species to £3,000 per hectare for afforestation which consists of over 75 per cent oak or beech.

(2) The Forest Premium Scheme applies to farmers and others who suffer a loss of income resulting from the afforestation of their land. It is payable only in relation to plantations which qualify for the Afforestation grant above. Premiums are payable annually for 20 years and the levels for farmers range from £130 per hectare for unenclosed land to £300 per hectare for oak or beech on non-disadvantaged enclosed land.

(3) Profits accruing to an individual or a company from the occupation of woodlands managed on a commercial basis and with a view to the realisation of profits are exempt from both income tax and corporation tax. Gains arising on growing trees and on the disposal of felled timber are not chargeable to capital gains tax. Forestry is regarded for VAT purposes as an agricultural activity: there is no VAT chargeable on timber. A person exclusively engaged in forestry is not required to register and account for VAT, though may elect to do so. It is not known what is the cost to the public purse of this tax subsidy. Other subsidies are given to promote the wood-based furniture sector, to aid the construction of forest roads, to courses for forest product marketing, and the like.

The annual real rate of return to forestry under the 1989-93 scheme has been calculated by several authors. On mineral soil, Farrell and Boyle (1990) estimate the rate of return to the forester to be 5.5 to 6.5 per cent, and 4.5 per cent on low-level blanket peats. Clinch and Convery looked at ten per cent of all forest investments grant aided in 1991. Assuming average historical prices, the expected real rate of return was just under 6 per cent in the presence of existing subsidies. However when afforestation subsidies are removed from the calculation, the real rate of return is decreased to 4.1 per cent. A rate of 5 to 6 per cent would be required for public investment. Under the more generous grants and annual payments introduced in 1994 the rate of return becomes 10.5 per cent, though in reality some of this return will be absorbed by higher land prices. An important question would be: what is the rate of return to public money, in terms of both private and public net benefits, and how does this compare with the cost of raising public funds to provide the subsidy?

Compliance with the guidelines concerning protection of fisheries, landscape and archaeology is a condition for grant aid. The extent to which this affects environmental behaviour is unclear as there are no reports, at least as yet. Afforestation over 70 hectare (reduced from over 200 hectare on 1 October 1996) requires planning permission from the relevant local authority, with submission of a formal Environmental Impact Assessment. If the afforestation is over 40 hectares and includes an aquatic zone the developer must consult the Regional Fisheries Board at least 6 weeks before start of operations - in a Designated Sensitive Area the threshold is 5 hectares. Grant approvals preclude the planting of archaeological sites, and forestry operations must cease on discovery of an archaeological object which must be reported to the Gardai or National Museum. Whether there are adequate resources to monitor and investigate these environmental issues is questionable, as there appears to be no automatic mechanism for their funding, apart from a 5 per cent administration charge on the value of grant payments, which might yield £10 million over the five years. The extra activity will put pressure on existing monitoring resources.

The guidelines for afforestation are published by the Forest Service (1995/6), outlining requirements for protection of fish, archaeology and landscape. A concern is the absence as yet of guidelines regarding wildlife, except that grants are not available for areas which are protected or qualify for protection under EU Directives 79/409 EEC and 92/43 EEC on the Protection of Birds and Natural Habitats. There are currently 75 protected areas under the Birds Directive and none as yet under the Habitats Directive. There is a marked disincentive to the retention of areas of natural and semi-natural vegetation, such as hedgerows and broad-leaved groves in properties under development according to Farrell and Kelly-Quinn (1991). These areas are sometimes deducted from the grant-assisted area. This is an example of the distorting effects of grants.

There are as yet no guidelines on procedures for harvesting and transport of timber. However, the Department's recent *Strategic Plan* (1996) heralds new procedures on notification to local authorities of proposals for over 25 hectares, new conditions on distance from dwellings, buildings and roads, and new guidelines on harvesting, wildlife, and use of chemicals. Also, premiums may be subject to attendance at training courses. With the present heavy planting programme, thought will need to be given to the staggering of felling.

A common theme running through the comment on forestry, as with agriculture, is the need for resources, that is, suitably qualified personnel and equipment, to ensure that the environmental conditions are adhered to. In the case of the requirement, for example, that development of forestry above 70 hectares have an Environmental Impact Study prepared by the developer, the procedure can only operate effectively if the County Councils, which have to assess these studies, have the expertise and the capacity to assess the projects. At the present time, few councils are suitably staffed for this work according to Farrell and Kelly-Quinn. If this is the case then the attachment of environmental conditions might have little meaning in practice. Another reason for concern is the absence of legal protection of Natural Heritage Areas, though amending legislation is currently in preparation by the Department of Arts, Culture and the Gaeltacht.

*4.B.3    Suggested use of economic instruments*

As with agriculture, forestry receives considerable subsidies from the state, but for development mainly. There is a further need for funds for checking and monitoring the environmental impact. In theory the forestry industry should probably provide these funds.

The underlying aim of the forestry programme is to enhance rural development and provide rural employment, especially in the context of reduced support to agricultural output. An informed outside observer might in fact suggest that these aims could be served just as well by a rural employment subsidy, or reduction in employment taxes, such as PRSI payments and income tax. At present the developer on the afforestation scheme enjoys a higher rate of return than if the grants were absent, but no change in employment costs per se. Hence the developer will want to continue to economise on labour.

However there is an area where subsidisation to forestry is strictly justified in economic terms for environmental reasons, and that is in relation to the external benefits bestowed on society, from carbon sequestration described at the outset. A figure for carbon fixation is quoted by Cannell and Cape. One hectare of new forest on good sites (in the Pacific Northwest and southern US) will sequester 6 tonnes of carbon per year. One could apply, in reverse, the EU's original proposed carbon tax by subsidising trees. In the proposed tax of $10 per barrel of oil, $5 is that part relating to carbon (see the chapter on Energy for more details). This is approximately £23.38 per TOE of oil, which contains 0.854 tonnes of carbon, and amounts to a subsidy of about £27 per tonne of carbon sequestered. The reasoning here is that oil users would be taxed £27 per tonne of carbon emitted and, in so far as this represents the marginal damage, the forester should be offered this sum for removing carbon. If a hectare of forest sequesters 6 tonnes per year, then the subsidy per hectare should be in the region of £150 per hectare per year. This would apply only during a certain phase of the trees' lives, though to overcome the aversion to risk some upfront phasing of the subsidy may be necessary. It ought not to be awarded to forest planted on peat soil where the net sequestration value may be zero or negative. If, say, half of the 474,000 hectares of forest in the state qualified, the total subsidy would amount to £38 million per year. The figures used here are for illustration.

This may be an upper limit, because there are other, cheaper, ways of reducing given amounts of carbon emissions[17] and Ireland may choose these rather than forestry, in order to achieve its emissions target. On the other hand, given that forest area will grow and it appears that 'the EU is committed to meeting contingent liabilities created pre-1997 in respect of premium payments of up to 20 years duration' (Department of Agriculture, Food and Forestry 1996 op. cit. para. 4.16.3), the funds may be forthcoming anyway. There should however be an obligation to use them optimally. An over-riding consideration is that the future of the CAP is uncertain and its price support aspects will be further phased out. The consequence will be a reduction in land prices, which should help to raise the internal rate of return on forestry and reduce the rationale for such widespread grants.

To the extent that mature forests, and broad-leaved forests in particular, provide habitats for wildlife, these should receive a habitats subsidy also. No evaluations of the habitat function of Irish forests has been undertaken, to put a figure on the desired subsidy. Such a habitats subsidy plus the £38 million carbon sequestration subsidy combined could amount to something over £40 million per year. Coincidentally, this rough estimate for environmental subsidies is similar to the existing subsidies, which amount to a total of £212 million over the five years 1994 to 1999, and should replace them. In other words, the existing pattern of subsidies for forests should give way to one that is based on subsidising their benign environmental external effects.

We have just dealt with the external benefits. The external damages, namely acidification, intrusion on scenery and detriment to some wildlife, are not generally amenable to pollution taxes and have to be regulated and monitored. Funds will be required to provide the resources for mapping, testing and analysis along with sufficient qualified personnel, including archaeologists, chemists, fisheries specialists et cetera. The existing administrative charge, which yields perhaps an average £2 million per year, possibly needs to be doubled.

# Notes

1    Lee (1996), who is the source of most of the environmental information in this sub-section.
2    Department of Agriculture, Food and Forestry (1996).
3    McNally (1995).
4    Sheehy-Skeffington et al. (1996), Douglas 1995, Whelan (1996), EPA (1996).
5    Marshall (1993) cited by Lee op. cit.
6    European Commission (1991).
7    80 per cent of the support went to 20 per cent of the farmers who produced 80 per cent of the output.
8    O'Connor (1995) has estimated Producer Subsidy Equivalents (PSEs) for Ireland which measure the proportion of the revenue of farmers which accrues as price support. The main PSEs are: 60 per cent for beef, 61 per cent for milk, 58 per cent for sheepmeat, 20 per cent for poultrymeat, 8 per cent for eggs and for pigmeat, 57 per cent for wheat, 62 per cent for coarse grains and 67 per cent for sugar.
9    Under Regulation 2078/92.
10   Fitz Gerald and Johnston (1996).
11   A rise in the price of fertiliser will generally decrease the output of agricultural produce. The profit maximising farmer will increase fertiliser application to the point where: Price of fertilizer/Price of output = marginal productivity (or change in output per unit increase in fertiliser use). An increase in the price of fertiliser in the absence of increased marginal productivity will cause a reduction in fertiliser application, reduced yields and reduced pollution. The relative reduction in output will be small in comparison to the reduction in input and pollution (Simonsen 1995).
12   As suggested by Johnston (1995).
13   Local Government (Water Pollution)(Amendment) Act, 1990, as amended by section 66(3) of the Waste Management Act, 1996.
14   Under the Local Government (Water Pollution) Acts of 1977 and 1990.
15   Phase Three, General principles of VAT, First package of formal proposals, mid-1997, (Commission of the European Communities, 1996).
16   A map showing the locations of acid-sensitive areas in Ireland is given on page 3 of Bowman (1991).
17   Fitz Gerald and Johnston (1996), cited in the chapter on energy.

# References

Allott, N. and Brennan, M. (1993), 'Impact of Afforestation on Inland Waters', in C. Mollan (ed.), *Water of Life, The Proceedings of a Conference on the Inland Waterways of Ireland*, Royal Dublin Society, Oct 7-9.

Baan, P.J.A. (1983), Baten Milieubeleid Water, (Benefits of Environmental Water Policy). Ministry of Housing, Physical Planning and Environmental Management: Leidschendam).

Baldock, D. (1995), 'Agriculture, CAP and Biodiversity', in J. Reus, K. Mitchell, C. Klaver and D. Baldock (eds.), *Greening the CAP*, Centre for Agriculture and Environment, Utrecht, and Institute for European Environmental Policy, London.

Barde, J.P. and Pearce, D.W. (1991), *Valuing the Environment, Six Case Studies.* Earthscan Publications Ltd, London.

Bowman, J. (1991), *Acid Sensitive Surface Waters in Ireland*, Environmental Research Unit, Dublin.

Boyle, G. (1995), 'An Applied Computable Equilibrium (ACE) Model of the CAP Cereal Policy Reforms: The Case of Ireland', *The Economic and Social Review*, Vol. 26, No. 2, January, Economic and Social Studies, Dublin.

Cannell, M. and Cape, J. (1991), *Forestry Expansion - A Study of Technical, Economic and Ecological Factors, International Environmental Impacts: Acid Rain and the Greenhouse Effect.* Forestry Commission Occasional Paper 35, Edinburgh.

Clinch, P.J. and Convery, F.J. (1996), *Assessing the Returns to Forestry Investment Stimulated by EU Structural Fund Support: A Note on the Case of Ireland*, unpublished paper, Environmental Institute, University College Dublin.

Commission of the European Communities (1996), *A Common System of VAT, A Programme for the Single Market*, 22.07 1996, COM(96) 328 final, Brussels.

Convery, F. (1994), 'Impact of Farm Retirement and Forestry Measures', in M. Maloney (ed.), *Agriculture and the Environment*, Conference Proceedings, Royal Dublin Society, 9-11 March, Dublin.

CSO (1996), 'Estimated Output, Input and Income in Agriculture, 1991-1995', *Statistical Bulletin, September 1996*, Stationery Office, Dublin.

Curtis, T.G.F. and McGough, H.N. (1988), *The Irish Red Data Book, No.1, Vascular Plants*, Stationery Office, Dublin.

Delpeuch, B. (1994), 'Ireland's Agri-Environmental Programme in the European Context' in Maloney, M. (ed.), *Agriculture and the Environment*, Royal Dublin Society, Dublin.

Department of Agriculture, Food and Forestry (1996), *Control of Farm Pollution Guidelines and Recommendations.* Dublin.

Department of Agriculture, Food and Forestry (1994), *Afforestation Grant Scheme, Forest Premium Scheme.*

Department of Agriculture, Food and Forestry (1996), *Growing for the Future - A Strategic Plan for the Development of the Forestry Sector in Ireland.* Stationery Office, Dublin.

Department of the Environment and Department of Agriculture, Food and Forestry (1996), *Code of Good Agricultural Practice to Protect Waters from Pollution by Nitrates,* Dublin.

Dixon, J. (1995), 'Regulation 2078/92 - An NGO View', in *Greening the CAP,* Centre for Agriculture and Environment, Utrecht, and Institute for European Environmental Policy, London.

Dollard, R. (1994), 'Combining Community Environmental Objectives and Standards with EU Agricultural and Environmental Measures in Ireland', in Maloney, M. (ed.), *Agriculture and the Environment,* Royal Dublin Society, Dublin.

Douglas, C. (1995), *Overgrazing in Ireland - Some Impacts.* Internal report for National Parks and Wildlife Service, Dublin. April.

DRI et al. (1994), *Potential Benefits of Integration of Environmental and Economic Policies, An Incentive-based Approach to Policy Integration,* in association with DHV, TME, IVM, ERM, ECOTEC, Travers Morgan and M+R. Report prepared for European Commission DGXI, European Communities Environmental Policy Series. Graham & Trotman, London, and Office for Official Publications of the European Communities, Luxembourg.

Dubgaard, A. (1991), 'Denmark', in D. Baldock and G. Bennett (eds.), *Agriculture and the Polluter Pays Principle, A Study of Six EC Countries,* Institute for European Policy, London.

Dubgaard, A. (1996), 'Agriculture and the Polluter Pays Principle', paper read at conference, *Economic Instruments Supporting Environmental Policy: The Polluter Pays Principle in Practice,* ESRI, 14 June.

Environmental Protection Agency (1996a), *Pesticides in Drinking Water, Results of a Preliminary Survey Dec. 1994 - Dec. 1995.* C. O'Donnell, Ardcavan.

Environmental Protection Agency (1996b), *Water Quality in Ireland 1991-1994.* Ardcavan.

European Commission (1991), 'Council Directive Concerning Urban Waste Water Treatment', 91/271/EEC, *Official Journal of the European Communities, L 135/40, 30 May 1991.*

European Commission (1995), *VAT Rates Applied in the Member States of the Community, Situation at 1st August 1995,* DG XXI, Customs and Indirect Taxation, Indirect Taxation, Elimination of tax frontiers, XXI.C.3. XXI/219/95 - EN.

Farrell, E.P. (1996), 'Sustainability of the Forest Resource', in F. Convery and Feehan, J. *Assessing Sustainability in Ireland.* Environmental Institute and University College Dublin.

Farrell, E.P. and Boyle, G. (1990), 'Peatland Forestry in the 1990s 1. Low-level banket Bog', *Irish Forestry,* Vol. 47, pp. 69-78.

Farrell, E.P. and Kelly-Quinn, M. (1991), 'Forestry and the Environment', in J. Feehan (ed.) *Environment and Development in Ireland*, The Environmental Institute and University College Dublin.

Fitz Gerald, J. and Johnston, J. (1996), *The Economics of Biomass in Ireland*, Seminar Paper, 29 February, Economic and Social Research Institute, Dublin.

Fitz Gerald, J. and O'Connor, D. (1991), 'Economic consequences of CAP Reform', in J. Bradley, J. Fitz Gerald and D. McCoy, (eds.), *Medium-Term Review: 1991-1996*, Economic and Social Research Institute, Dublin.

Forest Service (1995/6), *Forestry and Fisheries Guidelines, Forestry and Archaeology Guidelines, Forestry and the Landscape Guidelines*, Forestry Operational Programme, Department of Energy, Dublin.

Gren, I-M., (1994), 'Regulating the Farmers' Use of Pesticides in Sweden' in Opschoor, J.B. and Turner, R.K. (eds.), *Economic Incentives and Environmental Policies: Principles and Practice*. Kluwer Academic Publishers, Dordrecht.

Johnston, B. (1995), *Environment Project*, Submission to the Institute of European Affairs. 6 September.

Lampkin, N. and Measures, M. (editors), (1994), *1994 Organic Farm Management Handbook*. University of Wales, Aberystwyth and Elm Farm Research Centre.

Lee, J. (1996), 'Some Aspects of Sustainability in Relation to Agriculture in Ireland', in F. Convery and Feehan, J. *Assessing Sustainability in Ireland*. Environmental Institute, UCD, Dublin.

Leser, H. (1995), 'Payments for Environmental Benefits of Agriculture', in *Greening the CAP*, proceedings of a conference, Centre for Agriculture and Environment, Utrecht and Institute for European Environmental Policy, London.

McGarrigle, M. (1996), 'Eutrophication and the Environment', in Convery, F. and Feehan, J. (eds.), *Assessing Sustainability in Ireland*, Proceedings of a Conference held at University College Dublin, 18-19 April 1995, Environmental Institute, UCD, Dublin.

McLoughlin, J. (1996), 'Forestry, The Future', in Phillips, A. and Hogan, D. (eds.), *Seeking Partnership Towards Managing Ireland's Uplands*. Keep Ireland Open, Dublin.

McNally, S. (1995), *Policies to Prevent Nitrate Leaching from Agriculture*, unpublished Masters dissertation, Department of Economics, University College, London, June.

Magnussen, K. (1992), 'Valuing Reduced Water Pollution Using the Contingent Valuation Method - Testing for Amenity Misspecification' in S. Navrud, (ed.), *Pricing the European Environment*, Scandinavian University Press, Oslo.

Marshall, E.J.P. (1993), 'Exploiting Semi-natural Habitats as Part of Good Agriculture Practice', in *Agriculture - Scientific Basis for Codes of Good Agricultural Practice*, pp. 95-100. Ed VWL Jordan, CEC, Luxembourg.

Murphy, M., Scott, S. and Whelan, B. (1994), *Report on Attitudes to the Environment, A Survey Undertaken for the Department of the Environment*, Economic and Social Research Institute, Dublin.

Nutzinger, H.G. (1994), 'Economic Instruments for Environmental Protection in Agriculture: some Basic Problems of Implementation' in Opschoor, J.B. and Turner, R. K. (eds.), *Economic Incentives and Environmental Policies: Principles and Practice*. Kluwer Academic Publishers, Dordrecht.

Navrud, S. (1992), 'Willingness to Pay for Preservation of Species - An Experiment with Actual Payments', in S. Navrud (ed.), *Pricing the European Environment*, Scandinavian University Press, Oslo.

O'Connor, D. (1995), *The Use of the Producer Subsidy Equivalent (PSE) as a Measure of Support for Irish Agriculture*, Irish Economics Association 9th Annual Conference, May, Ballyconnell, Co. Cavan.

OECD (1991), *Communiqué*, Environment Committee Meeting at Ministerial Level. SG/Press(91)9, 31st January, Paris.

OECD (1994), *Managing the Environment, The Role of Economic Instruments*, Paris.

OECD (1996), *OECD News Release, Meeting of OECD Environment Policy Committee at Ministerial Level*, 19-20 February, Paris.

OECD (1996), *Making Markets Work for Biological Diversity: The Role of Economic Instruments*, ENV/EPOC/GEEI/BIO(95)1/REV1, Group on Economic and Environment Policy Integration, Expert Group on Economic Aspects of Biodiversity. Paris.

Pearce, D. (1993), *Blueprint 3, Measuring Sustainable Development*, CSERGE, Earthscan Publications Ltd, London.

Reynolds, J. (1996), 'A Study of the Lee Catchment', paper read to the conference *Eutrophication*, The Biology Society of Ireland, Royal Irish Academy, Dublin.

Sheehy-Skeffington, M., Bleasdale, A. and McKee, A.M. (1996), 'Research in the Connemara Uplands: Vegetation Changes and Peat Erosion' in Phillips, A. and Hogan, D. (eds.) 1996, *Seeking a Partnership Towards Managing Ireland's Uplands*, Keep Ireland Open, Dublin.

Sherwood, M. and Tunney, H. (1991), 'The Nitrogen Cycle: A National Perspective', *Irish Journal of Agricultural Research*, Vol. 30, 75-76.

Shortle, J. and Abler, D. G. (1996), 'Nonpoint Pollution', chapter in Folmer, H. and Tietenberg, T. (eds.), *International Yearbook of Environmental and Natural Resource Economics*, Edward Elgar.

Simonsen, J.W. (1995), 'Levies on Fertiliser-Nitrogen', in *Greening the CAP*, proceedings of a conference, Centre for Agriculture and Environment, Utrecht and Institute for European Environmental Policy, London.

Swanson, M. and Lloyd, R. (1994), 'The Regulation of Chemicals in Agricultural Production: A Joint Economic Toxicological Framework', in L. Bergman and D. M. Pugh (eds.), *Environmental Toxicology, Economics and Institutions*, Kluwer Academic Publishers.

Teagasc (1995), *National Farm Survey 1994*. Dublin.

Tunney, H. (1990), 'A Note on a Balance Approach to Estimating the Phosphorus Fertiliser Needs of Agriculture'. *Irish Journal Agricultural Research*, Vol. 29, No. 2: pp. 149-152.

Whelan, K. (1996), 'The Role of Peatlands in the Management of Freshwater Fisheries', in Phillips, A. and Hogan, D. (eds.), *Seeking a Partnership Towards Managing Ireland's Uplands*, Keep Ireland Open, Dublin.

Whilde, T. (1993), *Red Data Book: Vertebrates*, Office of Public Works, Dublin.

WRC/FHRC (1989), Water Research Centre and Flood Hazard Research Centre, *Investment Appraisal for Sewage Schemes: The Assessment of Social Costs,* Project Report. (Water Research Centre: Swindon).

**Appendix 4.1**   *Grant schemes to agriculture which have environmental impacts*

*Control of Farm Pollution Scheme*
The smaller farmer can receive grant aid for certain farm buildings, farmyards, storage facilities for fodder and agricultural wastes and slurry disposal equipment. (The scheme is currently suspended).

Two schemes which have had some adverse environmental effects should be included for completeness, as reforms have recently been introduced to modify their effects:

*(i) Livestock Headage Schemes in Disadvantaged Areas (for cattle, equines, sheep and goats in Disadvantaged Areas)*

Applicants must undertake to keep the animals for a minimum of two calendar months.

Some main schemes with annual payments are:

Cattle headage payments in handicapped areas range from £40 to £84.

Sheep or goat headage payments in disadvantaged areas are £10 up to a limit of £2,000.

This scheme has in fact had some adverse effects on the environment by causing over-grazing by sheep (discussed above) on commonage on hill areas designated as disadvantaged. In October 1995 new measures provided cash payments to farmers who agreed to reduce sheep numbers on hills, amounting to a payment of £31 per ewe for each ewe removed from the flock and an area-based top-up ranging from £60 to over £100 per hectare up to a maximum of 40 hectares. In addition there are incentives where two or more farmers owning at least 50 per cent of the sheep in a designated area agree to join REPS (see below).

*(ii) Livestock Premium Schemes*

Some main schemes are:

A suckler cow premium applying to the whole country amounts to £136.70.

A special beef premium of £87.88 per head, payable twice in the life of the animal, up to a maximum total of £15,818.

A ewe premium of £17.37 per ewe is paid, plus £5.37 in Disadvantaged Areas.

This scheme also has had some adverse environmental effects.

*Nutrient Management Planning via the Advisory Service*
This scheme is a subsidised service to help the environment. Nutrient Management Planning (NMP) has been developed by Teagasc, the State's agriculture and food advisory body, and is being applied at farm level through the Advisory Service, facilitated by the EU LIFE initiative. It is of relevance to the large farmer. Lee notes that recommendations not to apply nutrients at high soil test levels were

frequently ignored, especially for high value crops and products such as sugar beet and milk. This may be an indication of wrong incentives facing farmers.

*Rural Environment Protection Scheme (REPS)*
As mentioned, REPS is the agri-environment component of the CAP reforms. Operated by the Department of Agriculture, Food and Forestry, funding is available from the EU for 75 per cent of the cost to farmers wishing to implement environmental measures. This is the most radical environmental scheme to date, aiming to influence farming practice in its totality rather than just dealing with the 'end of pipe' problems. Farmers have to implement plans, drawn up by Teagasc or other approved agencies, for waste storage, management, liming and fertilisation plans for the farm and a grassland management plan which avoids over-grazing and poaching. Farmers in REPS will be paid annually a premium of 125 ECUs (£100) per hectare for five years up to a maximum of 40 hectares.

Extra payments are available for farmers who undertake additional environmentally friendly farming practices such as preserving Natural Heritage Areas (NHAs), organic farming (discussed below) and rearing animals of local breeds in danger of extinction. The Environmentally Sensitive Areas (ESAs) pilot scheme has been subsumed into the REPS.

The REPS in Ireland has an indicative allocation of £230 million for the period 1994 to 1999. While it might be claimed that the environment features rather modestly in the direct spending of the reformed CAP, Ireland in fact receives a significant amount under this.

*Early Retirement from Farming*
Farmers between the ages 55 and 66 can avail of an annual pension for 10 years (but not past the age of 70) provided at least five hectares are transferred and the transferee meets certain conditions, or the land is transferred to a non-farm use, including forestry and ecological reserves. Qualifying farmers receive a base payment of 4000 ECUs together with £244 per hectare up to a maximum of 24 hectares. Convery (1994) shows that the terms amount to a doubling of the value of poor quality land on farms of 24 hectares. The pension option will be favoured by farmers on small holdings or on poor land, but its environmental effects will depend in part on the uses to which the land is likely to be put.

*Organic Farming*
Organic farming is a system of farming which co-exists with, rather than dominates, other systems, sustains soil fertility and protects the environment, wildlife and non-renewable resources. Payments will be available to farmers who are already in, or wish to convert to organic farming under the REPS. Payments per hectare subject to a 40 hectare maximum are:

|  | Holdings < 3 hectares | Holdings > 3 hectares |
|---|---|---|
| Land in conversion | £195 | £146 |
| Land of organic status | £98 | £73 |

An additional 125 ECU (£100) per hectare per year for 5 years is already payable under REPS. Farmers will be paid £100 on completion of a 20 hour training course (Lampkin and Measures 1994).

Development of the organic farming sector is supported by grant aid to operators for packing and distribution etc. and to recognised bodies (e.g. An Bord Bia) for marketing and promotion. 50 per cent capital grants and 70 per cent marketing/promotion grants are available, co-funded by the EU. A minute proportion, some 0.015 per cent of agricultural output in Ireland is organically grown.

# 5 Environmental services

*J. Lawlor and S. Scott*

The three environmental services to be discussed in this chapter are:

1    Water supply
2    Waste water treatment and disposal
3    Solid waste collection and disposal.

These services are provided by local authorities, except in a few cases where parts of the service have been privatised under local authorities' direction. Central government, with support mainly from EU Cohesion Funds, provides almost the whole of the capital cost of water and waste water services, but, in the case of solid waste services, local authorities themselves fund capital investment from their various sources of income. Local authorities have a good deal of autonomy over their operations, subject to the usual budget constraints. Until the late seventies the remaining costs, which are largely operating costs, were paid for out of local Rates, but since the abolition of local Rates on households, the revenue shortfall has been made up out of a Rates Support Grant from central government. As funds are inadequate to cover the rising costs incurred in supplying environmental services, local authorities have had to levy charges for these services, often in the face of local opposition.

As will be seen, charges on business probably cover operating costs at least, while charges on households cover only perhaps one third of the total cost of these services. Thus society is paying for the services mainly via taxation raised by central or local government, or via EU funds.[1] This method of paying for services discourages careful use and recycling. In the case of water supply there is much wastage on the part of the user, which would not be so high if there were more widespread charging for water on a volume basis, according to the evidence described below. People tend to take more care if they are rewarded for doing so in lower bills.

The main economic instrument which will be considered in this chapter is total cost recovery from charges and extension of volume-based charging where it is economically justified. Why should one depart from the existing subsidised system of supply, a system which reflects the 'public goods' aspects of these services? Avoidance of epidemics and the like would be examples of public goods. The answer is that, while avoiding epidemics is still an objective, use of these underpriced services has grown rapidly and as with most underpricing, it gives wrong incentives; they in turn encourage excessive water demand, excessive emissions and pollution content of waste water, and excessive generation of solid waste. Underpricing puts at a disadvantage efforts to reduce, re-use and recycle, as well as discouraging technological developments in these fields. In the past there was an inadequate social welfare system, and so there was a strong argument for subsidised supply of these services, as there was no means for ensuring that low-income households could pay. This argument is less strong now.

It was noted that parts of the service have been privatised in a few instances. Were privatisation to become more widespread, we would witness an extension of full cost recovery as a matter of course. Indeed it could be argued that absence of full cost recovery from the supply of services to industry and commerce is a form of State aid, which the EU Treaty[2] describes as 'incompatible with the common market'. The Treaty includes here 'any aid..favouring certain undertakings.., in so far as it affects trade'. The shortfall in cost recovery may indeed be made up by local tax revenue from industry, but explicit payment would be less open to dispute.

We will see that volume-based charging will have good, though unquantified, environmental effects. It will reduce the amounts of water used and waste produced, as well as reduce or delay the need for capital investment in the future. It should also help in establishing correct benchmark prices to help the authorities to make comparisons of resource options. The requirement that costs be recovered means that utilities will have to produce explicit unit cost figures so that, after taking account of local conditions, comparisons of unit costs between regions are possible. Efficiency and careful resource allocation, such as leakage reduction, will be encouraged; it becomes more worthwhile to reduce losses if the 'retrieved items' can be sold. The benefits of accountability and efficiency will have to be weighed against the political obstacles and difficulties associated with change, and the requirement that the problems of low-income families and people with special needs be addressed.

Ideally charges should be set to reflect long run marginal costs (LRMC), in order to give the correct resource signals. LRMC is the marginal cost of providing the service, in the long run. It includes not only short run costs but also an element to account for the fact that increased usage of plant brings forward the time when the plant will have to be expanded or replaced. This has implications for the pricing of capital and need not conflict with the practice of cost recovery, which can be ensured in other aspects of the tariff, in a fixed charge for example. The absence of cost recovery at present means that extra funds have to be raised from central government taxation, which can be more distorting than local charges because of, among other things, the effects of grants on local authority behaviour. The demand for items that are 'free' tends to be higher than if the item is charged for; and this applies to all agents, including to local authorities. This is not to say that there is no case for central government grants. Grants from central government may be required where a local authority is supplying services to people who live elsewhere and are passing through, e.g. for trunk roads. Relative local deprivation is another instance. The image of the whole of Ireland may be tarnished, and people outside the region will be affected, if a region has a relatively serious litter problem, or a contagious water-borne disease, and so on. However, a large part of the benefits and disbenefits of the three services discussed here accrue to the people within the region. Furthermore, it is they who impose the costs, so application of the Polluter Pays Principle implies that local people should pay. Though costs may also have been imposed by others, such as the agricultural sector requiring for example extra treatment of drinking water, the aim would be to have these polluters pay also.

This chapter will look at each of the three services, and their supply to industry, commerce and households. There will be an overview of current charging practice and of the current extent of cost recovery. The environmental impact of the present situation and the options for improving the fiscal structure for each service will be considered. We discuss the implications of full cost recovery for the present levels of expenditure, and for the future situation, where more costly standards of environmental services will prevail in conformity with EU directives. A final section will give our conclusions and recommendations for all three services. We can envisage that full cost recovery will bring about a reduction in central government funding (and hence taxes) when compared to a continuation of the current charging levels. Later, when higher standards are provided, as required by EU law, there is the prospect of a correspondingly greater reduction in central government funding compared to what it would otherwise need to be.

## 5.1 Water supply

Some 1.3 million cubic metres per day are sent out to a population of 2.8 million who are served by public water supply schemes (McCumiskey 1991). Approximately 35 per cent of water is used for commercial or industrial purposes, the remaining 65 per cent being used by households. About 38 per cent of water production is apparently accounted for by leakage from the public distribution system, including leakage within private property, on top of unavoidable leakage of about 15 per cent (O'Connell 1992).

The eighties saw the coming on stream of large power stations and big industrial users, and the expansion of water consumption by dairies. All this was accompanied by rising incomes. Consequently costs of supplying water services have risen, as shown in Table 5.1.

**Table 5.1**
**Costs of supplying water 1981-1995 (£m)**

| *Current costs plus capital repayments** | | *Current costs only* | |
|---|---|---|---|
| 1981: | 51.7 | 1988: | 59.8 |
| 1982: | 63.7 | 1989: | 63.7 |
| 1983: | 75.5 | 1990: | 68.4 |
| 1984: | 87.6 | 1991: | 71.4 |
| 1985: | 99.0 | 1992: | 74.4 |
| 1986: | 101.6 | 1993: | 78.5 |
| 1987: | 110.9 | 1994: | 81.8 |
| | | 1995: | 88.1 |

*Source: Returns of Local Taxation*, various issues.
*Notes:* These figures are not adjusted for inflation.
* Capital repayments were made to the Local Loans Fund. The Fund was subsidised by central government, possibly to the tune of 50 per cent.

Note that inclusion of capital repayments up to 1987 makes the pre-1988 figures not comparable with those for 1988 and after. The pre-1988 figures give an indication of total costs. However on account of a subsidy to the capital costs, these earlier figures also understate total costs.

No direct means of obtaining total costs for water supply exist at present, and a figure for cost recovery cannot be calculated. Neither is a firm figure of total supply to hand, so that unit costs are also elusive. Efforts to put figures on these items yield the information given in Table 5.2 for 1994.

Total unit cost of water in Table 5.2, excluding finance charges, is £0.61 per cubic metre. The figure is speculative as several components are estimates. Judging from the figures for 1987 and 1988 in Table 5.1, financing charges could add considerably to the figure. Bearing this in mind, the estimate of £0.61 is broadly comparable with the cost of £0.70 per cubic metre in Wales and the South West of England (Fehily Timoney Weston, 1995), which include financing charges.

There is no formal or agreed procedure for setting tariffs for water supply with the result that there is considerable variation in tariffs between local authorities, depending on their circumstances. A consequence as we saw is that there are no national statistics of unit costs or cost recovery, with possible disadvantages for resource allocation and policy decisions.

**Table 5.2**

**Estimation of cost recovery from charges and unit cost of water supply in 1994**

*£ million*

| | |
|---|---|
| **Current Expenditure** (incl. administration) | 96 |
| Receipts: Charges[a] | 72 |
| Current cost recovery percentage | 75% |
| Current Shortfall | 24 |
| **Shortfall financed by:** [b] Local sources (mainly commercial Rates) | 9.6 |
| Central Govt (e.g. Rates Support Grant) | 14.4 |
| **Capital Expenditure** | 40 |
| Financed by: Govt grant [c] | 39 |
| Contributions from industry [d] | 1 |
| **Total Cost Recovery percentage** | 54% |
| Quantity supplied [e] | 223 million m$^3$ |
| Current unit cost | 0.43 £/m$^3$ |
| Capital unit cost | 0.18 £/m$^3$ |
| **Total unit cost** [f] | 0.61 £/m$^3$ |

*Notes:*

[a]   Of which £40 million and £32 million were paid by households and non-households respectively.

[b]   Figures for Local and Central Government sources are supplied only as totals (Appendix Table 2.1), so that the breakdown between local and central sources has been applied pro rata 40 per cent and 60 per cent.

[c]   *Local Authority Estimates, 1995,* p.31 and Department of the Environment.

[d]   Contributions from industry are estimates, therefore capital expenditure is also approximate.

[e]   This is an estimate of the quantity actually delivered to consumers. McCumiskey (1991) p. 48, and Environmental Protection Agency (1996a) p. 65 give 1.3 million m$^3$/day or 474.5 million m$^3$/year, sent out. O'Connell (1992) p. 53 gives leakage of 53 per cent. The household and non-household shares of consumption are estimated at 65 per cent and 35 per cent respectively.

[f]   Unit costs would be higher if financing charges were included.

*Sources:* Department of the Environment, *Local Authority Returns* and *Local Authority Estimates.*

### 5.1.1 Industry and Commerce

Industrial and commercial customers with demands above a certain level, which varies between authorities, are charged for water. A proportion, consisting mainly of large users, is charged on a metered basis. Only some 35 per cent of the water distributed is used for commercial or industrial purposes, though these users pay 44 per cent of the revenue from charges. As yet there is no firm breakdown of costs incurred for supply to households and non-households, but it would appear that current cost recovery from industry is above break-even level. However, water charges to non-households (more frequently than with households) include a contribution to waste water treatment, which is often not billed separately from water supply.

### 5.1.2 Households

There is again considerable variation between local authorities, depending on their circumstances. The costs of providing local water supply, as with other services, have risen and grants from central government have not kept pace. Domestic water charges are now raised by 86 out of 88 local authorities, that is, by all except Dublin and Limerick County Boroughs. These two authorities are relatively well endowed by central government, they have a wide base for business Rates and opposition to charges is strong in some quarters. Elsewhere charges raised annually range from £51 to £145 per household and tend to be a uniform flat fee across households within a local authority area. Some ten authorities impose a charge based on the old valuation of the property which was used under the now-extinct Rates regime. A few authorities charge by type of dwelling, for example according to whether it is terraced, detached et cetera.

The areas where there are higher water charges tend to be areas with no sewerage charges, charges for the two services being effectively combined in about 60 authorities. Local authorities report that it is easier to collect charges for water than for sewerage.

### 5.1.3 Subsidisation - who ultimately pays?

Nationally, revenue from charges for water supply covers but 75 per cent of *current* costs of supply, as shown in row 3 of Table 5.2. However this coverage is an improvement on the recent past. Taxpayers ultimately pay for this under-priced service. The immediate channels of subsidisation ought to be identified though only broad aggregates can be given.

The government provides a subsidy via the Rates Support Grant, paid to local authorities in lieu of the dismantled household Rates. Industrial and commercial enterprises would also claim to contribute to this subsidy, through the Rates which they have to pay on their property to the local authority (only household Rates were abolished in 1978). The government (and European taxpayer) subsidise practically the entire *capital* cost. A connection charge may however be raised from households, and non-households are increasingly required to pay a 'contribution' to the capital costs. To date, contributions have been very small in relation to total capital expenditure, at perhaps 2 per cent of the capital cost.

We estimate that *total* costs of water supply to households are possibly subsidised by some 55 per cent, and to non-households by 30 per cent, disregarding their payment of business Rates. Given that wasteful use is likely due to charging on an unmetered basis, the thrifty are subsidising the profligate. Low-paid and middle-income households may reckon that they are paying more than their fair share of general taxation, and may consider that they are subsidising the rich, who tend to be big users of water.

Low-income households which are deemed to be unable to pay local authority service charges are granted a waiver. Not being directly reimbursed by central government, the local authority has to finance waivers out of its grants from central government, out of commercial Rates or indeed out of other household and non-household charges. Figures from three local authorities on the proportions of revenue due from domestic charges that have been waived are 13, 20 and 24 per cent, the latter proportion relating to a town with very high unemployment. There is no information on this at central level. Some local authorities say that they are awaiting guidelines from central government on the operation of waivers.

*5.1.4 The decision to install household water meters*

From the point of view of equity it is desirable that households that consume large amounts of water make a higher payment. It is also preferable if households which reduce consumption pay lower bills. This is facilitated if payment is volume-based, which requires a meter to have been installed. However, owing to the considerable cost of meter installation, metered charging is probably not economic on a wide scale at present. To assess whether metering is desirable on economic grounds, it is necessary to estimate the costs and benefits of installing meters. As with any investment decision, domestic metering and unit quantity pricing are to be recommended from a national economic viewpoint if gains outweigh losses. Somewhat simplified, this condition can be expressed as follows (OECD 1987). After metering:

[Reduction in water use] x [long-run marginal cost of water supply]
+ external benefits >
resource costs of metering and volumetric charging + value of water use forgone.

In other words, if benefits are greater than costs, installation should proceed. Relevant items in the calculation can be expressed as annual equivalents, or as net present values. Owing to difficulties in estimation, the value of external benefits and of water use forgone are frequently omitted from the calculation, but as is now becoming evident the external benefits (or avoided damages of increased

91

abstraction) are considerations to be reckoned with. Potential damages are becoming greater as the most abundant and cheap sources are exploited already. Other benefits include the availability of management information which could help improve performance and forecasting. A by-product of metering is that some repair of leaks can be incorporated at small extra cost. The saved water can reduce costs and be sold for new uses. The resource costs include meter installation and maintenance, and billing costs.

We are witnessing two trends in the values of the figures which are used in the above calculation for assessing metering. Looking first at the benefits given on the left hand side of the equation, the long-run marginal cost of water supply is rising as water that is most easily accessed is already availed of. Obtaining new water supplies requires higher capital expenditure or removal of supplies from some existing use such as hydro-electricity, or rivers which have amenity value or ecological significance. The fact that money may not change hands is sometimes interpreted, incorrectly, to mean that such supply options are less costly than other options, including options which influence demand (Herrington 1996). Thus the benefits to be used in the above calculation from avoiding or delaying supply expansion are likely to rise, and therefore so are the benefits of metering. The National Rivers Authority (NRA 1995) reports that in the UK where water resource development costs have risen to £1.5 million per Megalitre per day, domestic metering would be only marginally more expensive than expanding supply. This takes no account of benefits to the environment of the reduced consumption. In fact, therefore, if the financial costs plus the environmental costs amount to £1.5 million to install capacity for a Megalitre per day, then metering is worth considering. This merely indicates the possible order of magnitude involved, and the sort of calculations that should be made.

Furthermore the external benefits are also likely to rise. We need hardly be reminded of the shortages of water in the world, with some 25 per cent or 1.5 billion people being seriously short of safe water, and the same again not having enough for daily needs, according to the UNDP (1990) and OECD (1993). Ireland's abundance of fresh water will make it increasingly attractive to foreign investors seeking locations for their water-using industry. The availability of water in certain regions is a known factor in attracting major companies. However, with strong growth in the demand for water in Ireland, this abundance cannot be taken for granted indefinitely and the value of water saved will rise. There are in fact 'water shortages' in some regions such as South Dublin, in addition to conflicts of use, such as between angling on the one hand and water abstraction for use by households or industry on the other. The Eastern Regional Fisheries Board, for example, is concerned that Dublin's claim to being the only European capital endowed with a healthy salmon river may become a thing of the past as the demand for water continues to rise (Evans 1996). In another county, extra supply is being sought from a salmon river in the face of environmental objections, to satisfy demand in a rapidly growing town. Owing to a historic agreement, the town at present is being charged but a fraction of the financial cost of water imported from a neighbouring authority.

It is worth noting that attitudes to various aspects of this issue are likely to alter over time and vary from place to place. For Waprog, the water company for the northern province of Groningen in the Netherlands, for example, the aim of meter installation in 1985 was to achieve a fairer allocation of what people paid for water. The 'motive of saving water hardly came into it' (Zweegman 1995). Benefits that were external to the utility were therefore the deciding factor. Installation of meters was carried out, reportedly to the satisfaction of all parties, by people who had been unemployed for a long time. This gave them the opportunity, after a brief training course, to gain work experience. More than 100 000 water meters were installed at a cost of little more than 150 guilders each (£45 in 1986/7, or £58 at 1996 prices).[3]

The second trend in the calculation to assess the desirability of metered charging arises in the costs on the right hand side of the inequality sign, namely in the improvements in metering technology. The meter itself now costs some £20 to £40. However it has to be installed in a meter box. The box is easily installed at the time of construction of a dwelling, when the overall cost of meter installation would be some £45. Installation at a later stage after the house is built might cost anything between £70 and £290, because there is the added requirement of reinstating the ground or pavement. The UK water regulator, OFWAT (1995), reports that in 1995/6 the average charge for internal installation was £120, and £176 for installation in the highway or on the pavement.

Measurement problems in meters (sometimes cited by opponents of metered charges) tend to result in under-recording rather than over-recording, due to jamming or inhibition of the propeller in the meter. According to the National Rivers Authority (1995) in the UK, while 20 per cent of meters in the National Metering Trials that were randomly tested failed to meet the in-service test requirements, incorrect registering 'was considered to be so minor that the effect on a customer's bill would be negligible'. In the UK the additional costs of metering of water and sewerage are £26 per customer per year. Meter reading technology is also advancing, with experiments underway in the US with hand-held data-loggers which can read the customer's meter from inside a van on the street. The advances in technology of the last few decades should alert us to the likelihood of further improvements, including the possibility of joint metering and charging of several services, such as fuels and water services, as in the Netherlands.

In sum, benefits of metering can be expected to rise and costs to fall, so that we will see increasing economic justification of meter installation in some areas. Early studies, such as those for Rotterdam in 1968 and for the UK in 1976 and 1985 concluded that metering was not viable (though in the latter case selective metering was recommended), but other studies show viability, such as for Perth in Australia in 1982. It depends on the circumstances of the region. If the cheapest leakage reduction options have been taken, it is possible that there is or will be economic justification for metering in some areas in Ireland where there is water shortage. Metering may be worthwhile if the next unit saved through leakage reduction would be relatively costly. NRA give a broad guide to demand management options including leakage reduction and universal metering in England and Wales, summarised in Table 5.3.

**Table 5.3**
**Demand management options in order of cost effectiveness, excluding environmental costs and benefits**

| Option | Costs | Cost/Benefit Ratio | | England and Wales |
|---|---|---|---|---|
| | Pence/m$^3$ | Low cost development[*] | High cost development[*] | Water savings Ml per day |
| Efficient washing machines | 0 | 0.0 | 0.0 | 440 |
| Controllers of urinals | 9 | 0.3 | 0.1 | 140 |
| Leakage control | 13 | 0.4 | 0.2 | 2,340 |
| Low flush WC | 18-28 | 0.6-0.9 | 0.3-0.4 | 850 |
| Universal domestic metering | 89 | 2.7 | 1.3 | 1,060 |
| Shower installation | 94 | 2.9 | 1.4 | 610 |
| Low volume shower heads | 102 | 3.1 | 1.6 | 40 |
| Lower flush WC (6 litres) | 172 | 5.2 | 2.6 | - |
| Domestic water recycling | 321-493 | 9.8-15.0 | 4.9-7.5 | 1,280 |

*Notes:* Ml is a megalitre, or a million litres. Costs include capital costs.
[*]    Assuming low and high development costs of water supply at £0.75 and £1.5 million per Ml per day, respectively.
*Source: NRA (1995).*

94

The first column of Table 5.3 shows the cost of saving a cubic metre of water by each option. The next two columns show the cost/benefit ratio of each option, a ratio of less than unity indicating that an option is financially feasible. As the table shows, universal domestic metering is not the first option which should be considered, as it is unlikely to be viable except in situations where there are shortages and high development (and/or environmental) costs, and where the options of efficient appliances and leakage control have been exploited. Based on these average calculations we can see that the cost per cubic metre saved by metering is 89 pence. In crude terms, if the cost of alternative options, including their environmental costs, is more than this, then metered charging should be considered. Obviously individual cases in Ireland would have to be considered on their merits.

The Appendix Table gives a brief summary of water charges in 17 European cities. It is noted that the charges vary a good deal as does the rate of VAT applied. About 7 per cent of households in the UK pay on a metered basis. Generally, households can opt for this method of payment and are given ready reckoners for calculating whether it is likely to be worthwhile in their particular circumstances. They pay for the meter installation costs. The Director of OFWAT believes however that where there is tight water supply, the costs of meter installation should be shared across all customers, as metered charging avoids supply expansion. There are also schemes for households which prefer a Do-It-Yourself arrangement for meter installation.

Different options for calculating the basis on which charges should be made were investigated in the UK by Rajah and Smith (1993). They assumed a switch from the existing charging method which would leave total revenue unchanged. The existing charging method for domestic water and sewerage in the UK was based on rateable valuation of the property, a method that is somewhat regressive, in that the proportion of household income taken in Rates rises as household incomes fall. Not surprisingly it was shown that a flat fee per household was rather more regressive than the Rates-based method. Interestingly, they found that a volume-based charge (i.e. metered), amounting to 91.8 pence per cubic metre, would be nearly identical to the rateable valuation method, in its incidence, the four middle income deciles paying very slightly more, the highest slightly less. In the absence of the rateable valuation method or of metering, they recommend charging on the basis of the numbers in the household. The charge per head worked out at £44.68 and would be marginally more regressive than the existing Rates-based system. They also recommended that targeted adjustments to the levels of social security benefits be made to address the distributional effects.

*5.1.5 Responsiveness of domestic demand to introduction of metered charging for water*

Apart from the benefit of 'fairness' invoked for metering in Groningen, it is important to see if metering has an effect on demand. If not, the gains in allocative efficiency may be rather small.

Studies applied to widely differing regions have shown that significant and enduring impacts result from metered charging. OECD (1987) listed twenty-two studies with reported consumption reductions usually in the range of 10 to 30 per cent as a result of metering alone. These studies referred to installations in Sweden, Denmark, Norway, Finland, France, the UK, Canada, the USA and Australia.

In the Netherlands, a considerable drop in individual consumption occurred in the Waprog jurisdiction, actually during the installation period, but was viewed initially as merely temporary. It was expected that the public would soon get used to the new but fairly low charges of 1.25 guilders (then 42 pence) per cubic metre. Now that six years have elapsed there has been virtually no subsequent change in individual consumption, the conclusion can be drawn that there has been a permanent drop in consumption of at least 10 per cent, and that this is probably conservative when viewed in relation to what consumption would have been by now. The ratios of maximum day to average day usage, and maximum hour to average hour usage, have also decreased as a consequence of the meter installation, by 11 and 9 per cent respectively.

The results of a study in the Isle of Wight have been analysed and published as part of the National Metering Trials, and they show that response to metering in the UK is in line with studies from elsewhere. The Isle of Wight was not in fact intended as a specific test of the impact of metering but rather to assess the problem of switching to metering on a large scale, so that there was no control area, and historic data had to be used instead. Again some 10 per cent reduction in household demand ensued, a further 10 per cent reduction being attributable to the replacement of defective supply pipes. From all trial areas, an average 30 per cent reduction was recorded in peak-month, week, day and hour demand. For a typical water company in the south east of England this could enable postponement of a new water source for 13 years, based on average demands, and an indefinite postponement based on peaks.[4]

On the issue of acceptability, 71 per cent of customers regarded metering as a reasonable system of charging. The majority of customers had lower bills, but 4 per cent suffered social or financial hardship as a result of the change, according to the National Rivers Authority (1995). These views on metering are consistent with the responses to a survey conducted by the Flood Hazard Research Centre (1993) in the UK, in which respondents were asked how households should pay for water. The results, with percentages of respondents who agree or disagree with each proposed method, are shown in Table 5.4.

The table shows that 41 per cent 'strongly agree' that payment for water should be according to the amount used, another 27 per cent 'agree'. These replies

96

**Table 5.4**

**How households should pay for water: percentages agreeing or disagreeing**

| Method of paying | Strongly Disagree % | Disagree % | Neither % | Agree % | Strongly Agree % | Number of Cases |
|---|---|---|---|---|---|---|
| According to the amount of water used | 9 | 9 | 14 | **27** | **41** | 994 |
| According to the number of people in the household | 15 | 13 | 18 | **26** | **28** | 995 |
| According to household income | 24 | 16 | 21 | 21 | 19 | 994 |
| According to the size of their house or flat | **28** | 24 | 17 | 18 | 13 | 991 |
| The same amount as any other household | **36** | **30** | 16 | 10 | 9 | 995 |

*Note:* Percentages of respondents above 25 per cent have been highlighted.
*Source:* Flood Hazard Research Centre (1993).

correspond quite closely to those for Ireland, given in the chapter on the General Background above, where 42 per cent of females and 51 per cent of males said that drinking water should be charged according to the amount used. Understandably, however, UK support for charging 'the same amount as any other household' is rather lower than support for this charging method in Ireland where the charge itself is quite small at present.

*5.1.6 Responsiveness to changes in the price of water*

Other studies have looked not alone at the effect of introducing metered charging while maintaining revenue constant, but at the effects of price changes on demand. International patterns of water consumption suggest that there is a significant price effect on demand. As a start, one should note that water prices in Europe are 50 to 350 per cent higher than in the US and per capita consumption is accordingly 50 to 75 per cent lower (OECD 1993). Econometric studies, quoted by the National Rivers Authority, undertaken in Australia, Canada, Israel and the USA show that domestic use decreases by between 3 and 7 per cent following a 10 per cent increase in the price of water.

Data from the American Water Works Association, derived from a survey of 430 US utilities, were analysed by Nieswiadomy (1992). The study showed that the response to a 10 per cent price rise would be a decrease in water demand ranging from 1 per cent to 6 per cent. Another US study (by Schneider 1991) indicates that short-run response to a 10 per cent price rise is in the 1 to 4 per cent range, but that long-run response is stronger and is in the 3 to 9 per cent range. Table 5.5 presents these results, and also shows responsiveness of demand to changes in income.

**Table 5.5**
**Estimates of price and income elasticities of demand for water supply**

| Type of user | Price Elasticity | | Income Elasticity |
| | Short run | Long run | Long run |
| --- | --- | --- | --- |
| Residential | -0.11 | -0.26 | 0.21 |
| Commercial | -0.23 | -0.92 | 1.97* |
| Industrial | -0.11 | -0.44 | n.a. |
| Government | -0.44 | -0.78 | 0.90 |
| School | -0.38 | -0.96 | 0.89 |
| Total | -0.12 | -0.50 | n.a. |

*Notes:* Figures show the percentage change in demand resulting from a 1 per cent rise in price or in income.
* Considered unreliable by the author.
*Source:* Schneider (1991).

The long-run response is generally double the short-run response, showing that behaviour and alterations to water-using equipment do occur. The high long-run response by schools is probably explained by the ease with which schools can switch off water during holidays, or adjust their appliances.

Further studies are summarised by Sanclemente (1995), for Spain. An analysis of nearly 3000 cases in the Metropolitan Area of Barcelona reveals that after the introduction of metered charging, some 24 per cent did not alter their consumption, but that the remaining 76 per cent reduced their consumption by nearly 17 per cent on average. This gives a 10 per cent decline overall. In Terrassa, it is observed that metered customers consume nearly 13 per cent less than customers charged a flat fee. In Mataro, progressive metered charging of customers in the decade to 1993 has reduced consumption per head by nearly 16 per cent 'enabling water resources to be released for industrial use without increasing the town's total water consumption'. In these three cases the structure of the tariff also played a role. The tariffs consisted of a mains connection fee and two or three consumption blocks charged at progressively higher rates. Other studies were undertaken of the effects of the installation of individual meters in blocks of flats in Paris, Nancy and Rennes, where the decreases observed were larger still.

There are many other worthwhile demand-side measures for constraining the growth in demand for water, which indirectly come within our scope. These measures include the imposition of a tax on appliances which use relatively more water, such as power showers. However, given that water supply constraints affect only certain regions, such measures could be viewed as crude. On the other hand, subsidies for installation of efficient appliances in some regions could be worthwhile.

*5.1.7 The impact of full cost recovery*

Table 5.6 summarises the possible impact of full cost recovery. This shows the present shortfall in financing the service, plus the likely increase in costs in the future – £19 million – to give the future shortfall in funding the system in the absence of full cost recovery – £82 million per annum. This is also, by definition, the improvement in public finances by moving to full cost recovery, though increased social welfare payments of perhaps £25 million per annum would be required to help low-income households. We assume no change in water usage

**Table 5.6**
**Impact of full cost recovery on public finances - water supply**

|  | *£ million* |
|---|---|
| Present shortfall in cost recovery (from Table 5.2) | 63 |
| *Add:* | |
| Expected increase in annual costs[a] | <u>19</u> |
| Future shortfall in financing the service, if full cost recovery is not introduced | 82 |
| = improvement in public finances if full cost recovery is introduced | |
| *Less:* | |
| Increased social welfare expenditure for low-income households if full cost recovery is introduced [b] | <u>25</u> |
| Net improvement in public finances if full cost recovery is introduced | 57 |

*Notes:*

[a]   KPMG (1996) indicates future increases in operating costs of £47 million per annum, for water supply and waste water services combined. We estimate later in this chapter that the figure relating to waste water is £28 million, leaving a balance of £19 million relating to water supply.

[b]   On the basis that future domestic supply will cost £100 million per annum (65 per cent of the total), and approximately 25 per cent of households will be unable to pay.

99

is likely that reductions by existing users would be compensated for by new firms or increased population, so we have not built any reductions into our figures.

## 5.2 Waste water

As with the other services, waste water falls into two main categories - domestic/municipal and industrial. For the purposes of this chapter agricultural waste is ignored, although it is also a very major source of waste water; it is dealt with in the chapter on agriculture. The level of waste water generation and treatment is given in Table 5.7. As can be seen, the majority of waste is generated by the industrial sector, and this sector also does most of the treatment currently carried out.

**Table 5.7**

**Estimated non-agricultural waste water arising and treated nationally ('000 tonnes BOD per annum)**

|  | Total | Of which - | |
| --- | --- | --- | --- |
|  |  | Industrial | Municipal |
| Waste water generated nationally | 114 | 69 | 45 |
| Reduction in waste by treatment |  |  |  |
| by industry | 46 | 46 | 0 |
| by local authorities | 12 | 3 | 9 |
| Waste discharged to the environment | 56 | 20 | 36 |

*Source:* Various, cited in Scott and Lawlor, 1994.

Municipal service levels vary by whether an agglomeration is inland or coastal. Most inland towns are serviced by secondary wastewater treatment, while no coastal town or city is as yet (of the latter, only Dublin currently has primary treatment). The coastal regions contain most of the large urban areas, which means that currently the bulk of the population (70 to 75 per cent) is not serviced by wastewater treatment plants. This situation is destined to change over the coming years, as the EU Urban Wastewater Directive is implemented. This will involve a major programme of expansion of municipal waste water treatment. Weston-FTA Ltd (1993) calculates that the current contributing population equivalent (PE) to existing sewerage and treatment facilities in the agglomerations affected by the Directive amounts to 2,715,000, while the future design PE for facilities in these agglomerations is 4,099,000. By the time of full implementation they estimate that 70 per cent of the population will be served by treatment plants.

Treatment conditions for industrial waste water are generally set out in the firms' water pollution licence. Because of the lack of treatment in the main urban areas, and the importance of agri-industry (many large food-processing plants are situated in rural areas or small towns), the majority of firms currently carry out their own treatment, as has already been stated. With the planned increase in treatment levels in urban areas, more firms are likely to become connected to municipal treatment plants in the coming years.

In terms of hydraulic flows, we estimate that the total quantity of waste water treated in municipal waste water treatment plants or conveyed in the public sewerage system is very roughly 240 million $m^3$ per annum.[5] The flow treated by industry is very difficult to estimate, since industrial effluent is of a far less uniform standard than municipal waste water.

### 5.2.1 Environmental impact

The potential impact of waste water entering open bodies of water is significant, in terms of oxygen depletion, eutrophication (these two factors are mainly responsible for fish kills and reductions in fish populations), health risks from human consumption of the water, loss of amenity, smells, etc. The actual impact depends on the level of treatment the effluent receives before release, and the assimilative capacity of the receiving waters. In relation to the latter point, one would generally be more concerned about discharges to inland waters than to open marine waters.

### 5.2.2 Existing fiscal structure

*Charging for public waste water collection and treatment services*  As with the other services, charges under-recover the costs of providing the service, especially in relation to the capital costs. Until recently, charges made no contribution to these costs, with 100 per cent being paid for by central government (with considerable aid from the EU). More recently, industry has been asked to make capital contributions to the cost of municipal treatment plants to which they discharge. The situation is summarised in Table 5.8 which shows 8 per cent overall cost recovery.

As regards charging practices, Table 5.9 summarises the results of a survey of Irish local authorities (to which 33 replied). As this survey was carried out in 1994 it is likely that it somewhat understates the current level of charging. Data for 1996 indicate that 31 out of 88 local authorities currently levy separate domestic waste water charges; in all cases the charge is fixed (i.e. not volume-related).

*Compliance incentives (i.e. financial penalties for non-compliance)* Local authorities have at their disposal several pieces of legislation which allow them to impose fines for non-compliance with regulations or for illegal releases of waste water. The degree to which these are used varies from authority to authority. The income from the fines is not known.

**Table 5.8**
**Estimation of total cost, unit cost and cost recovery of waste water in 1994**

*£ million*

| | |
|---|---|
| **Current expenditure** | 41 |
| Receipts from charges[a] | 7 |
| Current cost recovery percentage | 17% |
| Shortfall | 34 |
| Financed by[b]: | |
| Local sources (mainly commercial rates) | 14 |
| Central government (mainly Rates Support Grant) | 20 |
| | |
| **Capital expenditure** | 60 |
| Contributions from industry (estimate) | 1 |
| Shortfall financed by central government (with EU assistance) | 59 |
| | |
| **Overall cost recovery percentage** | 8% |
| | |
| Quantity supplied per annum | 240 million m$^3$ |
| Current unit cost | £0.17/m$^3$ |
| Capital unit cost | £0.25/m$^3$ |
| **Total unit cost**[c] | £0.42/m$^3$ |

*Source:* Department of the Environment.
*Notes:*

[a]  £6 million of this comes from commercial sources, and the remaining £1 million from households. Many more local authorities levy water supply charges than levy waste water charges; as already mentioned, in many cases the two charges are subsumed into one, and simply called water charges.

[b]  On a pro rata basis.

[c]  This is a rough indication of unit cost, based as it is on the hydraulic flow only. Other elements of waste water, such as BOD and suspended solids, are also important cost factors, and can differ from hydraulic flow considerably, especially in the case of industrial effluents.

**Table 5.9**
**Charging for waste water services**

| Type of charge | No. of respondents to survey | Basis of charge |
|---|---|---|
| Capital contributions from industry | 12 | Half were volume-related |
| Industrial effluent operating charge | 16 | Volume-related |
| Industrial effluent monitoring charge | 28 | Mainly related to the frequency of monitoring |
| Domestic charges | 10 | Fixed charges |
| Total number of respondents to survey | 33 | |

*Source:* Scott and Lawlor, 1994.
*Note:* In addition to those already levying industrial effluent charges, a further six respondents were considering adopting charges in the future.

*Environmental effects of the existing structure* The environmental impact of this fiscal structure - characterised by under-recovery of costs, and non-volume related charges - is that there is likely to be an excessive amount of waste water being generated. One would expect this over-generation mainly to occur at the industrial level (to the degree that firms are connected to the public waste water system), since the capacity to reduce waste water generation at the domestic level is more limited. This assertion is backed up by actual experience where some local authorities have introduced volume-related charges for industrial waste water services: firms responded by reducing their waste water generation quite significantly (Lawlor, 1996). Some reduction might be expected at the domestic level also, if volume-related charging were introduced: there would be an incentive, for instance, to buy domestic appliances that used less water.

*5.2.3 Options, from experience in Ireland and overseas*

*Charge the full cost of municipal waste water services* This would include the full capital and current cost on all users of their treatment plants and sewers. For industry, the charge could be made up of a LRMC (long-run marginal cost) charge, which would cover roughly 75 per cent of the capital costs, and the variable element of the operating costs. In addition there would be a fixed charge to recover the balance of the capital and operating costs. A possible design for a capital charging system for industry is given in Scott and Lawlor (1994).

At the domestic level, waste water volumes are of necessity proxied by water supply volumes. Thus volume-related charging would require the metering of water supply to each household. This has already been discussed in detail in the section on water supply, and we saw that the economic viability of domestic metering depends on regional circumstances.

*Introduce charging for discharges to water, even where no treatment is carried out*
This would be a pure pollution tax, based on the damage cost of the discharges. It would give an incentive to carry out the maximum amount of treatment, up to the point where further treatment is more expensive than paying the tax. It would be levied on discharges by industry *and* the local authorities, and would be administered by some central body, such as the Environmental Protection Agency (EPA). The amount of the tax would vary from place to place, depending on the sensitivity of the particular location. This approach is used in a number of European countries, including The Netherlands and France.

Another pollution tax would be a tax on the phosphate content of detergent. This could reflect the impact of the phosphates on receiving waters and waste water treatment plants.

*Subsidise or give grants for the capital cost of improved waste water treatment*
While in Ireland there is an implicit subsidy to users of municipal waste water services, in other countries the authorities often provide grants to industry to introduce improved treatment. However, the funding for these grants usually comes from general charges or levies on industry.

*5.2.4 The impact of full cost recovery*

What might be the impact for local and central government finances of full cost recovery? Two factors need to be considered:

1    Operating costs are due to increase significantly as new treatment plants come on stream. We estimate that operating costs will increase by very roughly £28 million per annum as a result of this.[6]

2    What would be the revenue from a pollution tax on waste water discharged to the environment? This depends on the extent to which the tax is levied (on all waters or just sensitive waters?), the level of the tax, and the level of pollution going into the relevant waters.[7] How much of this would be subject to a tax, and how much the tax would be are also unclear, so it is difficult from the current standpoint to estimate how much revenue this tax might raise.

Table 5.10 summarises the impact of full cost recovery. This shows the present shortfall in financing the service, plus the likely increase in costs in the future - £28 million - to give the future shortfall in funding the system in the absence of full cost recovery - £121 million per annum. This is also, by definition, the improvement in public finances by moving to full cost recovery, though increased social welfare payments of perhaps £20 million per annum would be required to help low-income households.[8] We assume no change in pollution levels, though it might be more appropriate to assume some reduction, especially by industry. However, it is likely that reductions by existing firms would be compensated for by new firms or increased population, so we have not built any reductions into our figures.

**Table 5.10**
**Impact of full cost recovery on public finances - waste water**

| | £ million |
|---|---|
| Present shortfall in cost recovery (from Table 5.8) | 93 |
| *Add:* | |
| Expected increase in annual costs | 28 |
| Future shortfall in financing the service, if full cost recovery is not introduced = improvement in public finances if full cost recovery is introduced | 121 |
| *Less:* | |
| Increased social welfare expenditure for low-income households if full cost recovery is introduced | 20 |
| Net improvement in public finances if full cost recovery is introduced | 101 |

*Note:* Any revenue from a possible pollution tax is ignored.

### 5.3 Solid waste

Industry is the major source of solid waste in Ireland, generating over 7 million of the 11 million tonnes or so arising each year (see Table 5.11). Commerce generates over 500,000 tonnes per annum, while households generate over 1.3 million tonnes. A further 245,000 tonnes of hazardous waste arises, and this is subject to various forms of treatment and recovery processes. We do not consider this waste here, as hazardous waste is more properly the subject of regulation than of fiscal instruments.

**Table 5.11**

**Solid waste arising and disposal routes in Ireland, 1995**

| Source | Landfilled | Incineration | Disposed to waters | Biological/ chemical treatment | Recovered/ reused | Other | Total |
|---|---|---|---|---|---|---|---|
| | Tonnes | Tonnes | Tonnes | Tonnes | Tonnes | Tonnes | Tonnes |
| Commercial | 443,339 | | | | 80,372 | | 523,711 |
| Domestic | 1,267,035 | | | | 57,486 | | 1,324,521 |
| Industrial non-hazardous | 5,855,217 | 8,014 | 357,681 | 34,412 | 1,207,392 | 226,093 | 7,688,808 |
| Industrial hazardous | 4,884 | 45,613 | | 70,590 | 103,481 | 19,186 | 243,754 |
| Municipal sludges | 493,323 | | | | | | 493,323 |
| Dredge Spoils | 784,600 | | | | | | 784,600 |
| Miscellaneous | 202,040 | | | | | | 202,040 |
| Total | 9,050,438 | 53,627 | 357,681 | 105,002 | 1,448,731 | 245,279 | 11,260,757 |

*Source:* Environmental Protection Agency, 1996b.

## 5.3.1 Environmental impact

The environmental impact of this waste is varied, and depends both on the type of waste and its disposal route. Considering industrial waste, the vast majority (almost 6 million tonnes) is landfilled. The major components are mining and quarrying waste (2.3 million tonnes) and construction and demolition waste (0.6 million tonnes). Much of these wastes are quite inert, however the mining waste would include some hazardous substances, and so has a potentially large impact, particularly on water quality. Also, the construction and demolition waste could possibly be put to a better use, if it were recycled into higher grade materials and reused directly for construction (see Box 5.1).

---

**Box 5.1 Demolition and construction waste.**

This represents a very significant proportion of the waste generated and disposed of annually. While most of this waste is used for land reclamation and site engineering, there appears to be scope for recycling it into higher grade material. A study of this issue in the UK (Department of the Environment, UK, 1994) indicates that in that country approximately 30 per cent of demolition and construction waste is reused on-site, 30 per cent is reused for landfill engineering, and a further 37 per cent is dumped in landfill. Only 4 per cent is recycled to secondary aggregate. The option of increased recycling is being pursued in a number of European countries, in the context of minimising waste going to landfill in general. For example, the French government proposes that by the year 2002, 40-50 per cent of this waste will be recycled, whilst in The Netherlands the target is 90 per cent by the year 2000.

A case in point is the city of Copenhagen (population approximately 1.3 million), where in recent years the percentage of the city's waste going to landfill has fallen from 48 per cent to 11 per cent of the total (Fonteyne, 1995). This has been achieved almost totally by a very substantial increase in the recycling of demolition and construction waste, encouraged by a high landfill levy (DKR195 or £20 per tonne) and restrictions on the type of waste allowed into landfill. There are indications that the main use of this recycled waste was for road construction (DRI et al., 1994). However, we do not know the economic cost of the Copenhagen approach; it may be that construction costs have had to be increased to pay for the recycling. The approach suggested in this paper, whereby the full LRMC of landfill disposal is charged, including a levy to cover the external costs, would automatically encourage construction and demolition waste recycling if this is the better option in economic and environmental terms.

---

The other substances that end up in landfill, from industry, commerce and households, are the usual range of solid waste materials - plastic, paper, metals, etc., and these will have various impacts on the environment, namely:

1    Land usage, visual impact, etc., through the existence and use of the landfill;

2    Air pollution and global warming through the generation of methane, from the anaerobic decomposition of organic materials;

3    Ground and surface water pollution from the leaching of liquids from the landfill into nearby waters; landfill leachate is highly toxic, and once again is generated from the decomposition of organic materials.

4    Transport impacts from the carriage of waste to the landfill.

### 5.3.2 Existing fiscal structure

*Charges for public waste collection services*[9]    We are concerned here with that element of solid waste that ends up in public landfills, i.e., approximately 2.2 million tonnes per annum (Environmental Protection Agency, 1996b). As already seen, the majority of industrial waste is dealt with on-site, by industry itself, and so this is not directly affected by the fiscal structure. There is no fixed approach for the entire country, as each local authority is free to set its own charges. Table 5.12 shows the total and unit costs of providing the service, as well as cost recovery levels.

Concerning the level and types of charging that local authorities use, complete data are not available, but Barrett and Lawlor (1995) provide some survey data, presented in Table 5.13. As can be seen from the Table, volume-related charges are quite widely used, especially for commercial users of the service, though the level of charge varies from authority to authority. It can also be seen that quite a sizeable proportion of households – 42 per cent – pay nothing for solid waste services.

In theory, it is preferable that the charge should represent the long run marginal cost (LRMC) of providing the service. We have seen already that charges do not recover the full costs of providing the service, but do they cover the LRMC? A number of local authorities have indicated that they do try to recover their (short run) marginal costs in providing services to the commercial/industrial sector. In general, LRMC will be higher than short run marginal costs, so it is probable that LRMC is not being recovered in most cases.

Two further considerations would lead us to suspect that public solid waste management services are being under-priced. Firstly, future waste management costs will be considerably higher than current levels, and when using LRMC we need to use future costs, rather than current costs levels, since the former is the ultimate cost to society of using up the existing facilities. Secondly, the above discussion relates only to internal costs – external or environmental costs are ignored. In Ireland external costs are estimated to add £4 per tonne to the LRMC and £7 to the average cost of disposing of solid waste to landfill (Barrett and Lawlor, 1995).

**Table 5.12**
**Estimation of total cost, unit cost and cost recovery of solid waste in**
**1994**

*£ million*

**Expenditure**[a]

| | |
|---|---|
| Collection | 35 |
| Landfill | 17 |
| Total [b] | 52 |
| Receipts from charges [c] | 12 |
| **Cost recovery percentage** | 23% |
| Shortfall | 40 |

Financed by [d]:

| | |
|---|---|
| Local sources (mainly commercial rates) | 16 |
| Central government (mainly Rates Support Grant) | 24 |

| | |
|---|---|
| Quantity landfilled per annum[e] | 2.2 million tonnes |
| Unit cost of collection[f] | £38/tonne |
| Unit cost of landfilling | £8/tonne |
| **Total unit cost** | £46/tonne |

*Source:* Department of the Environment.
*Notes:*

[a] Unlike the other environmental services, both capital and current costs of the solid waste service tend to be financed at a local level (i.e. there are no capital grants from central government). As a consequence it is difficult to split costs between capital and current.

[b] Total expenditure on solid waste services in 1994 was £73 million. This includes roughly £20 million for street cleaning and litter prevention, which are not included above.

[c] £5 million of this is from households and £7 million from commercial sources.

[d] On a pro rata basis.

[e] A certain amount of this waste is collected by individuals and firms other than the local authorities.

[f] A recent survey of the major local authorities (Barrett and Lawlor, 1995) indicates costs for collection ranging from £22 - 65 per tonne, with an average of £38 per tonne.

**Table 5.13**
**Local authority solid waste collection and disposal charges, survey results**

| Charge system | Percentage of respondents (weighted by population size) | | |
| --- | --- | --- | --- |
| | Domestic collection/disposal % | Commercial collection % | Landfill only %|
| Volume-related | 13 | 64 | 56 |
| Fixed charge | 30 | 14 | 0 |
| No charge | 42 | 3 | 9 |
| Privatised service | 15 | 19 | 1 |
| No landfills in area | | | 34 |
| Total | 100 | 100 | 100 |

*Source:* Barrett and Lawlor, 1995.

In relation to the increased costs of running the solid waste service, Barrett and Lawlor (1995) present a model of the expected future costs of modern landfill. This model indicates that the cost of replacing all the current landfills with modern facilities will entail a capital expenditure over the coming years of up to £400 million, depending on the number and size of facilities built. As a result annual expenditure on landfill facilities will increase to £45 million, from the present level of £17 million (from Table 5.12). On a per tonnage basis, landfill costs could increase from a current level of £8 per tonne to up to £25 per tonne. Assuming no increase in collection costs, total collection and disposal costs are likely to increase from their present average £46 per tonne to an average of perhaps £63 per tonne (excluding administration) in the coming years. This will obviously have major repercussions for local authority finances and levels of solid waste management charges. We are assuming that the public sector incurs the cost of building all new landfills. It may be that the private sector will build and operate at least some of these facilities. While this may or may not change the cost to the economy of providing solid waste services, it will take the financing burden away from the public sector.

*Grants and subsidies*    Apart from the implicit subsidy in the under-charging for public solid waste services, the central government and local authorities provide grant aid to a number of recycling projects. Most of these are aimed at recycling domestic waste, although some commercial and industrial waste would also be recycled in these projects.

*Compliance incentives (i.e. financial penalties for non-compliance)*    As with the other environmental services, local authorities have at their disposal several pieces of legislation which allow them to impose fines for non-compliance with regulations or for illegal dumping. The degree to which these are used varies from authority to authority.

*Environmental effects of the existing structure*    As with the other environmental services, the under-charging for solid waste services will tend to lead to an excessive amount of solid waste being generated. This will obviously have a detrimental effect on the environment. Artificially low waste disposal costs will also discourage reuse, recycling, and waste reduction, which are the main means by which solid waste can be avoided.

### 5.3.3   Options, from experience in Ireland and overseas

*Charge the full cost of public waste management services*    The charging system would be volume-related, and based on the LRMC of waste collection and disposal. In addition, the local authorities would want to recover the balance of costs (including administration) where LRMC is lower than average cost, and this would be achievable by applying an additional fixed charge. Volume-related charging is a practical option for both the domestic and commercial sectors, using systems such as tag-a-bag, or charges by reference to size of bin. In the future, more sophisticated approaches may be appropriate (see Box 5.2).

A concern with volume-related charging for solid waste services is that it gives an incentive to dump illegally. Indeed, this is often used as an argument for not introducing such charges. Discussions with local authorities that have introduced volume-related charges in Ireland indicate that while illegal dumping was an initial problem, the enforcement of anti-littering regulations and the threat of prosecution have been effective in discouraging such activity. In addition, the general public are becoming less tolerant of illegal dumping, and this is also discouraging the practice (Lawlor, 1996).

*Charge a landfill levy to cover the external costs*    This would represent revenue over and above the cost of running the service, and might be collected by a central agency. Given an average external cost to be £7 per tonne (Barrett and Lawlor, 1995), and the present quantity of 2.2 million tonnes landfilled annually, the revenue might amount to £15 million per annum.

The question of what to do with the levy revenue arises. Theoretically it should go into general revenues, to be used for the highest priority purpose. However, there are likely to be increases in exchequer expenditure related to the solid waste area, such as subsidies to recycling (see discussion later), and social welfare compensation for those households that are unable to pay the full charge for waste disposal as envisaged here. So the revenues from the levy can help to finance these.

**Box 5.2 Weighed refuse collection trials in Denmark (an experiment in pure weight-based charging).**

Specially designed vehicles are being used in Denmark which can weigh the refuse left out by households and can charge accordingly. In the trials to date, the vehicles are rear-loaded and the same amount of labour is employed as before (side loaded-vehicles are under development which will only require one person to operate them). The vehicles have two compartments, one for material that can be composted and the other for all remaining refuse which is landfilled or incinerated. The waste is collected from the household in 240 litre bins which are divided into two compartments, 40 per cent for compostible material and 60 per cent for the remainder. The new weight-based charge did not constitute a rise in price. If the household left out the same weight of refuse as before the trial, the average household's payment would be the same.

The result so far has been a 15 to 20 per cent reduction in weight of refuse collected. As the charge did not change, this reduction has been caused by the fact that payment was weight-based, rather than due to a price rise. One might say that households were responding to the opportunity to reduce their bills. Households can take their recyclables, that is bottles, plastics, paper et cetera to recycling centres.

It is hoped that economic analysis of the investment will be undertaken and that price responsiveness will be estimated. The question is: in present value terms, would the savings on the costs of landfill and incineration outweigh the extra capital costs of this equipment? As the vehicles are rather more expensive than traditional vehicles, the financial viability of the system would be more positive where there are high landfill and incineration charges, and strict regulations, as is the case in Denmark.

Another use may be to reduce labour taxes, as is being planned in the UK at present (Smith, 1995). France, which has an up-and-running landfill tax of FF20 (£2.50) per tonne of household and commercial waste, uses the revenues to finance a public body called the Modernisation Fund for Waste Management. This grant aids research into innovative methods of dealing with solid waste, the construction of modern waste management facilities, and the upgrading and restoration of existing landfill sites. However, as a result of lobbying, many elements of industrial waste are exempted from this tax, as are industrial on-site dumps (Fernandez and Tudenham, 1995). In return for this exemption, industry agreed to set up its own fund (which was subject to legal agreement) to finance the closure of illegal industrial dumps. A major proportion of solid waste in France, be it from household, commercial or industrial sources, goes to illegal landfill sites. Part of the aim of the law that introduced the landfill tax is to close down these sites, and to ensure that the direct disposal of waste to landfill is ended by the year 2002 (i.e. that waste would go through some other route such as incineration or recycling before going to landfill).

*Charge the landfill levy on industry's own landfill sites, to the degree that external costs exist*   The majority of industrial waste (over 5 million tonnes) is disposed of in industry's own sites. As mentioned, much of the waste is inert, but some would have an environmental impact. Given the quantities involved, this levy might raise considerable sums of money. The practical problems of calculating the amount of levy payable in each case may of course be large. More research would also be needed to consider the actual external cost applicable to these wastes, and the quantities involved.

*Privatisation*   An alternative approach, which would automatically lead to full charges being applied, is to privatise public waste management services. This is already done to varying degrees, especially in the area of collection of waste. Of course, the landfill levy would still be imposed, by some public agency.

*Subsidise recycling to the degree of its external benefit, or preferably introduce an energy tax*   Charging the full LRMC for disposal to landfill would give an automatic boost to the alternative disposal routes, i.e. recycling, re-use and reduction at source. In addition, these could be subject to a tax or subsidy to reflect their marginal external costs or benefits. The main alternative route currently in use in Ireland is recycling, so it would be important for this at least to have its environmental costs and benefits taken into account. The calculation of this is difficult, and Barrett and Lawlor (1995) take the approach of valuing the energy saved in the recycling of these materials, and treating this as an environmental benefit. They estimate rates per tonne of material recycled (see Table 5.14), but make the point that a general energy tax, equal to the marginal external cost of energy usage, would achieve similar results automatically, without the need for a separate bureaucracy to administer the subsidy.[10] Such an energy tax would also automatically benefit any other waste management route (e.g. re-use, reduction at source) that saved energy, and would improve the efficiency of the economy on an overall basis, not just in the case of waste management.

### Table 5.14
### External benefits of recycling, in terms of energy saved

| Material | Value of energy saving per tonne of material recycled £ |
|---|---|
| Aluminium | 186 |
| Glass | 2 |
| Paper | 24 |
| Tinplate | 16 |
| Plastics (average) | 148 |

*Source:* Barrett and Lawlor, 1995.

How much the subsidies would cost if implemented cannot be estimated, as the quantities of industrial recycling is not well known, and perhaps more importantly the reaction to the subsidy is unknown. A benefit of the energy tax in this context is that it raises revenues for the exchequer, which can be used to reduce other taxes.

*Product or packaging taxes*    Product or packaging taxes are taxes on goods or packaging which relate to their waste component, at the end of their useful lives. Such a tax can be used to achieve a number of objectives, but from an economic point of view the objective is to include the cost (internal and external) of the disposal of the product and its packaging, in its price. By making products with a higher 'waste content' more expensive, the tax provides an incentive for the consumer to alter consumption patterns, and for the producer to alter production patterns. As a result, one would expect the production and consumption of relatively waste-intensive products to decline, thereby reducing the total amount of waste arising. An example of a packaging tax is a tax on plastic bags, currently provided free in shops and supermarkets in Ireland. These bags tend to have a very high 'waste content', mainly in terms of their visual impact when discarded. Such a tax would seek to internalise the cost of this impact, encouraging the public to minimise their use of these bags or to switch to reusable packaging.

Apart from the economic objective of including waste costs in the purchase price, product taxes can be used with the specific purpose of encouraging industry to set up recycling schemes or deposit-refund schemes. For example, Norway taxes non-returnable beverage containers, thereby providing an incentive to operate a deposit-refund scheme. In order for the tax to be successful in achieving these sorts of objectives it must be sufficiently large to make the alternative worthwhile. In using product taxes for this reason, it needs firstly to be established that encouragement of re-use or recycling is an optimal objective. If the costs of re-use or recycling, both internal and external, are greater than the corresponding costs of landfilling, a product tax that creates a strong incentive towards recycling may not be appropriate. Alternatively, the revenue from the product tax could be used directly to set up recycling schemes (or similar schemes). Again, it needs to be established before a recycling scheme is set up that this is the environmentally optimal thing to do.

Another factor to keep in mind is the effect of such a tax on production costs. If the tax is levied only in Ireland, action would need to be taken to ensure that domestically produced goods are not put at a competitive disadvantage. Goods imported into Ireland would have to be taxed on a product basis so as to restore the competitive balance. Domestically produced goods sold abroad would require a tax refund. This would of course mean that the information requirements of the tax would become large. For this reason the imposition of such a tax may make more sense at a transnational level.

Finally, the design and coverage of a product tax depends on the trade-off made between administrative ease and effectiveness. For example, in order to internalise external costs correctly, a large number of tax rates must be used, reflecting the

114

contributions of different products to the waste stream. Clearly though, a higher number of rates will create greater administrative difficulties.

*Raw material taxes*    Raw material taxes come in two forms. First, virgin raw materials can be taxed while secondary (i.e. recycled) raw materials remain untaxed, thus creating an incentive for the use of secondary raw materials. The tax on virgin raw materials can be set so as cover the eventual disposal cost thereof. The logic then in leaving secondary materials untaxed is that their waste component has already been charged for. The second type of tax is where all raw materials are taxed but the rates differ according to the rate of recycling for the material in question. Thus, a raw material that is never recycled would face a higher tax rate than one which is recycled a number of times. In both cases, the incentive to use recycled materials is intended to lead to the diversion of waste from the waste stream. The provisos mentioned for the product tax would also apply here.

Another issue which arises in the context of foreign trade is the possibility that recycled materials could be imported into this country in an effort by firms to avoid a virgin material tax. If this recycled material makes its way into the waste stream following one use, the effect on the Irish waste stream is the same as if virgin materials were used, since no real diversion has occurred from the domestic perspective. It is true that waste is diverted from the country which exports the recycled material but it would seem unfair that Irish consumers and producers would bear the cost of waste diversion for another country. Again, for this reason, imposing the tax at a transnational level may make more sense.

*Deposit-refund schemes*    Deposit-refund schemes operate through an additional charge being placed on an item when it is purchased, and this charge being subsequently refunded when the item or its container are returned. Such schemes have been widely used in the US and Europe, although typically for a limited range of products such as beverage containers. Other applications have been for car hulks in Greece and Norway and vehicle batteries in the US (OECD, 1994).

These schemes can be used to internalise the costs of disposal. By setting the charge equal to the marginal social cost of disposal, a consumer who purchases an item and discards as opposed to returning it incurs the cost of disposal. A consumer who returns the item and thus keeps it from the waste stream avoids the disposal cost. Typically, however, the objective of these schemes has not been internalising costs but rather to generate high rates of return of materials, with a view to encouraging re-use and recycling and to reduce waste going to landfills and litter. The deposit rate necessary to achieve this may or may not be equal to the rate that would internalise disposal costs.

Finally, indications from Ireland and abroad are that while deposit-refund schemes may be appropriate at the commercial level or for the on-licence trade (pubs, hotels, restaurants), they are extremely expensive to operate at the domestic level (Barrett and Lawlor, 1995).

### 5.3.4   The impact of full cost recovery

Table 5.15 estimates the impact of full charging, as recommended here, on central and local government finances. Introducing full cost recovery (with compensating social welfare increases for low-income households) will reduce the revenue raising requirements of both central and local government by over £60 million at future cost levels, while the landfill levy will provide central government with a source of revenue over and above any financial costs. As an alternative, the private sector may become more involved in the provision of the service; this will have a similar effect on public finances as if the local authorities continue to provide the service, but use full cost recovery. We have not taken into account any reductions in waste quantities as a result of higher charges, though some reductions could be expected. However, without information as to elasticities of demand for landfill services, it is difficult to estimate the effect accurately.[11]

**Table 5.15**
**Impact of full cost recovery on public finances - solid waste**

|  | £ million |
|---|---|
| Present shortfall in cost recovery (from Table 5.12) | 40 |
| *Add:* |  |
| Expected increase in annual costs | <u>28</u> |
| Future shortfall in financing the service, if full cost recovery is not introduced<br>= improvement in public finances if full cost recovery is introduced | 68 |
| *Less:* |  |
| Increased social welfare expenditure for low-income households if full cost recovery is introduced (see note) | <u>12</u> |
|  | 56 |
| *Add:* |  |
| Landfill levy | <u>15</u> |
| Net improvement in public finances if full cost recovery, including a landfill levy, is introduced | 71 |

*Note:*   Expected future costs are £80 million per annum. 1.3 million tonnes out of a total 2.2 million tonnes landfilled per annum come from households, i.e. 60 per cent. Applying this percentage to the costs gives £48 million per annum chargeable to households. If 25 per cent of these cannot afford to pay, social welfare allowances would have to increase by £12 million to account for this.

## 5.4   Conclusions and recommendations

This chapter has looked at the current fiscal structure as it applies to environmental services provided by local authorities and used by households, commerce and industry. We have seen that, in general, these services are being under-priced, leading to over-usage and wastage, and consequent excess environmental damage. Present levels of cost recovery are 54 per cent for water supply, 8 per cent for waste water, and 23 per cent for solid waste. While the EU is at present paying a large share of the capital costs of these services (solid waste excepting), and will continue to do so until the end of this decade, beyond that date capital costs will have to be funded domestically. In view of this, our general recommendations are as follows:

1    Charges should be adjusted to achieve full cost recovery and removal of subsidies, on a volume-related basis where possible.  Over 95 per cent of Irish households say that they would prefer to pay for future improved environmental services by charges rather than through increases in central government taxes (according to the table in the General Background chapter) and there are sound reasons of efficiency for doing so.

2    This needs to be done *simultaneously* with reductions in central government taxes. If not operated as a package, the proposal might be strongly resisted.

3    Under full cost recovery, alleviation of hardship to low-income households will require an enhanced system of waivers which will put extra responsibilities on local authorities, or increases in social welfare payments. The latter is to be preferred, but whichever is adopted it should be paid for by central government.

4    The adjustments in charges, central government taxes and social welfare should be phased in over perhaps 10 years, and be announced and initiated immediately.

In addition, there are several recommendations that relate to the individual services, and they are listed now. For water supply, we would recommend that:

1    In areas where capacity is tight, or may become so, the viability of universal metering should be estimated. The calculated marginal cost of expanding water supplies should include environmental effects such as impacts on amenity waters, water levels in fisheries, environmental impacts on lakes, ponds, wetlands, habitats et cetera, not to mention the opportunity costs of reducing water for hydroelectricity generation and for other potential commercial and industrial uses.

117

2     In areas where metered charging is not deemed viable, equitable methods of domestic charging include basing the charge on the number of residents in the household, on rateable valuation or on type of dwelling.

3     All new houses being built, or areas where service work is being undertaken, should have water meter boxes installed to give occupiers the option of metered charging. Careful users and consumers of small quantities will tend to opt for metering. Non-metered domestic customers could be charged *their* average costs, i.e. their total cost averaged only over them. They would find their charges rising as smaller users opt for metering. As prices rise therefore, an increasing number would opt for metering.

4     All customers consuming above a certain calculated level should be charged on a metered basis (possibly above 500 m$^3$ per year, or 1370 litres per day).

For waste water services, we would recommend that a pollution tax be levied on discharges to bodies of water, whether or not treatment has already taken place on the discharges in question. This would apply equally to discharges from industry and municipal facilities, and might be administered by some central body.

For solid waste services, we would recommend the following:

1     The calculation of costs would be by reference to the next 'generation' of landfills, rather than existing landfills, since the new facilities will be very much more costly than those they replace.

2     There would be a landfill levy, equal to the external cost per tonne of disposal to landfill. We estimate that this would raise revenues of perhaps £15 million per annum.

3     There would be subsidies for recycling and re-use of materials, equal to the external benefits of these activities, vis-à-vis production from virgin materials. As an interim measure, these could be based on the external benefits of energy saved in the activity in question. The revenues from the landfill levy could help to finance these.

4     In the longer run, an economy-wide energy pollution tax would obviate the necessity to have a subsidy as described in 3 above. This, however, is an issue that affects much more than just solid waste management, and its implementation may require agreement at an EU or even wider level.

5     The option of increased privatisation could be explored, since this would automatically lead to full cost recovery, and it appears that private firms find

it easier to collect waste disposal charges than do local authorities. The landfill levy would of course still be charged on waste disposal.

*Implications for public finances of cost recovery for environmental services* Table 5.16 summarises the financial implications of full cost recovery for public finances. It shows the current shortfall on financing the services, and also the future shortfall, if full cost recovery is not implemented - an amount of £271 million per annum at future cost levels. This is by definition the saving to public finances from full cost recovery, though increased social welfare allowances of roughly £57 million per annum would have to be deducted. A landfill levy might bring in an extra £15 million annually. Note that the figures here do not incorporate any saving to the economy; they simply show the financial effect of moving from a system of paying for services mostly through general taxes, to one of paying for them by user charges. Society is paying for the services either way, although evidence of the incentive effects of use-related charges on quantities of the services demanded suggest that economic and environmental benefits will accrue from using this approach. In practice the incentive effect of charging may be considerable in the long run, given the very large rise in charges that is envisaged.

**Table 5.16**

**Present and future shortfalls in financing environmental services, in the absence of full cost recovery (expressed in present day prices)**

| Service | Total cost per annum £ million | Charges presently levied £ million | Annual shortfall /subsidisation £ million |
|---|---|---|---|
| *Present cost levels* | | | |
| Water supply | 136 | 73 | 63 |
| Waste water | 101 | 8 | 93 |
| Solid waste | 52 | 12 | 40 |
| Total | 289 | 93 | 196 |
| | | | |
| *Future cost levels* | | | |
| Water supply | 155 | 73 | 82 |
| Waste water | 129 | 8 | 121 |
| Solid waste | 80 | 12 | 68 |
| Total | 364 | 93 | 271 |

*Note:* Data on future cost levels assume that quantities of the services used are unchanged from present levels; i.e. the incentive effects of charging are ignored. The shortfall at future cost levels assumes no change in revenue from charges.

# Notes

1   As mentioned at several points in this document, EU funds ought not to be viewed as costless since there are many worthwhile projects competing for these funds and therefore expenditure on one project is expenditure forgone on some other project.

2   Article 92 of EU Treaty (OJ, 1992).

3   The chapter on Energy describes a method used in Sweden for encouraging installation of measuring equipment.

4   Installation costs in the majority of cases in this study came to £165 for internal meters (that is, meters positioned within the customer's property) and £205 per meter for external meters, at 1992 prices. Operating costs per meter came to £19.08 per year.

5   Weston-FTA (1993) indicate a total flow to the system of 2.7 million PE. The Dry Weather Flow per PE is 82.9 $m^3$ per annum (domestic sewage strength). 2.7 million x 82.9 = 240 million $m^3$.

6   Department of the Environment (1993) gives illustrative costs of operating new treatment plants of £11.38 per Population Equivalent (PE) per annum for a small treatment plant (capacity 15,000 PE) and of £4.06 per PE per annum for a large treatment plant (capacity 94,000 PE). If we take current municipal secondary treatment capacity from Table 5.7 of 12,000 tonnes of BOD per annum, this converts to 0.5 million PE (on the basis that one PE generates 60 grams of BOD per day). There is a further 700,000 PE of municipal primary treatment capacity in place. The planned future secondary treatment capacity as already mentioned is 4,099,000 PE. We assume that half of this is treated in small plants and half in big plants (including the upgrade from primary to secondary treatment, which we assume costs two-thirds as much as building a secondary treatment plant from scratch) and add 5 per cent for inflation.

7   Taking the estimated total waste generated from Table 5.7 of 114,000 tonnes of BOD per annum, this converts to 5.2 million PE. Existing municipal secondary treatment capacity is 0.5 million PE, rising to 4.1 million PE, and current industrial capacity is 2.1 million PE. This seems to suggest that the pollution load arising will be more than catered for by future treatment facilities, but treatment will only reduce the pollution (BOD) content by 80 per cent, future municipal capacity is likely to replace some existing industrial treatment capacity, and future industrial load and treatment capacity are unknown. Hence, it is not clear how much pollution will be released into the environment in the future, except to say that the quantity is not likely to be very large.

8   Future design PE is 4.1 million, while the human population covered is estimated to be 70 per cent of the total, i.e. 3.6 million x 70 per cent = 2.5 million. Therefore roughly 60 per cent of the future treatment capacity will relate to the domestic sector. Given future costs of £129 million per annum

(from Table 5.8 and above) full cost recovery will require the raising of £77 million per annum from households. If we assume that 25 per cent will be unable to pay, roughly £20 million per annum will have to be provided in increased social welfare payments.

9      This issue is considered in detail in Barrett and Lawlor (1995), and most of the following discussion is drawn therefrom.

10     Of course some extra bureaucracy would be needed to administer the energy tax, but the cost would not be as great, since much energy use is already subject to the tax system. Also, an energy tax would apply to a far wider section of the economy and hence the administration costs would be spread more widely.

11     Barrett and Lawlor (1995) review some international research into elasticities of demand, but the findings are incomplete. Those elasticities that have been estimated have tended to be not very large, though they have in general been short term elasticities, and it may be that long term effects could be greater.

**References**

Barrett, A. and Lawlor, J. (1995), *The Economics of Solid Waste Management in Ireland.* Dublin: ESRI Policy Research Paper No. 26.

Department of the Environment, (1990), *Water and Sanitary Services in Ireland -Policy and Programme for 1989-93,* Dublin.

Department of the Environment (1993), 'Operating Costs of Waste Water Treatment Plants'. Paper given by L. Kilmartin at County and City Engineers Annual Conference 1993.

Department of the Environment (1994), *Recycling for Ireland - a strategy for recycling domestic and commercial waste.* Dublin.

Department of the Environment (UK) (1994), *Managing Demolition and Construction Waste - Report of the Study on the Recycling of Demolition and Construction Wastes in the UK.* London: HMSO.

DRI, in association with DHV, TME, ERM, ECOTEC, Travers Morgan and M+R, (1994), *Potential Benefits of Integration of Environmental and Economic Policies - an Incentive-based Approach to Policy Integration.* Report prepared for the European Commission, Directorate-General for Environment, Nuclear Safety and Civil Protection. London: Graham and Trotman, Office for Official Publication of the European Communities.

Environmental Protection Agency (1996a), *State of the Environment in Ireland,* Ardcavan.

Environmental Protection Agency (1996b), *National Waste Database Report 1995.* Ardcavan.

Evans, D. (1996), 'Angling Notes', *Irish Times,* Saturday 18 May.

Fehily Timoney Weston (1995), *The Economic Appraisal of Environmental Projects Supported by the EU Cohesion Fund,* report prepared for the Department of the Environment.

Fernandez, V. and Tuddenham, M. (1995), 'The Landfill Tax in France', in Gale, R., Barg, S. and A. Gillies, A. (1995), *Green Budget Reform.* London: Earthscan.

Flood Hazard Research Centre (1993), *Customer Preferences and Willingness to Pay for Selected Water and Sewerage Services.* Publication No. 233, Technical Report, Middlesex University.

Fonteyne, J. (1995), Presentation at *Supply Opportunities in Europe's Environmental Industry* Conference, 15th June, 1995, Dublin.

Government of Ireland (1994), *Local Authority Estimates 1994.* Dublin: The Stationery Office.

Herrington, P. (1996), 'Sustaining Heaney's Gushing Taps: Demand Supply and Value of Water', paper read to the seminar *Economic Instruments Supporting Environmental Policy: The Polluter Pays Principle in Practice,* The Economic and Social Research Institute, 14 June.

KPMG, in association with Fitzpatrick Associates, and Murphy Ryan and Associates Limited (1996), *The Financing of Local Government in Ireland.* Dublin: Department of the Environment.

Lawlor, J. (1996), 'The Use of Economic Instruments for Environmental Services in Irish Local Authorities', in *Administration*, Vol. 44 (1) Spring 1996.

McCumiskey, L. M. (1991), *Water in Ireland, A Review of Water Resources, Water Supplies & Sewerage Services*, Environmental Research Unit, Dublin.

Nieswiadomy, M.L. (1992), 'Estimating Urban Residential Water Demand: Effects of Price Structure, Conservation, and Education', *Water Resources Research*, Vol. 28, No. 3, March.

NRA (National Rivers Authority) (1995), *Saving Water, The NRA's Approach to Water Conservation & Demand Management*, A Consultation Report, Worthing.

O'Connell, M. (1992), 'Water Supply, Domestic and Industrial', in C. Mollan (ed.), *Water of Life, The Proceedings of a Conference on the Inland Waterways of Ireland*, Royal Dublin Society, Dublin.

OECD (1993), *Water: An Impending Crisis?*, OECD Future Studies Information Base - Highlights, No. 6, November, OECD International Futures Programme.

OECD (1994), *Managing the Environment: The Role of Economic Instruments.*

OFWAT (1995), *1995-96 Report on Tariff Structure and Charges*, Office of Water Services, Birmingham.

OJ (1992), *Treaty on European Union, Together with the Complete Text of the Treaty Establishing the European Community*, Official Journal of the European Communities, C224, Vol. 35. 31 August. Office of the Official Publications of the European Communities, Luxembourg.

Rajah, N. and Smith, S. (1993), 'Distributional Aspects of Household Water Charges', *Fiscal Studies*, Vol. 14, No. 3, Institute for Fiscal Studies, London.

Sanclemente, C. (1995), 'Influence of Water Metering on Water Consumption', Special Subject 1 of the International Water Supply Association Congress Proceedings, Durban, Sept. IWSA, London.

Schneider, M. L. (1991), 'User Specific Water Demand Elasticities', *Journal of Water Resources Planning and Management*. Vol. 117, No. 1, Jan/Feb.

Scott, S. and Lawlor, J. (1994), *Waste Water Services: Charging Industry the Capital Cost*. Dublin: ESRI Policy Research Paper No. 22.

Smith, S. (1995), *'Green' Taxes and Charges: Policy and Practice in Britain and Germany*. London: The Institute for Fiscal Studies.

Sullivan, D. (1995), *European Water Charges: A Comparison of 17 Cities*. Centre for the Study of Regulated Industries (CRI), Public Finance Foundation, London.

UNDP (1990), *Annual Report 1989-90*. World Bank Water and Sanitation Program.

Weston-FTA (1993), *Strategy Study of Options for the Treatment and Disposal of Sewage Sludge in Ireland*. Dublin: Department of the Environment.

Zweegman, J. (1995), 'Positive Effects of Installing Individual Meters Greater Than Thought Previously', Special Subject 1 of the International Water Supply Association Congress Proceedings, Durban, Sept. IWSA, London.

**Appendix**

## Table 5.17
### The gross bill for water, for a consumption of 200 cubic metres

| City | Gross bill* | VAT rate (%) | Av consn $m^3$/yr |
|---|---|---|---|
| Amsterdam | £121.48 unmetered | 6% | 117 |
| Athens | £115.75 | varies | n.av. |
| Barcelona | £118.44 | 6% | 103 |
| Birmingham | £144.66 | 0% | 120 |
| | £75.12 unmetered | | |
| Brussels | £221.29 | 6% | n.av. |
| Copenhagen | £193.74 | 25% | n.av. |
| Dublin | none | n. applic | n.av. |
| Edinburgh | £69.06 unmetered | 0% | n.av. |
| Frankfurt | £271.96 | 7% | 109 |
| Helsinki | £93.90 | 0% | n.av. |
| Lisbon | £79.25 | 5% | n.av. |
| Milan | £19.60 | 9% | n.av. |
| Normandy | £199.72 | 5.5% | n.av. |
| Oslo | £64.18 unmetered | 22% | n.av. |
| Stockholm | £284.88 | 25% | 128 |
| Vienna | £231.00 | 10% | n.av. |
| Zurich | £208.45 | 0% | n.av. |

*Source:* Sullivan, D., (1995).

*Note:* * Based on metered consumption, unless otherwise stated.

It is estimated that in Ireland the average household consumes 164$m^3$ per year.

# 6 Energy

*S. Scott*

## 6.1 Environmental impact of the sector

The energy sector affects the environment in its production, transportation, transformation, use and residue-disposal phases. Here we will concentrate mainly on those aspects for which damage costs have been estimated and which are the main cause of concern in Europe. They are also highlighted in the report of Ireland's EPA, *State of the Environment in Ireland*. These relate to the transformation and use phases and include the emissions of carbon dioxide ($CO_2$), which constitutes about half of the Global Warming Gases, sulphur dioxide ($SO_2$) and nitrogen oxides ($NO_x$), the last two being implicated in respiratory problems and acid rain.

Global warming is a potentially serious issue for Ireland. The increased emissions of large quantities of so-called greenhouse gases, that trap solar heat radiation and prevent it escaping back to space, can lead to an increase in global temperatures. Given the wide natural variations in temperatures over the centuries, it is difficult to detect change and attribute it to the release of greenhouse gases. The recent report of the Intergovernmental Panel on Climate Change (IPCC, 1996) states, however, that studies have detected a significant change and show that the observed warming trend is unlikely to be entirely natural in origin, and that the balance of evidence suggests that there is a discernible human influence on global climate.

It is not clear to what extent Ireland would be affected by global warming. Higher temperatures and a rise in sea level of a few centimetres may not impose heavy costs, in terms of inland water depletion et cetera. However, the possibility of extreme climate changes in either direction, (a climate in Dublin like that of Spitzbergen in Norway is one prediction, in Scientific American (1995)), the small possibility of a spiralling effect, as warming leads to accelerated release of gases, and the existence of long lead-times – are a spur to take precautions and restrain growth in emissions. In fact Ireland's emissions, at perhaps 0.1 per cent of world emissions, have a negligible effect; but non-co-operation is not an option. Apart from the fact that Ireland would want many other nations to co-operate, the

125

emissions, have a negligible effect; but non-co-operation is not an option. Apart from the fact that Ireland would want many other nations to co-operate, the Environment Council's (1996) objective is for significant overall reductions of greenhouse gas emissions after 2000 to below 1990 levels. Ireland's agreed target for 2000 of stabilising emissions at 20 per cent above their 1990 level looks set to be met, while the target after 2000 is currently under negotiation and may be more restricting. Even in the absence of global warming, there would be no regrets at having reduced emissions, in so far as the costs of reduction are less than the cost of damage inflicted by emissions.

Several attempts have been made to measure the potential costs of climate change induced by man's release of greenhouse gases. These studies focus on what is expected to happen if the level of $CO_2$ in the atmosphere doubled compared to its pre-industrial level. The IPCC's earlier study estimated that such changes would cause a rise in global annual mean temperature of 2.5°C, with a range of 1.5°C to 4.5°C, and melting ice, which would raise the sea level by between 15 to 120 centimetres up to 2100.

Estimates of the costs of damage resulting from such climate changes have been made, based on extrapolated expected damage costs in the US. They are shown in Table 6.1, for illustrative purposes. While estimated climate effects have been revised downwards by the IPCC and these costs are clearly unrepresentative of other regions, they give some values to go on. Differences between the figures are largely accounted for by a higher figure being given to the value of a human life in some studies.

### Table 6.1
### Estimates of average global damage costs in the US resulting from a doubling of $CO_2$ emissions

| Study | Damage cost billion 1988 US$ | Damage cost % of GDP | Average unit damage cost 1988 ECU/tC |
|---|---|---|---|
| Fankhauser (1993) | 250 | 1.5% | 17 (range: 5 to 40) |
| Nordhaus (1991) | 220 | 1.3% | 15 |
| Tol (1993) | 415 | 2.5% | 28 |

*Source:* DRI (1994).
*Note:* tC = tonnes of carbon. One tonne of carbon emitted forms 3.6667 tonnes of carbon dioxide.

As can be seen from the table, estimates of the costs of damage arising from $CO_2$ emissions range from 5 to 40 ECU/tC, or £4 to £32/tC (where tC is tonnes of carbon). It is noted that the carbon part of the EU's proposed carbon tax, discussed later, falls within this range.

We now turn our attention to the other two emissions, $SO_2$ and $NO_x$. There is concern about these, especially on the European mainland. They have harmful effects on health, crops, building materials and monuments, forestry (see the forestry section in Chapter 4), on water in lakes and rivers, visibility (smog) and nature. Estimates of the damage to the first four items, health, crops, building materials and forestry are shown here in Table 6.2, aggregated by DRI (1994) into costs of damage per tonne deposited. These relate to the three countries for which estimates have been made, namely West Germany, the Netherlands and the UK.

**Table 6.2**
**Aggregated costs of damage of $SO_2$ and $NO_x$ deposited, in ECU/t**

|        | West Germany | Netherlands  | UK           |
|--------|--------------|--------------|--------------|
| $SO_2$ | 1202 to 3605 | 1062 to 3185 | 745 to 2234  |
| $NO_x$ | 683 to 2049  | 762 to 2286  | 394 to 1181  |

*Source:* DRI (1994).
*Note:* Only damage to health, crops, building materials and forestry are considered.

Again, these figures are highly preliminary and could be altered by an order of magnitude. In the case of Ireland, the effects of sulphur deposition are not all negative, since it can benefit some crops. However some areas in Ireland are vulnerable to acidification; waterways for example may be under threat, which are not covered in the above estimates. $NO_x$ on the other hand is becoming more of a problem in urban areas despite increased use of catalytic converters, owing to a rising number of vehicles.

Armed with these foreign valuations of partial damage costs per tonne, and with knowledge of the emissions per tonne of each type of fuel, it is possible to calculate the damage costs per TOE of fuel consumed, shown in Table 6.3. TOE stands for tonnes of oil equivalent, a common measure of calorific content to which all fuels can be converted. (1 TOE = $10^7$ kilocalories).

These figures for external damage costs of various fuels are shown here, because they give us an idea, and no more, for the sorts of costs that are envisaged. In theory then, according to Table 6.3, application of the Polluter Pays Principle implies that peat and coal be quite heavily taxed, even if only the carbon dioxide is considered to be the pollutant, and that oil and particularly gas be taxed somewhat less.

**Table 6.3**
**Emissions in t/TOE and damage costs in £/TOE, for main fuels**

|  | $CO_2$ | | $SO_2$ | | $NO_x$ | | Sum of damage costs |
|---|---|---|---|---|---|---|---|
|  | t/TOE | £/TOE | t/TOE | £/TOE | t/TOE | £/TOE | £/TOE |
| Peat | 4.34 | 4.73-37.88 | .0126 | 7.51-22.52 | .0042 | 1.32-3.97 | 13.56-64.37 |
| Coal | 3.7 | 4.04-32.29 | .0241* | 14.36-43.07 | .0021 | .66-1.98 | 19.06-77.34 |
| Oil | 3.01 | 3.28-26.27 | .0059 | 3.52-10.54 | .0021 | .66-1.98 | 7.46-38.79 |
| Gas | 2.07 | 2.26-18.07 | 0 | 0 | .0021 | .66-1.98 | 2.92-20.05 |

*Sources:* Emissions/TOE: McGettigan (1993), Scott (1992). Damage costs/tonne: Tables 6.1 and 6.2. above. Note that the lowest damage costs in Table 6.2 have been used, which relate to the UK. £1=1.25 ECU. t/TOE = tonnes per TOE.

*Notes:* For information, the EU's proposed carbon tax has (1) a carbon component at $5/barrel of oil = £23.38/TOE of oil = £27.37/tC = £7.47/tCO_2$, and (2) an energy component of £23.38/TOE for any fuel, except renewables, including hydroelectricity, as used in Fitz Gerald and McCoy (1992). Hydroelectricity is to be charged because it would be difficult to isolate and exclude from the charge.

*Lower if desulphurisation equipment is operating.

We said at the start of this chapter that we would only be dealing with the main aspects of the transformation and use phases of the energy sector. This is not to imply that production, transportation and disposal of residue are not matters of concern, or indeed that emissions of $CO_2$, $SO_2$ and $NO_x$ are the only environmental effects of transformation and use. Intrusion on views and impacts on habitats by power stations and windmills are a case in point. There is also some disquiet at the extent and manner of turf extraction in certain areas in Ireland and at its damage to scenery, ecosystems and species. The value of this damage has not been assessed. Turf cutting localities are, on the one hand, appreciated for their intrinsic value and depicted in art and poetry and, on the other hand, rejected as representing a hard and unrewarding life, such that any valuation would need to be mindful of this range of view. A similar kind of range of view was accounted for in Norway in the evaluation of bears in the chapter on agriculture (Navrud, 1992), where people who wanted them exterminated were also represented. Even after taking these precautions in valuations, the problem remains that perceptions are evolving quite rapidly with changing circumstances, as evidenced, for example, by growing support for organisations which aim to arrest the damage to ecosystems and scenery.[1] This is not to mention growing international concern for threatened ecosystems, displayed for example by willingness-to-pay on the part of individuals in the Netherlands to preserve a few unspoilt Irish bogs.

Transportation of oil is another important area not covered here, though oil spills have serious environmental impacts. A study of the effect of coast guard monitoring was recently undertaken to establish the extent to which increased monitoring resulted in reduced oil spills (Viladrich-Grau, 1994). The study seemingly indicated that increased monitoring resulted in increased oil spills. In other words, it showed that detection had previously not been very thorough. In sum, good mechanisms are needed for monitoring as well as for determining blame, apportioning costs and enforcing payment for clearing up oil spills. These need to be formulated in international fora in such a way that the incentives are right, in the face of much uncertainty concerning the weather, carelessness, human error and equipment failure. The final consumer ultimately pays to finance the mechanism, such as it is, but payment in the first round should be made by the potential polluter, the oil transporting companies, if the Polluter Pays Principle is to apply. At present the victims, the uncompensated inhabitants of affected coastal areas, pay a share.

## 6.2 Existing fiscal treatment of energy

The excise duties on transport fuels are not covered here as they are discussed in the chapter on transport. That chapter describes how in aggregate motorists pay for a large share of the costs that they impose, though not specifically *as* they impose them, and not sufficiently in cities. Therefore this chapter is concerned with non-transport fuels, meaning that jet fuel, petroleum and diesel oil are largely ignored here.

The most striking feature about the fiscal treatment is the reduced rate of VAT applied to heating fuel and light, at 12.5 per cent, a "reduced rate" which is allowed in the harmonised EU VAT rules. The incongruity is compounded by the high rate of VAT which is imposed on insulation materials which are charged at the standard 21 per cent. An energy audit is also charged at 21 per cent. Energy conservation work, of the nature of building repair and maintenance, is also charged at 21 per cent if the materials are more than 2/3 of the total cost. Only if labour constitutes a third or more can the work be charged at the building, repair and maintenance rate of 12.5 per cent VAT. This might in fact be the majority of jobs, since energy conservation work tends to be labour intensive. The UK has a similar situation, with energy charged at 8 per cent and conservation materials charged at 17.5 per cent. The intention in the UK to raise VAT on energy to 17.5 per cent was ineptly handled, not being accompanied by a corresponding rise in social welfare payments, so that such a move is deemed politically unacceptable for the near future. In Ireland, reduction of VAT on conservation materials would bring some consistency to the situation. However a general uniform rate of VAT was recommended by the

Commission on Taxation (1984) and harmonisation by Article 99 of the EU Treaty (European Communities, 1992). Therefore, in order merely to level the incentives, the reduced rate on fuel would need to be raised to the standard rate. It is recommended that discrimination, if necessary, be on the basis of explicit subsidies or grants.

At present there are two main grant schemes in operation in Ireland which aim to encourage energy conservation. These are (1) the Energy Audit Scheme and (2) the Energy Efficiency Investment Support Scheme, both administered by the Irish Energy Centre. They are available to organisations including industrial firms, commercial organisations, educational institutes, public sector organisations and local authorities. The objective of the schemes, which are funded by the EU, is to reduce national energy consumption and promote energy efficiency.

The Energy Audit Grant Scheme provides grant assistance, up to a maximum of £5000, to organisations that engage independent consultants to carry out site energy audits and surveys. The energy audit assesses how effectively and efficiently a company controls its energy costs. If approved, a grant of up to 40 per cent, is available towards the cost (excluding VAT which is charged at 21 per cent) of conducting an energy audit. The audit will identify the potential for energy and money savings and will recommend energy saving actions, many of which may be costless or low cost. Other actions "with longer paybacks" may be eligible for support under the second grant scheme.

The second grant scheme, the Energy Efficiency Investment Support Scheme, provides grant assistance, up to a maximum of £100 000, to organisations which propose to invest in technically proven energy conservation technologies or measures. Two of the criteria for approval are noted: one is that the project must have potential for widespread replication in other organisations, another is that "simple payback times (without grant support) must be realistically short". When there are investment opportunities with short payback periods, it implies that they have good internal rates of return or net present values. If individuals and organisations do not avail of seemingly good opportunities facing them, there is said to be market failure. Market failure can occur when there is ignorance about the investment and its potential benefits, where there are hidden costs, credit constraints and, perhaps, where the potential benefits are rather small anyway or very uncertain, or where behaviour is irrational. One suspects that the first two apply in the organisations targeted by the schemes funded by the Irish Energy Centre, namely ignorance and hidden costs. In so far as ignorance plays a role, it would be of benefit for the schemes to get feedback from persons working on the premises and ascertain their levels of understanding, attitudes and behaviour, with a view to rectifying these if necessary. In the nature of things, recipients of grants will have less commitment than people who paid for energy conservation measures themselves, and the benefits of technical improvements could easily be whittled away by adverse behaviour. It would also be desirable for there to be more firms offering energy conservation services, to present more competition in the supply.

There should also be analyses of the before and after situation, to see whether schemes were effective.

Subsidies are made available to charitable bodies, such as Energy Action, to enable them to undertake insulation work on dwellings of low-income households. The organisation also trains 25 unemployed people each year to UK 'City and Guilds' certification levels in house insulation. Lawlor's (1995) analysis of this scheme, which insulated approximately 1200 homes in the year 1993/4 at a cost of £232 000 to the government, reveals an internal rate of return of between 29 and 39 per cent (depending on labour cost assumptions), plus training skills, plus 344 tonnes of $CO_2$ saved annually.

Finally there may be subsidies aimed at non-energy objectives which have the effect of lowering price and perversely encouraging energy consumption. Such activities are sometimes not overt. The sort of activities which fall into this category would include the award of grants to private turf cutters, or charging fuel used as feedstock at a price that is below the world price.

## 6.3 Options based on information from Ireland and abroad

### 6.3.1 Indirect taxes

VAT rates on fuel tend to be higher elsewhere than in Ireland. For gas and heating oil, Ireland has the fourth lowest rate, at 12.5 per cent, in EU member states, after Luxembourg, Britain and Italy, six countries charging at 20 per cent or over. For electricity, Ireland has the fifth lowest VAT rate, with Portugal imposing a 5 per cent rate. Significantly, however, the UK charges only 8 per cent and may not make another attempt at raising it for a while.

The rate of VAT applied to heating fuels and lighting could be raised from 12.5 per cent to 21 per cent. However with a quarter of households receiving social welfare payments, compensation for the VAT rise would entail diverting some 20 per cent of the increased revenue to raising social welfare payments. This would enable low-income homes to be no worse off. Personal expenditure in 1995 on fuel and power was £862 million (from Table 13 of CSO, 1996). The rise in VAT rate would yield some £65 million in increased revenue, of which £52 million would be net of funds diverted to compensate social welfare recipients. To put it in context, the extra £52 million represents over $1^3/_4$ per cent of total VAT revenue and could be used to reduce the standard rate of VAT. The 7.6 per cent fuel price rise resulting from the imposition of VAT could be expected to reduce[2] consumption and revenue by about $2^1/_4$ per cent in the short term and over $4^1/_2$ per cent in the longer term, reducing the rise in VAT revenue to around £45 million after compensation.

Existing excise taxes tend to be viewed as revenue raisers, rather than as a means for internalising an external cost imposed on the rest of society. Ireland has, again, the fifth lowest rate of excise duty on home heating oil, after Belgium, Luxembourg, the UK and Finland (European Commission, 1995). Some countries levy carbon taxes on top of existing excises on fossil fuels. Table 6.4 is a summary of carbon taxes levied abroad.

## Table 6.4
### Explicit and implicit carbon taxes levied abroad

| Country | Rate per tonne of $CO_2$ | Implicit rate of existing excise duty | Incentive | |
|---|---|---|---|---|
| | ECU/t$CO_2$ | ECU/t$CO_2$ | Intended | Actual |
| Denmark | 5.5 (industry) 11.1 (households) | 26.3 | + | .. |
| Finland | 2.2 | 19.1 | # | .. |
| Italy | 1.7 (fuels producing thermal energy) | 39.9 | .. | .. |
| Netherlands | 1.6 (excl. feedstocks) | 15.9 | - | .. |
| Norway | 13.8-40.6 (many special allowances) | 32.5 | + | .. |
| Sweden | 9.5 (industry) 37.9 (households) | 38.2 | + | # |

*Notes:* + = yes   - = no ..   = no data available   # = unclear
*Source:* OECD (1994) p. 73.

As the above table shows, energy and $CO_2$ taxation are high in Sweden, to such an extent that some district heating plants are changing from fossil fuels to bio fuels.

Charges are raised on the sulphur content of fuels in Norway and in Sweden, as described by OECD (1994, p.74). The Norwegian charge is levied on oil and the Swedish charge is levied on oil, coal and peat. The charges are intended to be incentives to switch to low sulphur fuels and activities, and the revenues accrue to the general budget.

The Norwegian charge is levied per 0.025 S-weight percentage (S-weight is the share of sulphur in the weight of the fuel) at a rate of ECU 0.008/ litre of oil. It is not levied on oil with sulphur content lower than 0.05 per cent. The Swedish charge is levied per 0.1 per cent S-weight at a rate of ECU 3.2 per $m^3$ of diesel fuel and heating oil, and ECU 3.6 per kg for coal, coke and peat. An evaluation of the Swedish sulphur tax indicates that sulphur content of oil used has decreased by around 30 per cent, and emissions from burning coal and peat have also decreased considerably. The tax has made it profitable to clean flue gases to a larger degree than before. Administrative costs are probably less than 1 per cent of revenue. Repayment of the tax occurs if actual reductions of $SO_2$ emissions are demonstrated, and this occurs on a rather large scale. The success of the tax has resulted in an unexpected revenue shortfall. Finland has also imposed a sulphur tax towards the end of 1993.

In addition, Sweden has imposed a charge on $NO_x$, the incentive effect of which has surpassed all expectations. In 1992 the emission reduction was between 30 to 40 per cent compared to an expected reduction of 20 to 25 per cent. The charge is raised on $NO_x$ emissions of energy producers at a rate of ECU 4.7 per kg of $NO_2$ ($NO_2$ is the measure of $NO_x$ that is emitted). Small installations are not subject to the charge as the fixed cost of metering would be excessive and only final energy producers are charged. If emissions are not actually measured, standard emission rates apply which exceed what might be paid under the measured charge, encouraging the installation of measurement equipment. Charge revenues are in fact rebated on the basis of final energy production of installations, such that the total impact is zero, but with redistribution between high emitting and low emitting plants.

A tax on $SO_2$ in Ireland could be considered, in order to reduce emissions from households and small industries, which constitute about a third of emissions. The remainder is covered by quotas (discussed below) under the Large Combustion Plant (LCP) Directive. Much sulphur is emitted from high stacks, so that sulphur emissions tend to travel. Only 40 per cent of sulphur deposition in Ireland can be attributed to national emissions, and 40 per cent to other countries, the UK in particular (EPA, 1996). The tax could be added to the carbon tax. Coal being a high emitter of $SO_2$ and featuring prominently in the budgets of low-income households, compensation would be necessary. Unlike releases of $SO_2$, which are mobile across boundaries, the damage from $NO_x$ is more localised, with nearly a half arising from vehicles. With the growth in transport, the national quota for emissions may be overshot unless action is taken. A $NO_x$ tax could be imposed. If levied at the rate of tax in Sweden (ECU 4.7/kg $NO_2$), revenue from taxing fuels other than those in Large Combustion Plants would amount to some £280 million. If charged at the lowest damage cost given in Table 6.2, revenue would amount to some £30 million. Vehicles fitted with catalytic converters, however, are low emitters and their fuel ought not to be taxed, but it may be unduly complicated to distinguish between vehicles which do and do not have converters. Therefore it may be more sensible to encourage the adoption of catalytic converters in the manner discussed in the chapter on transport.

*6.3.2 The EU's carbon tax proposals*

The EU's carbon tax proposal of 1991, already referred to in Chapter 3, has been analysed by Fitz Gerald and McCoy (1992) to estimate its effects in the event of it being implemented in Ireland. The proposed tax, to be applied as an excise tax in stages, was $10 per barrel of oil, with half this amount being applied to the carbon content of the fuel and the remaining half to the energy content of the fuel. This works out at £27.37 per tonne of carbon contained in the fuel plus £23.38 per TOE for the energy component (using the exchange rates of September 1991). It is notable that the tax is not inconsistent with the estimated total damage costs which we saw in Table 6.3, albeit that the estimation of damage costs probably overstates damage to health in Ireland from sulphur deposition, but then omits damage to lakes and rivers. The tax on oil and gas might be rather high and that on coal and turf rather low. In the context of the Polluter Pays Principle, the EU's proposed carbon tax is far from unreasonable. If polluters are imposing these costs and victims are bearing them, there is a good argument for shifting this burden from the victim to the polluter. It would remove the lack of incentive to changes in behaviour and give encouragement to new technology, with less need for subsidies.

Despite having these commendable features, the tax in its original form has not been agreed and may be replaced by minimum excise taxes on fuels. Depending on the rates of excise taxes, the ultimate effects could be broadly similar to the effects of the carbon tax, and governments will still presumably be able to choose how to spend the revenues.

Using the ESRI's Medium Term Model (Hermes), Fitz Gerald and McCoy looked at the implications of the carbon tax for various options as to what the government might do with the revenue. The results of the simulation which assumes that the revenue from the carbon tax is used to reduce Pay-Related Social Insurance (PRSI) contributions, are quoted in Box 6.1. In this simulation it is assumed that Ireland unilaterally introduces the carbon tax. In summary, the results show the carbon taxes yielding an annual revenue of £460 million in year 1, rising to £740 million by year 10, which, on being used to reduce labour taxes (PRSI), increases employment, reduces emigration, has a minor effect on inflation and causes a small volume rise in GNP. Expenditure on fuel and power by manufacturing industries is less than 2 per cent of their total turnover. Therefore industry would be a net beneficiary, being quite a low energy user but a major employer of labour. Hence the compensation to industry in the form of reduced labour taxes outweighs its payment of carbon taxes.

Such a tax would stimulate the search for fuel economies. The power sector would be stimulated to strive for higher efficiencies. Heat recovery would receive a boost as would district heating schemes. Though the price rises would not be so high as they were during the oil price hikes of the 1970s, fuel efficient domestic appliances and vehicle mileage per litre would become the focus of attention again as they did then. The difference here is that the extra payments would not be leaving the country, and could be used to reduce the cost of employing labour.

Industry's gain from the carbon tax would be at the expense of households, which pay the tax and do not receive compensation. However households receive compensation indirectly through extra employment and lower emigration. The effect on households is to add about 1.5 per cent to the household budget, on average, unless they reduce energy consumption, which they can possibly do at a profit already by taking energy-saving measures. The carbon tax would make energy conservation more profitable. Low-income households however would be relatively adversely affected by the carbon tax which could add 2.5 per cent to their household budget. It is recommended that some of the revenue be diverted to give compensation via social welfare payments and Family Income Supplement (Scott 1992, 1996). The estimate of the reduction in carbon dioxide emissions resulting from the tax is about 3 per cent. This may seem rather small, the authors having taken care to base the estimated results on conservative response rates backed up by available empirical work. It is to be noted that the economy would benefit.

---

**Box 6.1:** *Results for Ireland of EU's Carbon Tax with Reductions in PRSI Contributions.*

The revenues from the tax are assumed to be used by the government to reduce the level of social insurance contributions (PRSI), which at present add to labour costs. The key to the impact of the revenue switch from labour to energy lies in where the incidence of the tax changes falls: who in reality pays the tax? In the case of energy taxes, because the industrial sector is not very energy intensive, it ends up paying a relatively small share of the tax. This happens in spite of the fact that industry cannot recoup the cost of the tax by raising prices. On the other hand, industry is a big employer of labour and, as a result, it would be a major beneficiary from a reduction in labour costs arising from lower social insurance contributions.

This switch in the tax burden from labour to energy would have a positive impact on the Irish economy. It is hardly a surprising result, given that Ireland is a net importer of energy, its industry is not very energy intensive, and it has high taxes on labour, a factor in excess supply. The net effect of restructuring the tax system is to improve the competitiveness of the industrial sector. Firstly there is some shifting of tax burden away from that sector to services or households. Secondly, because the elasticity of demand for labour is greater than that for energy in the medium-term, it is to be expected that the deadweight losses associated with the tax system would be reduced.

The change in relative factor prices results in higher employment and a limited fall in energy demand and $CO_2$ emissions of about 3 per cent. The improved competitive position of the sector leads to increased industrial output and exports and the benefits of the reduction in social insurance contributions are shared between employers and employees.

*Source:* Fitz Gerald and McCoy (1992).

---

The point must be stressed that a regulatory approach would aggravate the economy by imposing high, if disguised, costs. Similarly the subsidy approach on its own imposes costs on taxpayers, who are to some extent the victims of the polluters' activities. In view of experience from abroad, such as from Sweden's sulphur tax described above, the estimates of the resulting reductions in emissions are conservative and should be viewed as the minimum reductions in carbon dioxide.

Along with other studies (e.g., Capros, 1996), an analysis by the Norwegian Green Tax Commission (Moe, 1996) produces similar results to those for Ireland. The Commission calculated the effects of implementing green taxes of some 1 per cent of GDP combined with a reduction in payroll taxes of 2.3 per cent, over time, such that net government revenues are unchanged. The study again showed that both the economy and the environment benefit.

### 6.3.3 Tradeable pollution permits

Turning to an alternative market-based approach, there is some experience abroad with the use of tradeable pollution permits. They are also advocated by DRI as the best route for reducing $SO_2$ and $NO_x$ emissions in Europe. As already discussed in the chapter on economic instruments, such a method has the advantage that the desired reduction is achieved, the authorities do not need to know anything about the technical costs of abatement and, provided that there is sufficient monitoring to prevent cheating and that an unhindered trade in permits develops, a given level of abatement is achieved at minimum cost to society. Permits have an advantage over pollution taxes, when increases in pollution are likely to give rise to damage with steeply rising cost, that is when the marginal damage costs curve is relatively steep.

There are several examples of tradeable permits in operation in Australia, Canada, Germany and the USA, described by OECD (1994). Tradeable permit systems have been functioning in the USA since 1976. Initially, regulatory standards were laid down there on an emission-point basis, but later flexibility was afforded by allowing trade within a defined area or 'bubble'. New enterprises aiming to locate in such areas could buy permits off the existing permit holders, as an 'offset'. 'Netting' exempts modifications of existing sources from certain new standards, so long as no significant net increase in emissions occurs with a facility. 'Banking' enables firms to store permits for future use.

The offset and netting facilities have been extensively utilised, but most trade has been intra-plant, due in fact to the way that the trading system was only launched effectively after compliance deadlines for the previous regulatory approach. In February 1993 the US EPA issued proposed Economic Incentive Program Rules which expand upon the previous options for emissions trading.

As stated, compared with charges, permit trading has the advantage of a more certain reduction in emissions. However there is a requirement for enforcement which may be less easy than simply adding a pollution tax to an existing tax, for example. An information system is also needed to obtain data on potential buyers and sellers of permits and there has to be an agreed auction procedure. There needs to be agreement on the initial allocation of permits, because it amounts to a bestowal of income, and a clear definition of what is being traded. For example in the case of greenhouse gases, it could be fossil $CO_2$ emissions (total or just energy-related), or net $CO_2$ emissions, equivalent $CO_2$ including other gases, et cetera. It is important to have many operators in the market for permits, such that market power is reasonably shared. This might be a difficulty with international trading if permits are concentrated in the hands of a few countries. One solution to this is to limit the period during which emission permits can be hoarded, though in itself, such a limit would restrict trade.

In Ireland's case, trading of permits in $SO_2$ and $NO_x$ should be allowed within the island at least. Quotas have been allocated to Northern Ireland and the Republic. A subset of emissions has to comply with the levels specified in the Large Combustion Plant (LCP) Directive. The Republic is adhering to its national quotas, except possibly in the case of $NO_x$, where the increase in the number of vehicles is counteracting the increased number with catalytic converters. In fact quota transfer occurs at present but not by being traded. Britain recently transferred 17,000 tonnes of $SO_2$ and 1,000 tonnes of $NO_x$ to the existing quotas for Northern Ireland of 64,000 $tSO_2$ and 20,000 $tNO_x$, at zero price.

### 6.3.4 Subsidies

Because pollution taxes and tradeable quotas entail adjustments, countries have recognised that to smooth their introduction it is necessary to provide encouragement in the form of subsidies. One such example from abroad, which combines some useful features, is the scheme for encouraging people to install compact fluorescent light bulbs. These bulbs embody a new technology which is demonstrated to be worthwhile. However customers may be unaware of this. By buying CFL bulbs in bulk and with economies of scale in administration, the Energy Savings Trust in the UK sold 1.6 million bulbs in 1994. These normally cost £15 in the shops but, subsidised via the scheme and owing to administrative efficiency, they sell for £10, and save electricity which is worth £33.50 in present value terms. This saving does not include environmental benefits which make it even more worthwhile. The scheme also subsidises purchases by other categories of households to a higher extent. On account of improved market penetration, the free-market selling price has subsequently dropped from £15 to about £12.

Lawlor (1995) has undertaken a study of the costs and benefits of previous subsidy schemes for energy conservation projects in Ireland. The study also looked at pilot energy conservation projects in public sector office buildings and hospitals. The pilot project in a certain public building, undertaken in 1990 and 1991, effected savings of 23 per cent in the building's energy costs, despite the fact that the building was constructed as recently as the 1980s and was considered quite energy efficient at the time. The project entailed replacement of light fittings, installation of lighting controls and conversion from oil to natural gas central heating. Total costs were £56 000, private net present value is estimated at £82 000 with a 28 per cent private internal rate of return. Public benefits would include the reduction of 360 tonnes of $CO_2$ per year, which, for the sake of argument and based on the damage costs in Table 6.1, amounts to annual damage reduction of between £400 and £3100. In the other pilot project of energy conservation in a hospital, savings of 70 per cent of energy costs were achieved. Much of the saving arose in conversion from turf and oil to natural gas. Future savings may not be so dramatic - in keeping with the fact that marginal pollution abatement costs rise.

The main constraint preventing public bodies from availing of such efficiency investments is the inability to borrow. This forces them to undertake only those conservation measures with a short payback such as can be financed from annual energy and maintenance budgets. Furthermore savings made were subsequently absorbed by central government which constituted a further disincentive. In addition the scarce time of management and staff should probably be included as a cost; at least it would appear to be a restricting factor. Recent changes in budgeting procedures, whereby administrative budgets are set for three year periods, may see some improvement. Even then such artificial constraints on efficiency investments are short on justification if a high but drawn out financial return is denied. The Irish Energy Centre Grant schemes could address this problem, though grants might not be necessary if the underlying constraints were addressed.

Lawlor found a similarly large private net present value arising in the Attic Insulation Grant Scheme of 1980 to 1982, with an internal rate of return of 28 per cent. Expenditure of £7.5 million was incurred to which grants contributed £2.4 million. Not being targeted at low-income homes, many grant recipients would have been able to avail of these profitable investments without grants. The public benefit consisted of the reductions in emissions, which again using the damage costs above to give an idea of magnitudes, amounts to between £0.2 and £1.1 million annually. This public external benefit is the component that could justify awarding subsidies if one were pursuing the subsidy option. The net present value of such sums, assuming 5 per cent discount rate and a twenty year horizon, is £2 million to £12 million. The actual grant of £2.4 million at least fell within this range and, being at the lower end of the range, implies that this was a good investment.

In general, assessment of whether to award grants needs to take account of evidence which suggests that the total financial (including private) and external benefits arising should be considerably more than the nominal funds (Honohan, 1996). As stated, scrutiny is especially required where there are relatively large private gains from energy efficiency investments. It may be better to inform people about how to help themselves.

### 6.3.5  Grading the options

Having described the fiscal system and its consequences and having discussed a few options based on information from Ireland and abroad it is worth noting the results of a study which grades a selection of carbon reducing technologies. The list of technologies covered is very limited but it grades the few that have been addressed, in terms of cost per unit reduction of $CO_2$ (Fitz Gerald and Johnston 1996). The graded costs, starting with the cheapest option, are shown in Table 6.5.

The grading suggests that it is worth devoting attention to promoting (1) worthwhile energy conservation, (2) a carbon tax which replaces PRSI, (3) afforestation redirected from peat soils[3] to mineral soils, (4) electricity generation by gas replacing peat and (5) electricity generation by wind replacing peat generation. Well over three million tonnes are avoided at no financial cost to society as a whole.[4] There may however be environmental costs which are not included here, such as the placing of windmills or forests in scenic areas. As the table shows, an energy tax, similar to the carbon tax, should play a central role.

**Table 6.5**
**Cost of reducing $CO_2$ emissions with different technologies**

| Technology | Cost per tonne of $CO_2$ reduced, £ | Total tonnes of $CO_2$ which could be avoided |
|---|---|---|
| Energy conservation | Saves money | not avail. |
| Carbon tax replacing PRSI | Saves money | 800 000 |
| Redirect afforestation grants | 0 | not avail. |
| Electricity generation: | | |
| Gas replacing peat | -24.6 | 1,600.000 |
| Wind replacing peat | -1.7 | 900,000 |
| Wind replacing gas | 41.3 | 300,000 |
| Biomass replacing peat | 63.5 | 2,500,000 |
| Biomass replacing gas | 228.8 | 900,000 |

*Source:* Fitz Gerald and Johnston *et al.,* 1996), p. 25.


### 6.3.6 Low-income households

An important consideration is how would low-income households be affected by a carbon tax. Low-income homes would have characteristics requiring special attention. They are less in a position to borrow to finance efficiency investments and they are likely to take any improvements to the insulation of their homes in the form of extra comfort rather than as energy savings. Their homes tend to have few conservation measures (unless they are local authority homes built since the building regulations were upgraded) so that there would be high potential savings, except that they use very little energy anyway in most cases. Indeed some 15 per cent suffer hardship on a cold day (Callan et al., 1989). They also tend to use the more polluting fuels, coal and peat, for space heating in winter. A disproportionate number of them describe themselves as not being "energy conscious" and mistakenly would buy double glazing as a priority conservation measure, given the opportunity (Scott, 1996).

In the absence of action there is the prospect of further inefficiency if these households become well off without undertaking remedial measures to their homes. For the present however they are trapped into inefficient polluting fuels in poorly insulated houses. Investment is the only route to improvement. The lesson from the UK is that the regressive effect of increased fuel taxes on low-income homes needs to be demonstrably avoidable, by means of raised social welfare payments. Meanwhile in Ireland, the state pays out some £60 million annually in fuel allowances. In theory it would be possible for the state to use part of this to insulate homes, the home being level financially with its 'before insulation' situation owing to fuel saved. In practice, the household will spend 60 per cent of the potential for savings on increased comfort, since 'comfort' is now cheaper, so the home would be warmer and healthier. Also in practice it would be difficult for the government to remove the fuel allowances, though potential for compromise may exist, whereby people could opt to switch their fuel allowances to payment for efficiency improvements.

### 6.3.7 Behaviour and the market

A theme which reoccurs in discussions of energy conservation and grants is the enigma of seemingly irrational behaviour. Why should taxpayers subsidise energy users to install energy efficient technology (e.g., low-energy light bulbs and insulation) and reap a private gain, which if they were rational they would undertake anyway? Many investments in conservation have good net present values. In an attempt to prise an explanation from survey data, it is found that there are sound, though probably not insuperable, barriers to undertaking these profitable investments (Scott 1997). An important reason is found to be lack of information, with respondents saying that they 'don't know enough about it' or 'don't think it saves money in the long run', referring to clear money-savers, such as attic insulation, hot water cylinder insulation and low-energy light bulbs. High education levels are associated with high probability of ownership of energy saving items, as such people would be in a position to find out about energy efficiency more easily. Rented premises are less likely to have these items and it would not pay tenants to install them, unless they are permanent or long-term tenants. In the case of rented accommodation, regulation is required, or guidelines should be produced for negotiations between the tenant and owner to install energy saving items. A dominant requirement however is unambiguous information about the savings potential, and clear information on how to set about acquiring energy efficiency investments, because people are not aware that this is a better investment than many other investments that they undertake in their daily lives.

A final word in relation to economic instruments is in order. Economic instruments require a potential market situation to exist. This means that people have to be able to act in a manner which improves their perceived well-being. There has to be a free market with absence of monopoly elements, alternatives have to exist and people must be aware of them and of other relevant information. A simple but very beneficial recent move was the change by Bord Gais, the gas company, from charging per therm to charging per unit (i.e., per kWh). People could then observe that the price of gas was about half that of electricity. After taking efficiencies into account the price is still about 30 per cent lower. These are the aspects of information which are difficult for the ordinary customer to know. Another good move is the availability of pre-paid cards for electricity, like telephone cards. Any developments that encourage understanding of the amount of fuel used would be helpful, such as accessible positioning of meters, and bills that are easily understood. Similarly information on pollution from different fuels should be more accessible, with a selection of some of the more relevant magnitudes listed in Appendix 6.6 being presented in some user-friendly manner. Knowledge as to which fuels might be more polluting and how one's behaviour can have an effect is rather scant.

It should not need to be said that any vestigial subsidies to fossil fuel production ought to be phased out. There still exist damaging subsidies in some energy sectors in Europe, not to mention non-OECD countries. The French nuclear industry, for example, is suspected of operating cross-subsidies, given the obscurity of its accounts, and of not internalising the end-of-life plant costs, thereby incurring criticism by the International Energy Agency (*Economist*, 1996). A critical view should be taken here of pricing and subsidies which obscure the environmental implications of different choices of fuels, such as peat.

### 6.4 Suggested use of economic instruments

A package of tax changes is required to bring some logic to the VAT rates which, as we saw, stand at 12.5 per cent on heating fuels and 21 per cent on conservation materials. There is an argument for setting rates the same on all goods and services so that ultimately the standard rate can be reduced to a lower level. While it might be beneficial to reduce VAT on energy conservation materials to 12.5 per cent, this conflicts with the aim of harmonised rates. However, in so far as sales of conservation materials are not yet in a position to reap scale economies, some boost to sales would be in order which encouraged competition and efficiency. In these circumstances explicit subsidies are preferable and the amounts would be small. The same applies in relation to energy audits.

The rate of VAT applied to heating fuels and lighting should be raised from 12.5 per cent to 21 per cent. Households receiving social welfare payments would need to be compensated for the VAT rise by diverting some 20 per cent of the increased revenue to raising social welfare payments. The net extra revenue of around £45 million could be used to reduce the standard rate of VAT.

Something along the lines of the EU's proposed. carbon tax, in the form of increased excise taxes, should be gradually introduced, simultaneous with an enhanced programme for aiding efficient energy use on the part of those who cannot afford to undertake energy saving investment. According to the results of the ESRI's Medium Term Model, if the revenue from the carbon tax is used to reduce PRSI contributions, there is a net gain to the economy and to industry in particular. Total revenue from the carbon tax of £740 million is foreseen. It will be necessary to divert possibly 20 per cent of this to compensate low-income households. A few energy-intensive firms may also come under stress. By definition these will be polluting and not labour-intensive firms, and their case for receiving transitional aid would need to be scrutinised.

In so far as climate change is a global problem and everybody's emission imposes similar damage, a universal carbon tax should be aimed for. There is an argument for addressing greenhouse gases rather than merely carbon dioxide, since these are the problem. Methane emissions, mainly from enteric fermentation in cattle, are the other principal source of greenhouse gases in Ireland. However these are only likely to be reduced, world-wide, by reduction in demand for the animal products, otherwise products will be sourced from elsewhere.

The $SO_2$ and $NO_x$ quotas allocated to Northern Ireland and the Republic should become tradeable. If and when the quota limits are binding, quotas will have a value to the plants which can abate more cheaply than others. In addition to encouraging investigation of the costs of abatement for various options, this would achieve the specified targets at minimum cost.

Grant schemes need to be critically evaluated before they are adopted. In fact many grant programmes tend to be worthwhile in national terms, because many investments bring about net benefits. The stimulus which a grant gives also enables many new technologies to realise their potential, by achieving a critical volume of sales. With correct pollution taxes in place, the stimulus to technological improvements will also see price reductions come on stream. So, unless there are good external benefits or the conservation or new technology requires encouragement to get going, the case for financing grants, involving taxing the victims of pollution, requires scrutiny.

Knowledge is a prerequisite for markets and economic instruments to function. People may not be availing of opportunities because they are not sufficiently knowledgeable, or to do so entails using valuable management or leisure time to investigate the options, to choose the contractor who will supply the energy saving service, and to organise the investment. These are knowledge- and time-intensive activities. Yet much of the necessary information could be made available by central bodies, which can exploit economies of scale in information assembly and distribution. The Energy Audit Scheme can impart knowledge which helps the market to function. Activities which reduce other barriers to markets, or which actually provide external benefits ought to be encouraged, as ought renewables and other non-polluting technologies which come under the infant industry umbrella. In any event, the reality is that to make pollution taxes acceptable, some grants will be required, some of which may be strictly hard to justify. At least the grant level should be related to the ensuing societal benefits.

Procedures to enable the public sector to act 'rationally' need to be in place. A three-year administrative budget in the public sector still limits efficiency investments to those with roughly a three year payback. The audit and efficiency grant schemes address the problem to some extent but may not engender a sufficient level of commitment once the grant has been paid.

Areas where policy-makers require more information before economic instruments should be applied include the following. The best manner to overcome the income distributional effects of higher energy taxes needs to be addressed, in order to promote the taxes' acceptability. Valuation of some of the damage[5] costs, of $SO_2$ and $NO_x$ for example, would be helpful in setting the level of emissions taxes or subsidies for abatement. In this way it will not be necessary to resort to foreign valuations.

**Notes**

1   The number of people giving financial support through donations or membership to the Irish Peatland Conservation Council, for example, has more than trebled since 1991.

2   These reductions are based on the information on responsiveness of energy demand to price changes, derived from studies by Conniffe and Scott (1990) and Scott (1991).

3   Described in the chapter on agriculture and forestry. The EU-funded programme of afforestation should be directed away from acid-sensitive soils where there is some uncertainty as to whether the carbon sequestration by the forest compensates for the carbon losses resulting from oxidation of the peat during the development phase.

4   In other words, part of the nation's marginal abatement schedule, as shown in Figure 3.3 of Chapter 3, lies below the horizontal axis until pollution *reduction* has reached a certain level - a reduction of three million tonnes of $CO_2$ at least.

5   Work is underway on evaluation of the external costs of peat and coal fired electricity generation in Ireland, under DG XII's ExternE programme, by F. Convery, S. Rooney and D. Connolly, Environmental Institute, Dublin.

# References

Callan, T., Nolan, B. and Whelan, B.J., Hannan, D.F. with Creighton, S. (1989), *Poverty, Income and Welfare in Ireland.* ESRI, General Research Series Paper No. 151. Dublin.

Capros, P. (1996), 'Using the GEM-3 Model to Study the Double Dividend Issue', Baranzini, A. and Carlevaro, F. (eds.), proceedings of a conference, *Econometrics of Environment and Transdisciplinarity,* Applied Econometrics Association, April, ISEG (Lisbon) and CUEPE (Geneva).

Commission on Taxation (1984), *Indirect Taxation,* Third Report, Stationery Office, Dublin.

Conniffe, D. and Scott, S. (1990), *Energy Elasticities: Responsiveness of Demands for Fuels to Income and Price Changes,* ESRI, General Research Series, No. 149, Dublin.

CSO (1996), *National Income and Expenditure 1995.* Government Publications, Dublin.

DRI (1994) (in association with DHV, TME, IVM, ERM, ECOTEC, Travers Morgan and M+R). *Potential Benefits of Integration of Environmental and Economic Policies, An Incentive-based approach to policy integration,* Report prepared for the European Commission, European Communities Environmental Policy Series, Graham & Trotman and Office for Official Publications of the European Communities.

*Economist* (1996), 'How the French get power', 11 May; 'Electrifying news from Paris', 18th May.

Environment Council (1996), 'Climate Change - Council conclusions' 8518/96 (Presse 188 - G).

EPA (1996), *The State of the Environment in Ireland,* Environmental Protection Agency, Ardcavan.

European Commission (1995), *Excise Duty Rate Tables: Situation 29.3.95,* Commission for the European Communities, DGXXI, Brussels.

European Communities (1992), 'Treaty on European Union, together with the complete text of the Treaty establishing the European Community', *Official Journal of the European Communities,* C224 Vol. 35, 31 August.

Fankhauser, S. (1993), 'The Economic Costs of Global Warming: Some Monetary Estimates', in Kaya, Y., Nakicenovic, N., Nordhaus, W.D. and Toth, F.L. (eds.), *Costs, Impacts and Benefits of $CO_2$ Mitigation,* Proceedings of a IIASA Workshop, September 28, Laxenburg, Austria.

Fitz Gerald J. and McCoy, D. (1992), 'The Macroeconomic Implications for Ireland', in Fitz Gerald, J. and McCoy, D. (eds.), *The Economic Effects of Carbon Taxes,* PRS No. 14, The Economic and Social Research Institute, Dublin.

Fitz Gerald, J. and Johnston, J. (1995), 'Restructuring Irish Energy Utilities', in Fitz Gerald, J. and Johnston, J. (eds.), *Energy Utilities and Competitiveness,* Policy Research Series, No. 24, ESRI, Dublin.

Fitz Gerald, J. and Johnston, J. in conjunction with ESRI, TEAGASC and HYPERION (1996), *The Economics of Biomass*, Seminar Paper, 29 February, ESRI, Dublin.

Honohan, P. (1996). *Methodological Issues in Evaluation of Irish Industrial Policy,* Working Paper No. 69, The Economic and Social Research Institute, Dublin.

IPCC (1996), *Climate Change 1995, The Science of Climate Change.* Second Assessment Report of the Intergovernmental Panel on Climate Change, Cambridge University Press.

Lawlor, J. (1995), *The Costs and Benefits of EU Government Investments and Subsidies Applied to Energy Conservation in Buildings.* Report for DG XII of the EU Commission under the JOULE II Programme.

McGettigan, M. (1993), *CORINAIR 1990 Emissions Inventory for Ireland.* Environmental Research Unit, July, European Foundation for the Improvement of Living and Working Conditions, Dublin.

Moe, T. (1996), 'Ongoing Work in the Norwegian Green Tax Commission', in *Environmental Taxes and Charges: National Experiences and Plans,* Papers from the Dublin Workshop, European Foundation for the Improvement of Living and Working Conditions, 7-8 February, Dublin.

Navrud, S. (1992) (ed.), *Pricing the European Environment*, Scandinavian University Press, Oslo.

Nordhaus, W.D. (1991), 'To Slow or Not To Slow: The Economics of the Greenhouse Effect', *The Economic Journal*, Vol. 101, pp. 920-937.

OECD (1994), *Managing the Environment, The Role of Economic Instruments*, Paris.

Scientific American (1995), 'Chaotic Climate', W. S. Broeker, November, New York.

Scott, S. (1991), *Domestic Electricity Demand*, General Research Series, No. 151. The Economic and Social Research Institute, Dublin.

Scott, S. (1992), 'Theoretical Considerations and Estimates of the Effects on Households' in Fitz Gerald, J. and McCoy, D. (eds.) *The Economic Effects of Carbon Taxes*, PRS No. 14, The Economic and Social Research Institute, Dublin.

Scott, S. (1996), *Social Welfare Fuel Allowances... to Heat the Sky?*, Working Paper, No. 74, The Economic and Social Research Institute, Dublin.

Scott, S. (1997) (forthcoming). "Household Energy Efficiency in Ireland - A Replication Study of Ownership of Energy Saving Items", *Energy Economics*, North-Holland - Elsevier Science.

Viladrich-Grau, M. (1994), 'The Oil Spill Process: the Effect of Coast Guard Monitoring on Oil Spills' paper to the Fifth Annual Conference of The European Association of Environmental and Resource Economists (EAERE), June 22-24, University College, Dublin.

# Appendix

## Table 6.6
### Approximate costs of useful heat and $CO_2$ emissions from using different fuels

| Fuel used | Cost per unit of useful heat<br>*Pence/kWh of useful heat\** | Carbon dioxide emitted per unit of useful heat<br>*Kg $CO_2$/kWh of useful heat* |
|---|---|---|
| **Open fire:** | | |
| Machine turf | 5.12 | 1.49 |
| Baled briquettes | 8.52 | 1.49 |
| House coal | 7.00 | 1.27 |
| Coalite | 11.48 | 1.27 |
| **Open fire + high output b.boiler:** | | |
| Machine turf | 3.01 | 0.88 |
| House coal | 4.12 | 0.75 |
| Coalite | 6.04 | 0.67 |
| **Oil fired boiler:** | | 0.42 |
| Oil (gas oil) | 3.58 | |
| **Room heater or gas fired boiler:** | | |
| Bottle gas (11.35 kg butane) | 9.91 | 0.33 |
| Natural gas (first 585 kWh/ 2 months) | 6.59 | 0.25 |
| Natural gas (Double up discount: min. 5850 kWh/yr) | 5.49 | 0.25 |
| Natural gas (Supersaver: min. 16000 kWh/yr) | 3.29 | 0.25 |
| **Electric fire:** | | |
| Electricity (General dom. rate) | 7.65 | 0.88 |
| Electricity (Night saver): night | 3.05 | 0.88 |
| "      "          : day | 7.65 | 0.88 |

*Notes:* * Useful heat is a unit of actual warmth enjoyed by the consumer, rather than a unit bought. The prices in this column give a better indication of the true relative prices of different fuels. Midpoint efficiencies were used in these calculations.

*Source:* Prices from Forbairt, Scott (1995).

# 7 Transport

*J. Lawlor*

Transport is a vital part of a modern economy. It is needed to move raw materials and finished product to markets, to move wastes to places of disposal, and to move people to and from work and leisure. As an economy develops, its requirement for transport services generally increases, especially in the area of personal transport. This chapter considers two media of transport – road and air – and how the fiscal-transport interface impacts on the environment. These are chosen as being the areas of most concern in environmental terms, although the main focus is on road transport, which is the area most affected by the fiscal structure and through which most transport takes place.

The chapter is laid out as follows: the first section discusses the environmental and other external impacts of transport; the next section examines the existing transport fiscal structure, and the environmental effects thereof, and asks the question - do transport users pay the full costs of transport, i.e. to what degree are the external costs internalised; the next section explores the options that exist for adjusting the fiscal structure to internalise the externalities and make it more environmentally 'friendly', and the final section maps out a possible approach for future policy.

## 7.1 Road transport[1]

### 7.1.1 The external impacts of road transport

Road transport services have two elements - the vehicles themselves and the infrastructure on which they operate (roads and streets, parking facilities, maintenance facilities, etc.). Their environmental impacts are considerable, and can be listed as follows:

1    Air pollution, which impacts directly on human health, wildlife, building damage, and adds to global warming. Transport is now considered to be the biggest source of air pollution in Ireland (EPA, 1996).

2    Noise pollution, in both urban areas and on busy roads, which affects both humans and wildlife (Mead, 1996).

3    Water pollution and related impacts. Fuel and oil leakage, and other vehicle debris, have an impact on ground and surface waters, can contaminate land, and increase the cost of waste water treatment. Increased run-off of water from sealed road surfaces adds to storm and flooding damage.

4    Land use impacts from the space that the infrastructure takes up. Under this heading are loss of agricultural, urban,[2] amenity and natural land, community severance/barrier effects (where busy roads act as barriers to normal human and animal activity), planning blight, and visual impact.

5    Wear and tear to non-transport infrastructure from vehicle vibration.

6    The environmental impacts from constructing (and disposing of) transport vehicles, and from construction and maintenance of the infrastructure. The impacts from vehicle construction occur in other countries, whereas the other impacts are felt in Ireland.

In addition to the purely environmental impacts, there are three major non-environmental external impacts - accident costs, lost time due to congestion and damage to transport infrastructure. These are worthy of some extra discussion before we proceed, to consider the exact nature of the externalities in question.

*Accident costs*

These impose very considerable costs on society. However, where road transport insurance is compulsory (as in Ireland) the costs are largely paid for by road users. There would be some unpaid for costs if (1) some transport users were not adequately insured (though in Ireland this is covered by an insurance fund), (2) the insurance system did not deal with all costs related to accidents (for example if compensation for injury and death did not adequately cover the full cost thereof) or (3) the costs of enforcing the system were not borne by transport users. In addition, there are two ways in which insurance 'shields' motorists from the cost of accidents. Firstly, insurance premia are paid yearly - motorists are not faced with the cost of possible accidents each time they use the roads, and secondly, because insurance spreads the cost of accidents among all motorists, no individual motorist is faced with the full cost of the accidents he/she may be involved in.

When an extra motorist enters a busy road or street, his/her journey is slowed down by the other road users, and he/she in turn slows down all the other road users. In total, all motorists between them absorb the costs due to this (though at least some of the costs will be passed onto the customers of commercial road users). Indeed, if all road users shared the same characteristics, the delay suffered by each would exactly equal the delay each imposed on others (in economic terms, the marginal external costs each imposed would equal the marginal external costs each suffered, and every motorist would be confronted by the correct social marginal cost). However, there are a number of ways in which this is not the case:

1   Disaggregating between different road users, some motorists' journeys are more important than others, in the sense that time is more valuable to them, and hence lost time does not impose an equal burden on all. For instance, work-related travel or goods conveyance might be considered more important than other travel, and journeys by (say) fire brigades and ambulances are more important than journeys by other motorists.

2   Buses are slowed down considerably in heavy traffic, and their journey times become less predictable. Since buses are a more efficient method of road usage than private cars, this can have a detrimental effect on the efficiency of the transport infrastructure. It may also encourage the public to use private transport, thus worsening the problem.

3   Congestion reduces the general efficiency of the transport infrastructure, which has implications for the overall performance of the economy.[3]

Therefore, there are certain road users who impose more congestion costs on others than they themselves incur. From an economic point of view, the ideal solution would be to impose a tax on these motorists, equal to these 'excess' costs. Unfortunately we cannot determine *a priori* which motorists are imposing 'excess' costs, so we are forced to charge all road users by reference to some estimate of the gross costs they impose (i.e. without deduction for the costs they incur). This will encourage some motorists to use more efficient modes of transport or to reschedule their trips. These in general will be those motorists whose journeys are less valuable, and therefore who were likely to have been imposing 'excess' costs in the first place. This will eliminate the congestion problem, and leave the road for the other motorists, who are willing to pay the tax - they will in general be those whose journeys are more valuable, and hence were suffering more losses due to congestion than they imposed. Note that it is necessary to keep the tax in place even after congestion has been eliminated - a removal of the tax would result in the congestion re-appearing. Therefore the revenue from a congestion tax is a net tax on road users over and above any costs they impose on others.

*Infrastructure damage costs*

These costs are paid for on an overall basis by road users - motoring taxes more than pay for the maintenance costs of roads, streets, etc. However, the damage caused is not equal across all road users. In particular, Heavy Goods Vehicles (HGVs) cause an inordinate amount of the total damage. Therefore it is desirable that the tax paid by each type of road user reflects the damage they do.

*The Irish context*

There are two important factors relating to road transport in Ireland that are relevant in the present context. The first is the population density and distribution. Ireland is a sparsely populated country, and much car travel in Ireland is on rural roads. This accounts for 80 per cent of car fuel use in Ireland, as opposed to approximately 50 per cent in other European countries (O' Rourke, 1992). In other words, transport in Ireland is less than half as 'urban-intensive' as in other countries. Given that most transport/environmental problems are of concern in an urban context, this means that the environmental problems of transport in Ireland are not as great as in other countries. This is important when designing transport charges and taxes to pay for environmental damage - rural car users should not be penalised for damage they do not cause. Charges that do not distinguish between urban and rural car usage (almost all of those currently in place) penalise rural car usage unfairly. A further consequence of the demographic pattern is that the public transport system is neither very comprehensive nor very viable outside the main urban areas. So it is difficult to provide rural car users with an alternative mode of transport.

Secondly, although car ownership in Ireland is currently among the lowest in the EU (Eurostat, 1995), with the increase in disposable income expected over the coming years it is predicted that there will be a major increase in the private car fleet. Car ownership and traffic are expected to grow by 3 per cent per annum up to the year 2011 (DKM, 1994)[4] - at the end of this period there will be 55 per cent more cars on the road in Ireland than at present. This has major implications for the transport system, especially in relation to congestion. Congestion has been a growing problem in recent years, especially in Dublin.

### 7.1.2 Existing fiscal treatment, and environmental effects

The most important features of the Irish fiscal system as it impacts on road transport are as follows:

*Taxes on vehicles*

There are three main taxes on vehicles in Ireland - Vehicle Registration Tax (VRT), Road Tax and Value Added Tax (VAT). VRT is a once-off tax levied on vehicles which are being registered in Ireland for the first time (whether new or second-hand), and is estimated on the Open Market Selling Price (OMSP).[5] Rates of VRT for cars are 23.2 per cent for vehicles of up to 2,500cc, and 29.25 per cent for larger-engined vehicles. Car-derived vans incur a 13.3 per cent rate, while buses and lorries pay a fixed sum of £40.

Road Tax must be paid in order for a vehicle to be used on public roads. It is an annual tax, and is based on the cubic capacity, type and use of the vehicle. For example, rates on private cars range from £92 per annum for a car less than 1,000cc to £800 per annum for a car of greater than 3,000cc. Goods vehicles are taxed by unladen weight of vehicle and trailer (in the case of an articulated lorry), and the annual tax ranges from £150 for a vehicle of not more than 3 tonnes to £1,390 for a vehicle of 14 tonnes. For vehicles in excess of 14 tonnes an extra £135 per tonne is added. Buses are taxed at annual rates ranging from £150 to £375, depending on the number of seats. Taxis and hackneys are taxed at a fixed £60 per annum, and motorcycles are taxed at a fixed £20 per annum.

VAT on all road vehicles is levied at the standard rate of 21 per cent, on the price of the vehicle, including VRT. VAT on lorries is deductible from VAT on business sales, but VAT on cars is not deductible. Public passenger transport services are VAT exempted activities, and therefore VAT paid on these vehicles (including taxis) is generally not refundable. However, a recently introduced scheme allows the VAT on the purchase of buses to be reclaimed. This concession has been granted because of the importance of bus transport to the tourist sector.

*Taxes on fuels, oils, parts and maintenance*

Transport fuels are subject to excise duties and VAT. Excise duties are variable by fuel type (see Table 7.1). VAT is chargeable at the standard rate of 21 per cent on

### Table 7.1
### Excise duties on transport fuels and oils, 1996

| Fuel type | Duty per 1,000 litres £ |
|---|---|
| Leaded petrol | 307.65 |
| Unleaded petrol | 282.05 |
| Diesel (general) | 243.75 |
| Diesel for use in licensed public passenger transport* | 17.90 |
| Diesel for use in agriculture | 37.30 |
| LPG and methane | 56.75 |
| Recycled waste oils | nil |

*Source: Revenue Commissioners.*

\* Net of rebate. The main beneficiary of this reduced rate is the state public transport company, CIE.

most fuels, except diesel for use in tractors, which is chargeable at the reduced rate of 12.5 per cent. VAT is not reclaimable as a business input on petrol.

VAT is chargeable on road vehicle parts at the standard rate of 21 per cent. However, road vehicle maintenance is charged to VAT at the reduced rate of 12.5 per cent, provided parts supplied as part of the maintenance do not exceed two-thirds of the total value. Tyres and batteries are chargeable at 21 per cent, even when supplied in the course of maintenance.

*Charges for infrastructure use*

Charges for infrastructure use exist mainly in the urban areas. Parking meters and disks, and pay-for-use carparks are examples. There has been a recent administrative development in this area. Revenues from meters and disks are administered by the local authorities, however, until recently, the revenues had to be handed over to the general exchequer. Now, the local authorities can retain the revenues, but must spend them on road-related projects. The amount involved is currently £1 million per annum. It will be interesting to see whether this change will encourage the local authorities to charge more (or more extensively) for on-street parking. In addition, a small number of privately owned and operated toll roads and bridges exist in the Dublin area.

*VAT on transport services*

The main point of note is that public passenger transport services are VAT exempt. Hence there is no VAT charged on the supply of the service, but the business cannot reclaim VAT on its inputs (except for the purchase of buses, as mentioned already). VAT is chargeable on short term car hire at a rate of 12.5 per cent. VAT is charged on the carriage of goods at a rate of 21 per cent.

*Business profit tax treatment*

By and large, transport-related expenses are fully allowable against taxable profits. Capital expenditure on vehicles is allowable as a capital allowance, at 20 per cent per annum. There are two exceptions to the general rule. Firstly, there are restrictions on tax-allowable running expenses and capital allowances relating to cars costing more than £14,000 (£10,000 if they are second-hand). Secondly, capital allowances on vehicles used for taxi and car hire businesses are at a rate of 40 per cent per annum (with no restriction relating to the purchase price).

*Personal income tax treatment*

By and large, private transport costs are not allowable against income tax. This applies even to the costs of travelling to and from work, which is not considered a work or business expense. Where an employee is provided with a company car, his/her taxable income is increased by 30 per cent of the car's original market value. This percentage is reduced if the employee pays for private petrol, insurance, road tax and maintenance. The resultant amount of tax is further reduced if business mileage travelled exceeds certain amounts. Cars in car pools provided mainly for business use by employees do not give rise to any income tax charge on the employees.

*Other features*

1    There is a 2 per cent levy on car insurance premia.

2    There is a wide range of financial penalties for non-compliance with transport laws and regulations. These include fines for parking offences and non-display of tax/insurance disks, the charge for recovering a car that has been towed away, and fines imposed by the courts for insurance, drink-driving and other offences.

3    There are incentives for the construction and operation of multi-storey carparks, which run from 1/7/95 to 30/6/98. Similar incentives have been in place in the past for the building of toll roads, however these provisions have now expired.

4    There is a £1,000 VRT Repayment Scheme, where cars of ten or more years old are scrapped and replaced by new cars, attracting a refund of £1,000 in the VRT on the new car. This scheme ran for a limited period - 1st July 1995 to 31st December 1996, and was renewed for another year.

*Environmental effects of the existing structure*

In a number of ways the Irish fiscal treatment of transport is quite environmentally positive. Cars are taxed quite heavily, and taxes increase with cubic capacity. Tax allowable business expenses are curtailed on cars costing more than £14,000, and the provision of company cars is taxed heavily on the employee (see Box 7.1). All these discourage the use of cars, and especially of larger cars.[6] Unleaded petrol and LPG are taxed at lower rates than leaded petrol, which should encourage the use of these less polluting fuels. That said, there are features of the fiscal system that have an ambiguous or even negative impact. For example, the 2 per cent levy on car insurance may help to internalise some of the external costs of accidents, but may also exacerbate the problem of uninsured driving. Favourable tax treatment for the construction of multi-storey carparks effectively subsidises car parking in urban areas, thus encouraging air pollution, congestion and other problems of urban car use. Other such issues are:

**Box 7.1: The taxation of company cars**

This is a controversial issue. As stated, company cars are taxed quite heavily in Ireland, as a benefit-in-kind in the hands of the employee. Revenue from this was £50 million in 1994. Many motoring lobby groups (e.g. SIMI, AA) have called for the level of taxation to be reduced, claiming that the tax base (30 per cent of the original market value of the car) overstates the real value of the provision of the vehicle. This is probably strictly true, given that such cars usually depreciate rapidly in value. However, there are a number of arguments for maintaining taxation levels on company cars in excess of the strict market value of the use of the car:

(a) The provision of such cars is often accompanied by free car-parking space. In a built-up area this amounts to a valuable 'perk', which is not subject to tax. It also blunts the effect of restricting or charging for on-road parking as a method of dealing with congestion. A recent study of 17 UK cities found that 43 per cent of urban parking was provided free to drivers of company cars, and that 4 out of 5 cars coming into London at peak hours were company cars (*Economist*, 1995). Company cars in the UK are taxed similarly to the system in Ireland, although the applicable income tax rates and car prices are lower.

(b) Company cars are generally seen as status symbols, which gives companies an incentive to provide them, and their drivers an incentive to use them, even when alternatives are available. These vehicles also typically carry only the driver, without any passengers.

(c) The business mileage rule, which reduces the level of tax as business mileage increases, encourages drivers to drive more business miles, or at least to claim that they do so. A recent study in the UK found that this was a major source of tax evasion. It found that 48 per cent of company car drivers travelled less than 2,500 miles on business annually, whereas less than 10 per cent declared this as their business mileage (*Economist*, 1995). It is quite possible that this applies to some extent in Ireland also.

(d) Company cars tend to be larger than the average, and may well be larger than the vehicles chosen by employees if they were buying them from their own resources (notwithstanding that their salaries would be increased to replace the benefit-in-kind). This effect increases fuel consumption, pollution and congestion.

1   High vehicle taxes on cars, while discouraging car ownership, also discourages car replacement, leading to an older car fleet. The car fleet in Ireland has been ageing considerably over the last decade: in 1985, 9 per cent of the cars in Ireland were over 10 years old; at the start of 1995 this percentage had risen to 25 per cent (Hamilton, 1995). This has a positive impact, if it means that cars' useful lives are extended - there is a better

return on the initial investment in the car, and the considerable environmental impact of new car construction is lessened. However, an older fleet creates other problems, including that cars are less fuel efficient, more polluting, possibly less accident-resistant, and require more maintenance to operate properly. It is not clear where the environmental balance lies, but it is likely that there is a point where it makes sense to encourage the replacement of the fleet, from an environmental point of view. The £1,000 scrapping subsidy for replacement of 10 year-old cars appears to be an attempt to do this. Whether this measure has a positive or negative impact on the environment depends in the first place on the net effect on the number of cars sold and scrapped,[7] and in the second place on the environmental pros and cons of vehicle replacement.

One way of looking at such a scheme is to take as a starting point that only vehicles worth less than the scrapping subsidy (i.e. £1,000) would be scrapped as a result of it. We can then ask the question, is the fleet of 10-year-old and older vehicles, worth less than £1,000, a good proxy for the fleet of vehicles that it is environmentally worthwhile to replace? A survey of such vehicles would assist in answering this question. However, a system of compulsory vehicle testing (as is planned for the start of 1998) might be more effective in maintaining the efficiency and safety of the motor fleet, and at identifying the optimal point at which vehicles should be replaced.

2    The high taxation of the purchase of new vehicles has another impact, arising from the fact that this encourages an older fleet, and that older vehicles require more maintenance to operate properly. In this context, it makes sense to encourage proper maintenance. We have seen that car maintenance services (the cost of which can include up to 2/3 parts) are subject to VAT at the lower rate of 12.5 per cent. However car parts on their own (and tyres and batteries even when supplied as part of repair services) are subject to the standard rate of 21 per cent. These taxes make it more expensive to maintain cars properly, which would have a detrimental effect on the car fleet, especially if it is likely that the older vehicles are owned by less well-off people, who are less able to pay for maintenance.

3    Ireland has the lowest excise duty on petrol, and the lowest differential in favour of unleaded petrol, in the EU. Notwithstanding that the Irish VAT rate is among the highest, and that VAT on petrol is non-deductible, Irish consumers face the lowest level of tax (with Luxembourg) on leaded petrol and the third lowest level of tax on unleaded petrol (after Greece and Luxembourg).

4    Diesel receives a substantial tax benefit vis-à-vis petrol, both in terms of lower excise duties (especially for public passenger transport) and the fact that VAT can be reclaimed on diesel. The reason for this is the

preponderance of its use for commercial transport. Until recently, it was considered that diesel was in many ways less polluting than petrol, and hence this differential appeared somewhat justified on environmental grounds also. However, more recent research indicates that diesel pollution is quite damaging, particularly in an urban context (Smith, 1995). In addition, the use of catalytic converters in petrol-engined cars erodes diesel's advantages. Hence, the case for treating diesel preferentially on environmental grounds is now less solid. Indeed, the commercial justification is also weaker than it used to be, as there is a considerable percentage of the private car stock now running on diesel (undoubtedly encouraged by the tax differential).[8] One could argue then that the preferential tax treatment of diesel is no longer justified. There is certainly a strong argument for increasing the rate of excise paid on diesel used in public passenger transport. The current extremely low rate is a discouragement to fuel efficiency; if it is felt that public transport deserves a subsidy, it can be given in some other way.

*Do transport users pay their way?*

Another way of looking at this issue is to ask the question, do motorists pay the full costs of transport (i.e. is the Polluter Pays Principle being adhered to)? We could disaggregate the question further and ask does each type of transport user (cars, taxis, vans, buses, lorries; urban, rural) and indeed each *individual* road user pay their fair share of the costs. Answering the latter question would require a greater level of information than is available, but we can keep the question in mind. The relevant costs would include not only the market costs of vehicles, fuel, infrastructure, etc., but also the costs of the environmental impacts, already listed.

From an economic point of view, the question would be rephrased as follows: do transport users pay the full marginal costs at the point of use? Economic theory tells us that the use of a resource will be efficient only if costs are paid on this basis. In reality, although transport users pay a wide range of taxes and charges, many (e.g. road tax, VRT, insurance) are only indirectly use-related. From a practical point of view, of course, charging full marginal costs would be hugely problematic, as these costs vary with vehicle, time of day, location, the precise level of congestion, and many other factors. Information technology may help us to achieve this in the future, and there is a discussion on this later in the chapter. In the meantime, we might wish that the Polluter Pays Principle is adhered to, as much as possible on a marginal cost basis, and that sub-groups within the transport sector pay their fair share of the costs.

This dichotomy between the average and marginal costs leads to another question: if marginal costs are greater than average costs (which may be the case if marginal costs rise with levels of usage), and we apply marginal cost pricing, what is to be done with the excess revenues? One argument would be that they should be returned to the transport sector, for instances through a reduction in non-use-related taxes, or by an increase in expenditure on transport infrastructure. While this might be the politically most acceptable approach, it is not the economically optimal one. In theory, the revenue from a tax would be put to the highest priority use, which might not necessarily be related to its original source. This optimal use might be the reduction of other distorting taxes in the economy, the most obvious candidate being taxes on labour. Indeed, there is an argument (made by Maddison, 1996, among others) for imposing taxes on transport beyond the marginal cost, if the dead-weight losses generated as a result are less than the dead-weight losses avoided by reducing labour (or other) taxes. In other words: which is less damaging to the economy and environment - to over-tax transport or to over-tax labour? These questions are wide-ranging, and apply to all sectors, not just transport. However, they can be kept in mind as we proceed.

Transport users pay a range of taxes and charges, as we have seen, and the amounts paid annually are presented in Table 7.2. We consider road users as a body, and in keeping with the foregoing discussion, amounts are shown on an overall or average basis and a marginal or use-related basis.

### Table 7.2
### Taxes paid by road users

| Revenue item (year) | Annual revenue £ million | |
|---|---|---|
| | Average basis | Marginal basis |
| Taxes on vehicle purchase (1995) | 433 | |
| Road Tax (1994) | 249 | |
| Taxes on fuel (1995) | 788 | 788 |
| VAT on parts and maintenance (1995) | 18 | 18 |
| Car insurance levy (1994) | 8 | —— |
| Total | 1,496 | 806 |

Source: Revenue Commissioners, Irish Times, 29/11/95.


Comparing this to the costs of supplying the road transport infrastructure,[9] the Local Authority Estimates (Government of Ireland 1995b) indicate that the local authority Road Transportation and Safety Programme in 1995 (excluding expenditure on new roads) amounted to £203 million. It can be seen that, in terms of internalised market costs, the transport sector pays significantly in excess of the costs it imposes (even when only the use-related payments by the transport sector are considered). However, to determine whether transport users truly pay the full costs of transport, we must attempt to put values on the many related external costs. Considering them as follows:

158

It is extremely difficult to value these costs, and no estimates currently exist for Ireland. Feeney (1993), quotes Quinet's (1990) estimation for air and noise pollution of 0.2 to 0.5 per cent of GDP (excluding acid rain and global warming). More recent estimates by Quinet, quoted in DRI et al. (1994), puts the cost of air and noise pollution at an average of 0.6 per cent of GDP, for a number of EU countries (again, global effects are excluded). Using this in an Irish context is not ideal. Other EU countries are more densely populated, meaning that the damage is higher than it would be in Ireland, but their GDP is also higher. A further factor is that Ireland's GDP is inflated by the very high degree of foreign direct investment in the country. Hence the actual cost figure for Ireland might be quite different from 0.6 per cent of GDP. However, without detailed research it is impossible to tell. For want of better data, we have used this percentage, and applied it to GNP in Ireland for 1995, (£33.4 billion), to get a figure of £200 million per annum.

To this we must add some estimate of the cost of the global effects of air pollution. We can take total $CO_2$ emissions relating to road transport in Ireland in 1990 as 4.047 million tonnes (McGettigan, 1993) and add 3 per cent per annum for the interim, to get 4.8 million tonnes. Converting this to carbon gives a quantity of 1.3 million tonnes. Fankhauser (1994) has estimated an external cost of £13 per tonne of carbon emissions, based on the Resource Cost method, assuming a doubling of atmospheric carbon over pre-industrial levels.[10] Applying this value to the total tonnage gives a value of £17 million per annum. This valuation is low by comparison with some others, but our calculation of localised air and noise pollution is probably on the high side, given that road transport in Ireland is less urban-intensive than in other countries, so overall our estimate is probably reasonable. The total then for the external cost of air and noise pollution is (say) £220 million per annum.

*2   Water pollution impacts, from vehicle debris, and also from increased flooding*

Studies that value these are very limited, and again no estimates exist for Ireland. OFWAT (1990) indicates that in the UK highway drainage is estimated to account for almost a quarter of total sewerage costs - in an Irish context this might represent up to £10 million per annum - but no estimate is given for water treatment costs. Including a reasonable estimate for the latter costs might bring the total up to perhaps £30 million for Ireland. Research from the USA (Washington DC) indicates costs of $0.01 per vehicle mile for water quality and flood damage (Maddison et al., 1996). Given an annual vehicle mileage total for Ireland of 15.47 billion (ERU, 1990), and an exchange rate of £=$1.60, this would suggest a cost for Ireland of as much as

£100 million per annum. Applying such a number to Ireland is not appropriate, not least because of differences in geography, climate and water quality, but it at least gives an indication that a figure of £30 million per annum might not be an overestimate.

3    *Land use impacts*

These are many and varied. Comprehensive studies of the costs of these are not available. However some research has been carried out in Scandinavia of the cost of the barrier effects of transport. Applying these to Ireland would put the costs at roughly £100 million per annum. Barrier impacts in Ireland might be lower than this, but the other impacts would probably (at least) make up the difference.

4    *Wear and tear to infrastructure*

Wear and tear to transport infrastructure has already been considered above, so we are only concerned here with damage to other infrastructure such as buildings. No estimates of the cost of this are available.

5    *External impacts of vehicle construction and maintenance, and of infrastructure maintenance*

These have not been quantified; however, vehicle production certainly imposes significant costs, as this sector is a major user of energy. These costs will affect the country of manufacture rather than Ireland (global impacts excepting), but they still exist.

6    *Non-internalised accident costs*

The Department of the Environment (1996) indicates that total accident costs in 1993 were £784 million. Adding say 3 per cent for inflation gives an estimate for 1995 of roughly £830 million. As against this, road users pay insurance to cover at least some of these costs. Total motor insurance paid in 1994 amounted to £625 million (Government of Ireland, 1995a), and indications are that the 1995 value would be around the same. This suggests uninternalised costs of (say) £200 million per annum. On a marginal basis the amount is different, because insurance payments are not directly use-related. Hence the marginal cost is the full £830 million.

The Department of the Environment valuation is consistent with using a Value Of a Statistical Life (VOSL) of roughly £800,000, and is based on UK 'Willingness To Pay' surveys. This is an area of controversy. The standard used internationally varies, but is roughly £1 million. However, a recent study prepared for the EU

Commission (DRI et al., 1994) has suggested using a VOSL of ECU 2.6 million for all European inhabitants. This translates into £2 million roughly, and if used would add up to £500 million to our estimate of social costs of accidents.

## 7    Congestion costs

Congestion costs, by their nature, vary by country (standard of roads, population densities, economic activity/wealth), location, time of day, and other factors. There have been no studies carried out of these costs in an Irish context, and it is not appropriate to extrapolate from findings in other countries, because the factors affecting congestion are so variable. We can, however, look at one or two findings from other countries, to get some indication of the overall levels of costs. Quinet (1994) estimates that congestion costs about 2 per cent of GDP in western industrialised societies; this would give a value for Ireland of perhaps £670 million per annum. This is probably an over-estimate, given the relatively low population densities and small urban areas in Ireland. A closer approximation to Ireland might be Sweden: Maddison et al. (1996) quotes Swedish research which puts the cost there at 0.35 per cent of GDP. For Ireland this would be £120 million per annum; however, it is not possible to quantify the congestion problem in Ireland properly without carrying out research here.

As mentioned earlier, one can argue that congestion costs are absorbed in overall terms by the body of road users, and therefore, while they are a cost on a marginal basis, it is not appropriate to include them on an average or overall basis. Against that, the economy as a whole does suffer when the road infrastructure is over-used, as slower transport times lead to increased production costs. So at that level at least there is an overall cost.

In summary, and notwithstanding all the uncertainties, we can list the external costs of road transport in Table 7.3.

**Table 7.3**
**External costs of road transport**

| Cost item | Annual cost £ million | |
|---|---|---|
| | Average basis | Marginal basis |
| Air and noise | 220 | 220 |
| Water pollution/flood damage | 30 | 30 |
| Land use/severance impacts | 100 | 100 |
| Wear and tear to other infrastructure | NQ | NQ |
| Vehicle construction and maintenance | NQ | NQ |
| Accident costs | 200 | 830 |
| Congestion costs | NQ | NQ |
| Total quantified | 550 | 1,180 |

\* NQ = not quantified

We can compare these costs with the balance on internalised costs and revenues, as shown in Table 7.4.

**Table 7.4**
**The balance of internal and external costs of the road transport sector**

| | Average basis £ million per annum | Marginal basis £ million per annum |
|---|---|---|
| Revenues from the transport sector (from Table 7.2) | 1,496 | 806 |
| Less: | | |
| Internalised costs of transport | 203 | 203 |
| Quantified external costs (from Table 7.3) | 550 | 1,180 |
| Net position - transport sector overpays/(underpays) by | 743 | (577) |

It can be seen that the transport sector in Ireland is more than paying its way, *on an average basis*. However, on a marginal basis, road users are significantly underpaying. It is also important to keep in mind that several externalities are not quantified in the above calculations. The inclusion of these would certainly reduce the balance in the transport sector's favour. In view of this, and the discussion at the start of this section, it would appear that there is scope for improving transport taxation in Ireland, from an environmental and economic point of view, by making it more marginal-cost based.

**Box 7.2: Are there external benefits of transport?**

We have considered in detail the external costs of transport, but there is a debate also about the external benefits thereof. If such benefits exist there is an argument for deducting them from the costs of transport, in estimating whether road users pay the full social costs of transport.

These benefits are in the nature of positive spin-offs in the economy from the transport system, in terms of increased consumer surplus from lower goods prices, improved mobility and access of people and goods, increased opportunities in the economy, and general industrial development benefits. These benefits are often referred to as pecuniary externalities (i.e. they are processed through the market system).

There is a debate as to whether these benefits should be deducted from external costs. Rothengatter (1993) makes the argument against considering them. He argues that many products, e.g. electricity, generate positive economic spin-offs, but that we do not generally consider that their supply should be subsidised. This is the general economist's attitude to pecuniary externalities - because they are processed through the market system and do not alter the efficient allocation of resources, there is no need for government intervention in their supply.

In reality, governments do often subsidise products such as electricity, because of the economic (or social) benefits referred to above. This is justified where private firms could not easily capture these benefits, and hence the market would be inclined to under-supply the product. However, this justifies subsidising only the provision of *infrastructure* for supplying the product. Once infrastructure has been provided, the full marginal cost of supply (including upkeep of the infrastructure) should be paid by the user.

In the context of roads, cost-benefit analysis is generally carried out to determine whether a new road will generate benefits greater than the cost of its construction (needless to say, this procedure should consider the external as well as internal costs). Where the benefits exceed the costs, and a private firm could not easily capture these benefits, it is justifiable for the state to subsidise construction of the road. Once constructed, however, users of the road should pay the full marginal cost of its use (see INFRAS, 1994).

In summary, all the internal and external costs and benefits of road construction and use (including pecuniary externalities), need to be considered when a new road is being planned. Once the road is built, however, only the full (internal and external) costs of its *use* should be taken into account.

---

### 7.1.3 Options from experience in Ireland and overseas

We have already considered the environmental impacts of transport, and the existing fiscal structure and its environmental effects. The next step is to consider some of the options that are available to adjust the fiscal system, to improve its environmental impact. Our aim is to move the fiscal structure more closely to a situation where transport users pay the full marginal costs at point of use. We would also wish to remove specific anomalies in the tax structure that are injurious to the environment, and to ensure that sub-groups within the transport sector pay their fair share.

The main areas of concern are air pollution, congestion, and wear and tear to the transport infrastructure. We will consider each of these in turn, along with how to encourage the use of public transport, and the proper maintenance of vehicles. Where information is available, we also discuss how effective the measures in question might be in reducing external damage from transport (i.e. the price elasticities).

### 1. Reducing air pollution damage

*Fuel taxes* Fuel taxes are an obvious approach to trying to reduce air pollution from transport usage. By making fuel more expensive there is an incentive to use less, which will reduce pollution. Differentiating taxes by reference to the polluting potential of the fuel also helps. As mentioned, Ireland has among the lowest petrol taxes in the EU, and the lowest differential in favour of unleaded petrol. There is also a lower excise tax on diesel than on petrol. A number of countries, notably the UK, have committed themselves to regular real increases in fuel prices over the next number of years. The OECD and European Conference of Ministers of Transport (ECMT) have recently recommended an increase of 7 per cent per annum in the full price of fuel over the next twenty years, in the context of reducing $CO_2$ emissions by 60 per cent over the same time period (OECD/ECMT, 1995).

There is scope therefore to increase fuel taxes here, and to increase the differential on unleaded petrol. There is also a strong argument for reducing the gap between petrol and diesel, especially for diesel used in public passenger transport. One approach, introduced in the UK in 1994, is to bring the tax on diesel into line with that on unleaded petrol. Further options relate to favourable tax treatment of other fuel types, some of which are at various stages of development. Those already available include cleaner forms of petrol and diesel (which have lower sulphur and carcinogenic content and lower particulate emissions than conventional fuels), while fuels at the development stage include liquefied natural gas and crop-based fuels.[11] In the case of new fuels, favourable tax differentiation in Ireland is unlikely on its own to encourage commercial development; however, it would encourage the adoption of new fuels which had already been developed in other countries. Another consideration with new fuels is the need to develop a refuelling infrastructure.

It is worthwhile considering what is the effect of increasing fuel taxes on consumption. International evidence suggests that in the short run this is modest: price elasticity of demand for petrol in the short run is thought to be about -0.2.[12] In the longer run it is higher, at -0.4 (Smith, 1995). However, where there are close

164

substitutes (e.g. leaded versus unleaded petrol), the elasticity is much higher. For example, the relatively modest price differentiation between these fuels in Ireland has lead to a major switch to unleaded fuel in recent years, and this is reflected in the experience in other countries (Schnutenhaus, 1995). A similar tax differentiation on 'reformulated gasoline' (unleaded petrol with lower sulphur content and fewer carcinogenic substances, among other improvements), and on various grades of less polluting diesel, introduced in Sweden in recent years, has also had considerable success.

*Vehicle taxes* One approach is to differentiate road taxes or excise by the fuel efficiency of the vehicle. This is already done indirectly by calibrating the tax by reference to the cubic capacity of the engine, but this may not fully reflect fuel efficiency. Several US and Canadian state/provincial governments have in recent years operated 'gas guzzler' taxes, which are a direct sales tax on fuel-inefficient vehicles. These promote fuel efficiency directly by affecting consumer choice and indirectly by encouraging manufacturers to improve the fuel efficiency of their models.

A variation on the theme is a 'feebate' system, whereby fuel inefficient cars are taxed and fuel efficient cars receive a rebate. This approach has been used in North America, notably in Ontario.[13] The Ontario system is on an overall basis revenue-generating, although it could of course be designed to be revenue neutral. US studies of 'feebate' systems indicate that while they can have a positive impact on fuel consumption, the bulk of this comes from manufacturers' responses rather than consumers' choices (Davis et al., 1993, cited in Bregha and Moffet, 1995). This would suggest that such taxes are most effective if applied in large jurisdictions - large enough to force manufacturers to react. It is possible therefore that such a scheme applied in Ireland alone might not have a significant effect on fuel consumption.

Apart from the amount of fuel used, the combustion efficiency and state of repair of vehicles also impact on the amount of pollution generated. Regulations, which for example require catalytic converters and impose regular maintenance on vehicles, have been the main approach used internationally in this area. Certainly there is a strong case for introducing compulsory vehicle testing in Ireland,[14] as will be required by EU regulations from the start of 1998. A lower road tax or VRT on cars which have specific pollution-reducing devices is another approach. Germany operated a tax differential on cars with catalytic converters (and on unleaded petrol) from the mid-eighties to the early nineties, with the result that currently more than 40 per cent of all petrol-engined cars in Germany are equipped with converters (by 1993, 99 per cent of all new cars had converters). During the period of the incentive, the government gave an exemption from the annual car tax for all new cars bought with a catalytic converter installed (and gave grants to have the devices retro-fitted). This exemption ranged from one to almost seven years, depending on the engine capacity of the vehicle. The measures were very generous, but were seen as necessary to bring about a rapid change in the emission standards of the vehicle fleet, given the low level of use of catalytic converters at the start of the process.[15] However the measures were designed to be revenue-neutral, and involved an increase in tax on cars without converters, and substantial increases in the tax on petrol (while maintaining the differential in favour of unleaded petrol). As stated, the incentives have now been eliminated; they have effectively been replaced by regulations at EU level which require all new cars to have catalytic converters fitted. Measures to encourage the use of converters of course also further encourage the use of unleaded petrol, since cars with converters can only be operated with this fuel - unleaded petrol now has 89 per cent of the market in Germany (Schnutenhaus, 1995).

*Tradeable permits*  An approach taken in the US combines regulation with economic instruments, by imposing stringent emission standards, but allowing car manufacturers that produce cars that go beyond the standards to trade their 'excess' emission reductions with other manufacturers. This 'tradeable permits' approach applies for instance in the case of the Californian Zero Emission Vehicle (ZEV) requirement. By 2003, 10 per cent of all cars sold in California must be ZEVs,[16] but individual manufacturers can trade so that if one firm sells more than its 10 per cent quota it will be able to trade its excess to another firm, which can then sell fewer than the quota. This means that firms with a technological advantage in this area will have an incentive to go beyond the quota, while those for whom the quota is onerous can 'pay' others to meet their quota for them. Overall, the quota will be achieved at lower cost to the economy. Such a system would only be applicable over a very wide jurisdiction, for example the EU. It would not be practical for a small country such as Ireland to impose standards significantly higher than those applicable internationally, as it would be very expensive for manufacturers to meet the standards purely for such a small market. Manufacturers would either pass on these large costs to Irish consumers, or withdraw from the market. The net effect would be that the existing fleet would continue to be used and the replacement rate would slow down, with no impact on air pollution, and eventual increased pollution as vehicles became older. In addition, the benefits of improvements to vehicles designed to meet standards in other countries would be forgone.

As a final note on measures to reduce air pollution damage, whether a journey is through a congested area will also have an effect, as slow-moving traffic causes more pollution, and the pollution in such areas will tend to do more damage to humans. The measures aimed at reducing congestion will help this.

### 2. Dealing with congestion

*A discussion of the regulatory approach*  Congestion costs can be dealt with in a number of ways. Using the regulatory approach, several options are available, ranging from 'do nothing' (i.e. let the congestion itself act as a constraint on road users), to various restrictions (including bus and cycle lanes, and bans on certain vehicles[17] and on-road parking at peak times[18]) to the increased use of information technology (which provide motorists with better route information, and improve the control of traffic flows), to pedestrianisation. However, the disadvantage of these approaches from an economic point of view is that they do not in general differentiate between journeys - a journey that is very important or has a high economic value is restricted equally as much as a less important journey. Economic measures which charge for road use get over this problem, because those whose journeys are valuable will be willing to pay for making them, while those whose journeys are less so will find alternative transport modes, or make their journeys at another time.

*Economic measures* Using economic incentives, there are several ways of charging road users in relation to the differing congestion costs they impose, and the main ones are discussed below.

*Tolling* Tolls have the advantage of simplicity, and the fact that they can be differentiated by vehicle type and time of day. Toll roads and bridges are widely used, though usually they are privately built and the tolls reflect the need to earn a return for investors - the charges are therefore not necessarily equal to the marginal cost of road use. Toll systems also have problems in that they themselves cause delays and traffic tailbacks, take up space, and may simply displace traffic to other areas. In the context of considering a toll system for Dublin city centre, it has been suggested that the two canals in Dublin form a natural toll barrier around the city centre, and that the bridges thereon form suitable sites for toll booths (or for the type of electronic systems discussed later).

*Supplementary licence fees* Another approach is to charge a supplementary licence fee or road tax to enter the congested area. The city of Singapore introduced such a system in 1975 (in conjunction with increased parking fees, tax increases and a park-and-ride public transport scheme). Motorists entering the city centre between 7:30 and 10:15am had to pay an additional licence fee of roughly £20 per month or £1 per day (in 1996 values). Between 1975 and 1979 a reduction of traffic of 33 per cent was achieved. At the same time car pools increased by 143 per cent (Barrett and Walsh, 1983). This system has the considerable advantage of simplicity, but suffers from the disadvantage that once the license has been bought there is no further disincentive to travelling in congested areas.

*Electronic systems* A more recent approach is to use electronic systems (often referred to as Automatic Vehicle Identification or AVI) that take into account vehicle type, journey route, and possibly the actual level of congestion and pollution. Vehicles communicate with a central computer via roadside terminals, and users are charged by reference to their use of congested routes. Such a system gets over the short-comings of the alternative approaches, and is a step in the direction of true marginal cost pricing, but has considerable problems, not least the costs of set-up and public opposition. However, it has been used in practice, notably in a number of US and Norwegian cities.

In the Norwegian cases (Oslo and Trondheim), an electronic card system is used, though motorists also have the option to pay cash at manual tolling booths (cards generally cover a fixed time period - year or month - and are sold at a considerable discount over the cash charge). Jones and Hervik (1992) review the Norwegian experience with both manual and electronic tolling systems. The evidence indicates a moderate price elasticity to tolling, ranging from -0.2 to -0.45, with more car sharing and little increase in public transport use. They state that the impact of tolling might be greater if charges were accompanied by improvements in public transport and other disincentives to car use. They also state that the discount on charge cards - mostly availed of by frequent travellers - reduces the ability of these systems to control traffic flows.

Electronic charging has also been attempted in Hong Kong, and this is an interesting case: the technical and economic viability of the scheme was established in extensive testing prior to the introduction of the scheme in 1985; however, a combination of economic recession and public opposition led to its abandonment shortly after introduction (Hau, 1990). Financial costs were high for the Hong Kong scheme also, estimated to be 40 per cent of the revenues collected. This compares with only 10 per cent for the Singapore system mentioned already (DRI et al., 1994).

*Parking charges - on-road parking* Another economic approach is more extensive (and expensive) metering of on-road parking, with differentiated rates depending on time of day. A study carried out in a number of British cities recently concluded that doubling parking charges and halving the number of parking spaces in these cities would reduce traffic by 30 per cent (*Economist,* 1994). However, metering of on-road parking has weaknesses in that much rush-hour traffic parks for free at car parks provided at work, a reduction in on-road parking may encourage through traffic, and effectiveness generally requires increased policing and enforcement (Button, 1993). So the net impact of the measure may not be as much as hoped for.

*Parking charges - private parking* In addition to on-road parking, off-road or private car parking spaces encourage car usage in urban areas. This is particularly the case with commuting to work, where employers provide free parking spaces to employees. A solution is to tax car park spaces, either directly, or to make them a basis for calculation of local property taxes (known as Rates in Ireland). The latter option has the advantage that the overall level of Rates need not increase, simply that the basis of calculation would change. The adoption of such a system would encourage employers to charge employees for the use of car parking spaces. There might be an 'incumbent' problem, with employees who have traditionally enjoyed free car parking complaining that this 'condition of employment' had been changed. However, in new office and apartment buildings car park spaces are increasingly being treated as marketable assets. As time goes on, and on-road parking becomes more expensive, this trend is likely to strengthen. So the market will automatically put a value on parking spaces; with the external costs of parking included in Rates or a tax, this will feed through to the cost of spaces. The final report of the Dublin Transport Initiative recommended that car parking spaces be taxed. As mentioned already, the Irish fiscal system subsidises the building of multi-storey carparks in urban areas, and there is a strong argument for removing this provision.

*Other economic approaches* There are a few other approaches which merit brief mention. One is to have higher fuel taxes in particular areas. This has been used in Tromso in Norway, a city remote from other urban areas. Alternatively, although less direct, there can be a higher annual road tax for urban as opposed to rural cars. This approach is used in Malta, where there is a higher road tax in Valetta than outside (Button, 1993). In Singapore, vehicles that are used only at weekends are subject to lower purchase taxes. These measures are quite blunt, and would have major boundary and evasion problems. The tax differentiation could not be too great for these reasons, so the impact of the measures would be limited.

*The Irish context* As mentioned already, there are no estimates of the costs of congestion in an Irish context, though it is likely to be a lower figure than in other more densely populated countries. Also, as mentioned, the costs of (particularly electronic) systems to control congestion can be quite high. Whether the benefits would justify the costs in an Irish context is open to question, although costs will doubtless fall as technology advances.[19]

*3. Relating taxes to road damage done*

A disproportionate amount of road damage is caused by HGVs. To quote Feeney (1983): 'vehicles with heavy axle loads are estimated to account for 94 per cent of the structural damage to roads'. The damage depends on weight per axle (rather than overall vehicle weight), distance travelled, and strength of the road surface. There is therefore an argument for replacing the current road tax on HGVs, which is based on *unladen* weight, with a tax based on laden weight per axle, and a kilometre tax. Kilometre taxes are currently used in a number of countries for HGVs, e.g. New Zealand, Finland, Sweden and Norway. A weight per axle system has been in consideration by the EU since the late seventies (EC, 1978) and indeed a recent EU Directive (EU, 1993) provided for the introduction of such a system (with a temporary 50 per cent derogation for Irish hauliers). This Directive was annulled by the European Court of Justice in 1995, on a technicality, but a replacement is planned for the near future. On the strength of this Directive several EU countries (Benelux, Germany and Denmark) have introduced a common 'Eurovignette' system, whereby all hauliers wishing to travel on roads in these countries must purchase a ticket, which is valid for a set time period (day, week, etc.). In line with the provisions of the Directive, Irish hauliers enjoyed a 50 per cent discount until the end of 1996.

The UK currently taxes commercial freight vehicles on the basis of weight and number of axles. Germany recently tried to introduce a tax based on weight, number of axles and kilometres travelled. However, the European Court ruled that the application of the tax to foreign-registered vehicles would have adverse effects on competition, and the measure was suspended (Smith, 1995).

### 4. Encouraging the use of public transport

There are two aspects of this - firstly to remove elements of the fiscal system that unfairly penalise public transport, and secondly, actually to subsidise public transport. While the first is always appropriate, the only justifications for subsidies are if other forms of transport receive subsidies which for some reason cannot be removed - the most important element here is the failure to internalise the external costs of car transport - or if there is some public good element to the service. Whatever the reason for subsidies, they need to be:

1       As explicit as possible, i.e. not hidden in rebates or some other device. An example of this is the provision in Ireland of large rebates in fuel taxes. This masks the true level of subsidy, and, as mentioned already, discourages fuel efficiency.

2       Where possible related to particular disadvantages that public transport suffers, or to particular routes which are not commercial but which are worthwhile maintaining for other reasons.

There is also a concern with subsidies where competition is restricted, as is the case with urban public transport in Ireland. In such circumstances the benefits of subsidies may not be passed onto consumers. In total, public transport in Ireland receives considerable subsidies, and it is not clear whether this fully compensates for the implicit subsidy that private cars receive. Further research on this would be useful, though the best option is to internalise all costs for all modes of transport. This would obviate the necessity to subsidise public transport, except where uncommercial but worthwhile routes are concerned. In the meantime, other options for encouraging public transport include:

*Making public transport services (including taxis) zero-rated for VAT purposes*
Such services are currently VAT exempt; the change would allow the operators of these services to reclaim VAT on their inputs, thus reducing their costs, and making them more competitive with private transport. There is a difficulty with this, however, as changes in VAT provisions are very much circumscribed by EU provisions on VAT harmonisation, and the measure described here may not be allowed. In addition, allowing taxis to reclaim VAT on inputs would need to be tied

**Box 7.3: Distributional impacts and political aspects**

These are a major concern for any attempt to introduce economic instruments in the environmental sphere. On the face of it, any proposal to shift the financing of a service from income taxes to use-related taxes is regressive. In addition, it is politically easier to maintain an existing tax or charge than it is to introduce a new one. Also, the imposition of a tax regime significantly different from that of neighbouring countries has implications. In the case of the transport sector, there are a number of issues which arise from these general observations:

*(a) Urban versus rural drivers*

As mentioned earlier, one could argue that rural car users should be taxed less heavily than their urban counterparts, since rural road usage generates fewer environmental problems. Some of the options discussed in this paper (e.g. congestion pricing) would enable this to happen. Of course any measure that would hurt one group of drivers while helping another might not be publicly acceptable.

*(b) High income versus low income groups*

High income groups use cars more extensively than low income groups, so higher motoring taxes would cause the former to pay more taxes. However, these taxes would also hurt low income car users more severely, especially if they have no alternative to driving, and would also put car ownership out of reach of a certain number of low income households. Given the ease with which 'hard cases' can be identified, and the perceived desirability of car ownership across all income groups, even those proposals which on the face of it are progressive might have difficulty in generating wide support.

*(c) Transport lobbies*

These lobbies are powerful in all countries, in the spheres of both personal and freight transport, and Ireland is no exception. Their influence is important at two levels -

1. In terms of the general level of transportation taxation. For example, freight transport is an important part of a modern economy, and its efficiency is crucially important for economic development. It is appropriate therefore that any proposal to increase taxes on this sector would raise concerns about the effect on the wider economy, and the transport lobbies use this argument to their advantage. This is not just confined to Ireland: in The Netherlands, freight transport is taxed very lightly, due to the importance of this sector to the economy.

2. Where a new tax or charge is being introduced, which as we have stated is always a difficult task. A case in point is the proposal to toll motorways in the Dublin region, which is being vociferously opposed by the AA amongst others. Again we can find parallels in other countries: the failure of the Hong Kong Electronic Road Pricing system has already been mentioned; similarly a recent proposal to toll the road system electronically in the Amsterdam/Hague/Rotterdam region of Holland was defeated, though it was replaced by increases in fuel taxes. In 'T Veld (1991) gives a good description of this case.

*(d) Border problems*

Having a border with Northern Ireland, any Irish tax or policy proposal must consider the equivalent position in the UK. Measures which are significantly more 'draconian' than those in the UK, may simply encourage transport users to e.g. buy their fuel or register their businesses in the North. The net result would be a loss of revenue to the Irish exchequer, with no environmental benefit. This may be less of an issue than it was in the past, as the British government has committed itself to increase fuel taxes considerably in future years, as well as other measures designed to internalise transport cost more fully. However, it still needs to be considered when new measures are proposed in Ireland.

to measures to improve competition in the taxi sector.

*Making commuting by public transport a tax deduction* This is done in Germany, although relief is also available there for commuting by private car (expenses deducted are either a fixed lump sum, actual public transport costs, or a fixed rate per kilometre for private cars[20]). There might of course be administrative difficulties in implementing this, especially in ensuring that commuters were genuinely using public transport. Tickets would have to be identifiable with the user and be non-transferable. However, non-transferable weekly and monthly tickets are already available from the public transport companies, and confining tax relief to these tickets might be appropriate.

*5. Encouraging proper maintenance of vehicles*

This will improve the fuel efficiency and pollution characteristics of vehicles, and help to reduce accidents. There can be no doubt that the single most effective method of doing this is to introduce mandatory vehicle testing for private cars, including the testing of emissions. Another option would be to reduce the VAT on vehicle parts, possibly from the standard to the low rate; this might 'soften the blow' of mandatory testing. Most vehicle maintenance services are already taxed at the low rate, including the parts - this anomaly may disadvantage low-income car owners, who might be more likely to do their own maintenance. However, as mentioned already, strict EU rules on VAT apply, and it appears unlikely that the suggested change would be allowed under these rules.

*7.1.4 Recommendations*

Having discussed the various fiscal options for improving the environmental characteristics of the transport sector, we now consider a possible approach for incorporating some of these options into the Irish fiscal system. We would recommend the following:

*1    Air pollution:*

(a)    Increase the tax advantage of less polluting fuels, especially cleaner forms of diesel and possibly natural gas; this would be paid for by increasing the tax on regular fuels.

(b)    Give grants for the retro-fitting of catalytic converters, for LPG conversion (it appears that with LPG the tax differentiation on the fuel is not sufficient to encourage large-scale use), and possibly for conversion to natural gas; this would be paid for by increases in car tax on cars without catalytic converters, and increases in the price of fuel.

(c)    In the longer run, consideration might be given to moving from a cubic capacity-based road tax to one based directly on fuel efficiency, possibly using the feebate approach.

*2    Congestion costs:*

(a)    The first step would be to estimate what the congestion costs are in an Irish context. Contingent valuation methods, which ask the public what they would be willing to pay for a reduction in travel times (as well as the other benefits of reduced traffic), would be appropriate. Researching the viability of the various congestion control approaches - tolling, electronic systems, etc. - would be the next step. These investigations would tell us whether such approaches would be viable in Ireland.

(b)    In the meantime, increasing parking costs, through increased on-road metering, perhaps (partially) basing local authority Rates on the number of parking spaces on a premises, and removing the tax benefits for building multi-storey carparks, would be appropriate first steps.

*3    Relating road taxes to damage done:*

Change the tax on HGVs to one based on laden weight per axle and distance travelled. This may require an EU-wide approach.

*4    Encouraging the use of Public Transport:*

If it is not possible to internalise fully all costs of other modes of transport, there is a justification for measures to encourage the use of public transport. However, it is necessary to keep in mind the problems and concerns with subsidising public transport, already discussed. One possibility is to make commuting by public transport a tax deduction; this could be paid for by increasing the road tax on cars. In addition, there is a strong argument for replacing the public transport rebate on fuel tax with a subsidy calculated on some other basis, as the present situation discourages fuel efficiency.

*5    Reducing the cost of vehicle maintenance*

If it is possible under EU regulations, it is desirable that all costs related to vehicle maintenance be subject to a uniform low rate of VAT. This of itself would encourage more maintenance, which would partly pay for the measure. Mandatory vehicle testing for private cars, due to be introduced at the start of 1998, will generate more of a market for maintenance services, which will also generate more tax revenue. Any shortfall in revenue could be made up by increased road tax, petrol tax or VRT.

## 7.2 Air transport

This part of the chapter briefly reviews the fiscal structure as it applies to air transport. Although perhaps of less concern than road transport, there are important issues relating to the environmental impacts of air transport, which are worthy of consideration, especially in the light of expected increases in air traffic world-wide, and concerns about global warming.

### 7.2.1 The external impacts of air transport

In many senses these are similar to road transport. The main impacts are as follows:

1    Air pollution; of particular concern are the global impacts, mainly $CO_2$ emissions and ozone depletion.

2    Noise pollution and visual intrusion in the vicinity of airports.

3    Accident costs.

4    Congestion costs (i.e. lost time), especially for take-off and landing at large, busy airports.

$CO_2$ emissions and noise pollution are the major causes of concern. Air transport produces twice as much $CO_2$ emissions as cars, and the effects of these and other emissions at high altitudes are largely unknown, due to the difficulty and high cost of carrying out research in this area (INFRAS, 1994; Netherlands Ministry of Housing, Spatial Planning and the Environment, 1995).

### 7.2.2 Existing fiscal treatment, and environmental effects

In contrast with road transport, international air transport is subject to few taxes, and in many senses is actually subsidised. Three factors drive this:

1    Air transport is the subject of a high degree of international competition, and firms are highly mobile. Therefore it is difficult for one country to impose higher taxes on its air travel firms without hurting their competitive position.

2    Many airlines are state-owned and have traditionally benefited from a high degree of protection and regulation. While this has changed substantially in recent years, especially in North America, some elements still remain in the European industry.

3      International and bilateral agreements governing the industry forbid taxes on international air travel. EU rules also forbid countries from introducing unilateral taxes, such as VAT, on domestic air travel.

As a result of these three factors, governments have been slow to impose taxes on the air transport sector, and Ireland is no exception.
The main features of the existing fiscal system are as follows:

1      Supply, modification, repair and maintenance and hiring, fuelling and provisioning of large passenger aircraft are zero-rated for VAT purposes.

2      Aviation fuel for commercial airlines is not subject to tax (aviation fuels for other users is subject to excise duty at a rate of £153.82 per 1,000 litres, and is subject to VAT at a rate of 12.5 per cent).

3      Air travel, like other transport services, is VAT exempt, so there is no VAT on airline tickets.

4      Air travellers pay a travel tax of £5 each time they leave Ireland on an international flight.

5      Air transport (in common with sea transport) is substantially subsidised by the concession of duty free shopping, both in airports and in flight.

6      In addition, Shannon airport is aided by the fact that trading activities carried on within the airport are subject to the 10 per cent corporation tax rate. This concession may indirectly reduce the cost of running the airport, and hence the cost of air travel therefrom.

7      Companies involved in the repair and maintenance of aircraft are subject to corporation tax at the 10 per cent rate. This is designed to attract such activities to Ireland, but also acts as a subsidy to air travel.

8      Unlike road travel, where use of the infrastructure is largely free at the point of use, airlines must pay directly for the use of airports and air traffic control services. Aer Rianta, the state-owned body that operates Irish airports, charges aircraft landing and passenger load fees. The company is profit-making, but recent annual financial reports indicate that the duty-free concession contributes as much to these profits as do the landing and passenger load fees. In the absence of the concession these fees would possibly need to be higher than they currently are. The Irish Aviation Authority operates the air traffic control system for Irish airspace, from Shannon. Seventy per cent of North Atlantic traffic flies through Irish

airspace, and these flights are charged the full cost of operating the air traffic control system.

From the point of view of the environmental impact of the fiscal system, it is necessary to ask whether the taxes paid by the sector, less the subsidies it receives, pay for the external costs imposed. It can be seen from the foregoing that commercial air travel is untaxed, apart from the £5 travel tax, which raises less than £10 million annually. Taxes forgone on duty free concessions certainly outweigh this. The only other taxes are on aviation fuel used for non-commercial purposes, which raise less than £0.5 million annually.

There is a general problem with valuing the external costs of air transport, in that very few studies have been carried out in this area, and large uncertainties exist, especially in relation to high altitude emissions. INFRAS (1994), in reviewing the literature, could only find three relevant studies, and only one which put a value on all elements of costs. This was Kågeson (1993), who estimated costs of £14-15 per 1,000 passenger kilometres. However, costs such as congestion and noise are location specific, so it is not appropriate to use this generalised estimate in an Irish context.

To summarise, while it is difficult to cost the external damage from air travel in Ireland, we know that it is certainly positive. At the same time, the air travel sector makes little contribution to these costs, through the taxes it pays.

### 7.2.3 Options for air transport

Notwithstanding the uncertainties cited above, we can examine the options that exist for internalising the external costs of air travel. There is another barrier to internalising costs, which is that international co-operation will be required to do so. North America is opposed to any change in the current position, though there have been some recent moves in Europe. In 1994 the EU Environment ministers called for measures to be taken 'provided this happens on a global scale' (Netherlands Ministry of Housing, Spatial Planning and the Environment, 1995). In the short run such global action is unlikely. The two areas where action is possible in the short run are in landing fees and for domestic flights, although even for the latter EU rules would have to be changed to allow tax measures to be introduced. Subject to these problems, we can explore what the options are, under the various external costs headings.

### 1. Air pollution

Ideally the tax here would be directly on the emissions from aircraft. It is difficult to see how this would be operated, however. Therefore, as a proxy, a tax on fuel might be the only practicable option. As already mentioned, more research is needed at an international level to determine the cost of damage from this pollution.

## 2. Noise pollution and visual intrusion

Many airports internationally differentiate their landing fees or have charges or taxes based on the noise performance of different aircraft. Luton airport in the UK has a scale of charges related to excess noise (Pearce, 1993). In Heathrow airport in London, aircraft that deviate from their assigned flight path are subject to a fine. In Schiphol airport in Amsterdam, aircraft with noisy engines pay a tax, and the government uses the revenue to insulate homes near the airport. Research into the cost of noise and visual intrusion at Irish airports is needed, in order to determine the appropriate level of tax here.

## 3. Accident costs

The scope for fiscal instruments here is limited. Regulations that ensure that airlines have sufficient insurance, and that proper safety requirements are met for airlines, airports and air traffic control, help to minimise accident costs.

## 4. Congestion costs

Congestion is a major problem at busy international airports. These airports are generally operating at or close to full capacity, which means that take-off and landing procedures are slowed down, and delays for one aircraft can have knock-on effects for others. Whether congestion is a significant cost at Irish airports is not known. Research into the level of delays, and the cost of these to passengers, would need to be carried out. Greater differentiation of landing fees to reflect congestion levels is one way of dealing with this. Another option being considered in a number of countries is to auction landing 'slots' at airports to the highest bidder. This would mean that those airlines that wished to provide services at peak times would have to pay more for doing so, and this would be passed onto their passengers. Those passengers who wished to travel at peak times and whose journeys were sufficiently valuable would then be able to do so, at a higher price. Others, who were not prepared to pay the higher price, would be encouraged to fly at less congested, cheaper times. There may be a problem, however, if operators are encouraged to fly at night, thus increasing noise pollution effects.

### 7.2.4 A possible approach

As already mentioned, there are many uncertainties about the external damage caused by air travel, and these would need to be resolved before firm recommendations could be made about fiscal measures. In an Irish context, research could be carried out on the extent of noise pollution and congestion costs at Irish airports, and measures could be designed on the basis of the findings.

It might be appropriate to introduce increased fees on noisy aircraft in advance of research, since we know that some damage is being caused. The increase could be fairly modest, but enough to send a signal that might encourage the use of quieter aircraft on Irish routes. A tax at Irish airports on its own would be unlikely to encourage airlines to switch to quieter aircraft, but in concert with similar measures in other countries it might be effective. Also, given that other airports are already implementing such charges, the absence of charges in Ireland might actually encourage airlines to use their noisier aircraft on Irish routes, so a charge here might be necessary to prevent this.

A tax on fuel would also appear to be justified, since we can be confident that some damage is being done, even if we do not fully know its extent. The Irish government could lend its support to EU moves in this direction.

# Notes

1    We broadly exclude cyclists and pedestrians from this analysis of road transport, because their environmental and external impact is negligible, in comparison with that of the users of motorised means of transport. The one exception is where pedestrians and cyclists cause traffic accidents.

2    Typically 30-35 per cent of urban space can be devoted to transport infrastructure (MacNicholas, 1991).

3    In 1989 the Confederation of British Industry estimated that the direct costs to British industry of lost time due to congestion in London and the surrounding area was in the order of Stg£10 billion per annum, in 1989 prices (cited in Jones and Hervik, 1992).

4    Increased car ownership is expected across Western Europe over the coming years (Jones and Hervik, 1992).

5    This is a notional value calculated by the Revenue Commissioners, not necessarily the actual selling price.

6    The effectiveness of the high road tax on large cars is dampened somewhat in the case of second-hand cars, since the market prices of such vehicles tend to reflect the high tax. Ironically these older, larger cars are probably the worst environmentally. It is difficult to see how this can be counteracted by fiscal measures, since any extra tax on second-hand larger cars might simply be reflected in a lowering of the market value thereof.

7    It could be that the scheme attracts motorists who are going to replace their cars anyway, or that it encourages motorists to bring forward their car replacement decision to take advantage of the scheme. However, in both cases the measure does ensure that the old car is scrapped, and to the degree that car replacement is brought forward there is some net effect. The government expects this scheme to be revenue neutral, which given that the tax on a new car is greater than the scrapping subsidy, suggests that it expects that some of the vehicle replacements would have occurred without the subsidy scheme.

8    Between 1986 and 1991 the share of diesel cars in the total fleet grew from 6 per cent to 11 per cent. By 1991 one in six new cars was diesel fuelled (Feeney, 1993). In the UK the stock of diesel vehicles now makes up 20 per cent of the total, while in some continental European countries the percentage is up to 50 per cent. These countries also have a tax advantage in favour of diesel.

9    An issue here is whether the costs of maintaining roads as listed above makes good the actual damage done to those roads by road users. If the maintenance carried out keeps the roads in a constant state of repair, then the cost thereof is an adequate measure of the cost of damage done. If however, the road system is deteriorating over time, this is not the case. In this circumstance, all road users suffer the consequences of the road deterioration; however, it is the case that heavy goods vehicles (HGVs) cause

a disproportionate amount of road damage, so there is the question of sharing the costs fairly among road users. Also, the use of deteriorating roads adds to noise pollution, which non-transport users must suffer.

10    The Resource Cost method values the damage caused by a particular outcome or event. It should be noted that there are very wide uncertainties in this calculation. Other estimates, based on the Prevention Cost approach (which puts a cost on preventing the damage) are considerably higher (INFRAS, 1994).

11    Further into the future, power sources such as electricity and liquefied hydrogen may become available.

12    That is, a 10 per cent increase in the fuel price will cause a 2 per cent decrease in fuel usage, in the short run.

13    It is noteworthy that this system was implemented in Ontario, given that the province is a major automobile-manufacturing region. However, it was introduced in the context of severe budgetary problems, and there was extensive public consultations in the design of the system. The government was amenable to adjusting the scheme in response to public and industry concerns, so long as any changes were revenue neutral.

14    Especially where catalytic converters are used, as these devices require high levels of maintenance, and poorly maintained converters are ineffective. Indeed, since the use of these devices slightly reduces fuel efficiency, cars with poorly maintained converters are likely to cause more pollution than cars without converters installed (Timoney, 1992).

15    In order to make the incentive for catalytic converters operable, the German government effectively had to ensure that unleaded petrol was available throughout the EU. This has been the main impetus for regulations promoting unleaded petrol and converters at the European level (Schnutenhaus, 1995).

16    A requirement that by 1998 2 per cent of vehicles sold be ZEVs has recently been dropped.

17    One famously unsuccessful approach is the ban on cars with odd and even numbered licence plates on alternate days, tried in Athens and Mexico city. This encouraged many people to buy a second car, often an 'old banger', to get around the ban. The net result was an increase in the car population, little reduction in traffic flows, and worse air pollution.

18    It has been claimed that the introduction of parking restrictions along busy routes in London has reduced journey times by 20 per cent and increased bus passengers by 10 per cent (*Economist*, 1994).

19    Europe-wide systems are being envisaged at EU level, which would reduce the cost of introduction in Ireland.

20    Smith (1995) quotes research in Germany that found that the rate for private commuting - DEM0.50 or 20p per kilometre - was greater than the marginal cost of driving, and therefore encouraged excess commuting by car.

# References

Barrett, S.D. and Walsh, B.M. (1983), 'The 'User Pays' Principle: theory and Applications', in Blackwell, J. and Convery, F.J. (eds.), *Promise and Performance - Irish Environmental Policies Analysed*. Dublin: Resource and Energy Policy Centre, University College Dublin.

Bregha, F. and Moffet, J. (1995), 'The Tax for Fuel Conservation in Ontario', in Gale, R., Barg, S. and Gillies, A. (1995), *Green Budget Reform*. London: Earthscan.

Button, K. (1993), *Transport, the Environment and Economic Policy*. Aldershot: Edward Elgar.

Davis, W.B. et al. (1993), *Feebates: Estimated Impacts on Vehicle Fuel Economy, Fuel Consumption, $CO_2$ Emission, and Consumer Surplus*. Draft Report, Lawrence Berkeley Laboratory.

DKM (1994), *Forecast of Vehicle Numbers and Traffic Volumes*. Report for the Department of the Environment.

DRI, in association with DHV, TME, ERM, ECOTEC, Travers Morgan and M+R. (1994), *Potential Benefits of Integration of Environmental and Economic Policies - an Incentive-based Approach to Policy Integration*. Report prepared for the European Commission, Directorate-General for Environment, Nuclear Safety and Civil Protection. London: Graham and Trotman, Office for Official Publication of the European Communities.

EC (1978), *Draft Council Directive on the Adjustment of National Taxation Systems for Commercial Road Vehicles*. R/2904/78 (Trans 165), Brussels, November 1978.

*Economist* The (1994), *London's Fuming*, November 12th, 1994, pp.45-46.

*Economist* The (1995), *Company Cars - A Suitable Target*, November, 25th, 1995.

EPA (1996), *State of the Environment in Ireland*. Wexford: Environmental Protection Agency.

ERU (1990), *Traffic Station Counts and Road Travel*. Dublin.

EU (1993), 'Council Directive on the Application by Member States of Taxes on Certain Vehicles Used for the Carriage of Goods by Road and Tolls and Charges for the Use of Certain Infrastructures', 93/89/EEC, *Official Journal of the European Communities*, L 279/32, 12 November 1993.

EUROSTAT (1995), *Basic Statistics of the European Union - Comparison With the Principal Partners of the European Union*. Luxembourg: Office for Official Publications of the European Communities.

Fankhauser, S. (1994), *Evaluating the Social Costs of Greenhouse Gas Emissions*. London: CSERGE.

Feeney, B. (1983), 'Paying for Road Damage', in Blackwell, J. and Convery, F.J. (eds.), *Promise and Performance - Irish Environmental Policies Analysed*. Dublin: Resource and Energy Policy Centre, University College Dublin.

_____ (1993), *Transport and Air Pollution*. Dublin: Goodbody Economic Consultants.

Government of Ireland (1989), *National Development Plan, 1989-1993*. Dublin: The Stationery Office.

_____(1995a), *Insurance Annual Report 1994*. Dublin: The Stationery Office.

_____ (1995b), *Local Authority Estimates 1995*. Dublin: The Stationery Office.

Hamilton (1995), 'A Major Boost for the Industry', in *Irish Times*, 29th November, 1995.

Hau, T. (1990), 'Electronic Road Pricing Developments in Hong Kong, 1983-1989', in *Journal of Transport Economics*, May 1990.

In 'T Veld, R.J. (1991), 'Road Pricing: a Logical Failure', in Kraan, D.J., and In 'T Veld, R.J. 1991, *Environmental Protection: Public or Private Choice*. Dordrecht: Kluwer Academic Publishers.

Infras (1994), *Comparative Evaluation of a Number of Recent Studies (Undertaken on Behalf of Various Bodies) on 'Transport External Costs and Their Internalisation', Suggestions on the Most Appropriate Methods for the Internalisation*. Report for the European Commission, DG VII.

Jones, P. and Hervik, A. (1992), 'Restraining Car Traffic in European Cities: an Emerging Role for Road Pricing', in *Transport Research*, Part a, Vol. 26A, No. 2, pp. 133-145.

Kågeson, P. (1993), Getting the Prices Right - a European Scheme for Making Transport Pay its Full Cost. Stockholm: European Federation for Transport and Environment.

MacNicholas, M.J. (1992), 'Environmental Impacts and Equity in Transportation Planning', in Feehan, J., (ed.), 1992. *Environment and Development in Ireland*. Dublin: The Environmental Institute, University College Dublin.

Maddison, D. (1996), 'Economic Instruments to Reduce the Environmental Impacts of Road Transport'. Paper given at Seminar *Economic Instruments Supporting Environmental Policy: The Polluter Pays Principle in Practice*. ESRI, Dublin, 14th June, 1996.

Maddison, D., Pearse, D., Johansson, O., Calthorp, E., Litman T. and Verhoef, E. (1996), *The True Costs of Road Transport*. London: Earthscan.

McGettigan, M. (1993), *Corinair 1990 Emissions Inventory for Ireland*. Dublin: Environmental Research Unit.

Mead, C. (1996), 'Rage Against Roads', in *IWC News*, Spring 1996.

Netherlands Ministry of Housing, Spatial Planning and The Environment (1995), *Environmental News from the Netherlands*, No. 6, 1995. The Hague.

OECD/ECMT (1995), *Urban Travel and Sustainable Development*. Paris: OECD.

OFWAT (1990), *Paying For Water - A Time for decisions; Annex 3 Current Water and Sewerage Charges*. Birmingham: Consultation Paper.

O' Rourke, K. (1992), 'Overview of Energy Trends and Prospects', in Feehan, J. (ed.), 1992. *Environment and Development in Ireland*. Dublin: The Environmental Institute, University College Dublin.

Pearse, D. (1993), *Blueprint 3 - Measuring Sustainable Development*. London: Earthscan.

Quinet, E. (1990), *The Social Cost of Land Transport*. Paris: OECD Environmental Monographs No.32.

Quinet, E. (1994), *The Social Costs of Transport: Evaluation and Links with Internalisation Policies*. Paris: ECMT/OECD.

Rothengatter, W. (1993), 'Externalities of Transport', in Polak, J., and Heertje, A. (eds.), 1993, *European Transport Economics*. Oxford: Blackwell.

Schnutenhaus, J.O. (1995), 'Tax Differentials for Catalytic Converters and Unleaded Petrol in Germany', in Gale, R., Barg, S. and Gillies, A. 1995, *Green Budget Reform*. London: Earthscan.

Smith, S. (1995), *'Green' Taxes and Charges: Policy and Practice in Britain and Germany*. London: The Institute for Fiscal Studies.

Timoney, D.J. (1992), 'Internal Combustion Engines and Exhaust Emissions - an Irish Perspective on Existing and Prospective EC Policies', in Feehan, J. (ed.), 1991. *Environment and Development in Ireland*. Dublin: The Environmental Institute, University College Dublin.

# 8 Tourism

*A. Barrett*

In this and the following chapter, we discuss the possible use of economic instruments in two sectors which have received less attention in this context relative to the sectors we have already discussed. For this reason, the approach in these chapters is more exploratory and less definitive than earlier chapters. While we do identify scope for the use of economic instruments, it will be seen that the points made in Chapter 3 about the limits to their use apply in these sectors.

## 8.1 Introduction

There is a growing recognition that although a good environment attracts more tourists (i.e., a positive link) it is also true that increased numbers of tourists can damage the environment (i.e., a negative link). Tourists put pressure on the environment in a number of ways which will be discussed below but for now we can say the following: just as the economic benefits of industrial production bring with them costs such as pollution, so too is tourism development not without costs. And as the number of tourists coming to Ireland is on the increase, the relevance of these costs is growing.

In this chapter, we want to discuss these costs, to explore the conditions under which it might be optimal to restrict tourist numbers and to examine how this might be achieved using economic instruments. While it might appear strange to talk in terms of restricting an industry that has contributed to the economic growth enjoyed in recent years, such thinking has entered policy documents on the subject of tourism, where reference is now made to 'optimal' as opposed to 'maximum' tourist numbers. There is a concern that the environmental consequences of tourism could impact negatively on the industry itself, in addition to imposing costs on domestic residents. However, given the economic benefits which accrue from tourism, pressure is likely to remain for policies to pursue the maximum as opposed to the optimum.

The approach we will take is as follows. With the growing interest in using economic as opposed to regulatory instruments for environmental protection, it is appropriate that the possible use of economic instruments in this particular sector be explored. As that is the ultimate objective of the chapter, we want to pose the problem in terms of the concepts of the branch of economics most suited to its analysis, public economics. With the growing discussion of the possible negative environmental implications of tourism, it is important to have an economic model in mind so that the discussion of economic instruments is carefully placed.

Having looked at the issue in principle, we will then consider the economic incentives that are currently used in the tourism sector. The approach will be to examine these incentives in the light of the earlier discussion and to think in terms of the environmental impacts being generated. We will then suggest the type of incentives that may be appropriate given our discussion in Section 8.2.


## 8.2 The environmental pressures of tourism

To begin the discussion, let us consider the environmental pressures associated with tourists.[1] Essentially, these pressures can be broken down into two main categories, although one of these can then be further broken down into three sub-categories. The first main category of environmental pressure arises on the production side of the industry and is associated with a tendency for additional construction to be undertaken in order to facilitate the influx of tourists. The construction can be of two types. One type is the building of new hotels and guesthouses which seek to cater for the accommodation needs of tourists. In a rural setting environmental damage occurs if the developments intrude in such a way that the environmental attractions of rural areas, such as the lack of visual blemishes on the landscape, are reduced. The other main type of tourism construction is that which seeks to provide facilities which contribute to the activities of tourists. In Ireland, possibly the most familiar examples of this are the proposed interpretative centres in places such as the Burren, a natural area of considerable botanical importance in the west of Ireland. In the language of public economics, what we are describing are production externalities. By this we mean that those producing the tourism service impose costs for which they are not charged. This fits into the general class of problems called externalities and so we shall draw on that area in suggesting market based solutions.

The second main category of environmental pressure arises through the consumption by tourists of the tourism product or, more simply put, through large numbers of people visiting an area or a specific tourist attraction. There are three such pressures. First, large tourist numbers put additional pressure on the environmental services of an area such as solid waste collection and disposal, waste water treatment and disposal and water provision. The problem can be particularly acute when the extra pressure comes in a concentrated way, as is the case when an area is popular with tourists for a certain limited period over the year. The dilemma for local planners is that expanding the capacity of these services to cope with this short-term high demand may not make economic sense if there will be excess capacity for the remainder of the year. This problem has been recognised as having arisen with regard to water in the Aran Islands, Achill Island and Westport.[2] Those familiar with public economics will recognise this as a case of the peak-load problem and below we will outline the proposed solution.

The second consumption-side environmental impact is the simple damage or environmental degradation that large numbers of tourists inflict on an area. One recently highlighted example of this effect is the damage being done to Newgrange, an ancient burial site.[3] Similarly, motoring tourists bring with them their fuel emissions and noise. The third consumption-side effect is similar in the way it is dealt with in public economic theory so we will mention it here. Large numbers of tourists generate congestion and so reduce the pleasure in visiting an area or in living there. In both the degradation and congestion effects, we can say that a consumption externality exists. By this, we mean that tourists through their consumption of the tourism product impose a cost, be it in terms of degradation or congestion, for which they are not charged. Again, we are well within the territory of public economics and so we will draw on the solutions proposed.

It should be noted at this point that concerns over the environmental impact of tourists can be viewed from two perspectives. First, to the extent that individuals in a community, visited by tourists and subject to their associated environmental pressures, view these pressures as a cost, the concern can be with the quality of life for those effected. Thus, we can consider this as a consumption-side impact. Second, as the negative effects of tourists can reduce the attraction of the tourism product, there is also a production-type impact.

### 8.2.1 Carrying capacity

Although we have been talking about tourist numbers and environmental pressures, it would be wrong to think that there is a simple linear relationship between the two so before proceeding we should examine this issue more fully. In economic discussions of pollution,[4] account is normally taken of the fact that not all emissions constitute pollution. The reason for this is that the environment has a certain "assimilative capacity" which allows it to absorb a certain amount of emissions before environmental damage is done. Beyond this point, additional emissions do inflict damage and so it is really only the emissions above the assimilative capacity that constitute pollution.

A similar distinction arises in discussions of tourism, although rather than talk about 'assimilative capacity' the term 'carrying capacity' is more usually used. The idea behind carrying capacity is that an area can absorb a certain amount of tourist activity, up to which no negative environmental effects arise. Beyond that point, however, extra numbers do indeed inflict environmental damage, be it in terms of congestion, degradation or whatever.

The implication of this is that if tourist numbers are within the carrying capacity of an area, we should not be worried about them and so no policy is required to restrict numbers. In fact, if the numbers are within the carrying capacity, additional tourists should be sought as they will bring with them economic benefits without inflicting environmental damage. As such, before deciding that it is necessary to restrict tourist numbers, it is desirable that we have some notion as to the carrying capacity of an area.

In practice, however, this is a difficult task. As Coccossis and Parpairis (1992) put it: '...it is recognised that a single and absolute measure of carrying capacity of an area is difficult to estimate since the factors involved are not all quantifiable or even measurable'. For example, if the trampling through the Burren of a large group of people is damaging, how is the damage to be measured? And while environmental economists might feel that the damage, once measured, can be quantified through, for example, contingent valuation methods, will others be prepared to accept such a measure?

Even if we do not have a single index of carrying capacity, it is still important that we have some notion of the level of tourist pressures. Towards this end approaches have been used which aim to get at least a partial view of how many tourists an area can handle without suffering environmentally (see Coccossis and Parpairis, 1992). Some such approaches focus on the ecological issues and attempt to model how specific actions might have adverse environmental impacts; others look at the built environment of an area and assess the capacity of environmental services or accommodation services.

*8.2.1.1 Some figures on tourist numbers*    While it is beyond the scope of this chapter to put together a measure of carrying capacity and to see if that capacity is being breached, we can at least look at some of the evidence as to whether tourists may be putting parts of the country under any strain. The first thing to look at is the extent to which tourist numbers have been rising and whether they have been spread over the year or over the country. This is done in Figure 8.1 and Tables 8.1 and 8. 2 using figures from Bord Failte (the Irish tourist board).

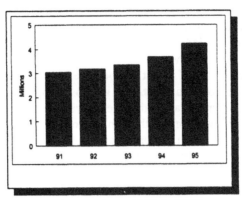

**Figure 8.1    Overseas tourist numbers, 1991 to 1995**

In Figure 8.1, the rise in overseas tourist numbers since 1991 is clear. In 1991, there were 3.051 million overseas visitors and this rose to 4.231 million in 1995, a rise of 38.7 per cent. It is difficult to say whether or not this represents an encroachment upon carrying capacity, but we can certainly be less comfortable relative to a situation in which tourist numbers were static or growing at a more moderate rate. While these numbers may be a concern, they would be less of a concern if they were becoming more dispersed over time. Clearly from Table 8.1, however, this is not the case.

**Table 8.1**
**Timing of arrival (per cent)**

|             | '91 | '92 | '93 | '94 | '95 |
|-------------|-----|-----|-----|-----|-----|
| Jan/Feb/Mar | 13  | 12  | 13  | 14  | 13  |
| April       | 7   | 9   | 9   | 8   | 8   |
| May         | 10  | 9   | 9   | 9   | 9   |
| June        | 10  | 10  | 10  | 11  | 10  |
| July        | 15  | 16  | 16  | 15  | 15  |
| August      | 15  | 14  | 15  | 14  | 15  |
| September   | 10  | 10  | 9   | 10  | 10  |
| Oct/Nov/Dec | 20  | 20  | 19  | 20  | 20  |

There is a remarkable similarity in the proportions arriving in the various months, with 30 per cent almost always arriving between the months of July and August.

**Table 8.2**
**Regions visited - stayed at least one night (per cent)**

|              | '91 | '92 | '93 | '94 | '95 |
|--------------|-----|-----|-----|-----|-----|
| Dublin       | 45  | 45  | 46  | 49  | 49  |
| South-East   | 20  | 20  | 21  | 22  | 22  |
| South-West   | 35  | 35  | 33  | 30  | 30  |
| Mid-West     | 24  | 25  | 24  | 23  | 23  |
| West         | 25  | 27  | 25  | 25  | 25  |
| North-West   | 11  | 11  | 11  | 11  | 11  |
| Midlands-East| 15  | 16  | 17  | 17  | 17  |

Finally, we see in Table 8.2 that the build-up in numbers has affected all areas. Although the proportion spending a night in the South-West has declined from 35 per cent to 30 per cent between 1991 and 1995, in absolute terms there has been a rise in visitor numbers to that area from 1.067 million in 1991 to 1.269 million in 1995, a rise of 202,000.

While these aggregate numbers provide evidence of a possible problem, it is more instructive to consider specific areas. We can do this by looking at a recently circulated interim report on the islands off the Irish coast (Gill and Cullen, 1996). In this study, the permanent resident population of Ireland's off-shore islands was estimated to be 3,095. Taking this as a baseline figure, a headcount was taken on the islands on the first Saturday of August in 1995, a day which the authors describe as a 'typical high-season summer's day'

This headcount found that the population of the islands rose roughly from 3,000 to 13,000, meaning that 10,000 visitors were on the islands. The authors express this increase in terms of a pressure factor of 3.36, and point out that pressure factors ranged from 0.6 on Innishbiggle, County Mayo to 12.6 on Heir Island, County Cork. Of the approximately 10,000 visitors, about 4,000 were day-trippers and the remainder over-nighters.

The authors conclude that 'it is obvious that the gradual decline of the resident population, or especially, its decreasing proportion of the total throughflow population, involves serious planning decisions which may include active restriction'. They go on to conclude that 'there are also immediate and important environmental considerations', a conclusion which seems reasonable given the numbers presented.

As a further example of the pressures being felt because of tourism, we can consider the problems of water supply that arose in Westport and Achill Island in the summer of 1995.[5] The water supply service to Westport from Moher Lake can provide 750,000 gallons per day. While the winter-time water demand of the town is about 640,000 gallons per day and so within capacity, demand rose to 830,000 gallons per day for a number of weeks in the summer, a rise of almost 30 per cent. In Achill, demand is generally about 300,000 gallons per day but this rose to about 500,000 in the summer of 1995, a 60 per cent increase. While it was possible to deliver 420,000 gallons per day along the usual mains, it was also necessary to tanker 80,000 gallons per day to the reservoir serving the island.

## 8.3 Existing fiscal treatment of Irish tourism

Having established a framework in which to think about tourism, the environment and economic instruments, it is interesting to take a brief look at how fiscal incentives are currently employed in Irish tourism. While it is beyond the scope of this chapter to perform any sort of environmental analysis of the effects of these incentives, it is of interest to consider the possible effects.

### 8.3.1 The Operational Programmes

By far the most significant fiscal incentives in recent years have arisen through the Operational Programmes for Tourism, one which ran from 1989 to 1993 and the other which began in 1994 and will run until 1999. Based largely on EU money, these programmes have sought to develop the Irish tourist industry through direct government spending and also the subsidising of private sector tourism spending. Focusing on the latter element, we can ask if the projects which were subsidised generated the type of production externalities which were discussed above. If it did then the question must be asked as to whether the economic return on the spending was sufficient to outweigh the environmental cost.

One study that has considered the environmental impact of the Operational Programmes is that of Meldon (1992). Writing about the 1989 to 1993 Operational Programme, she sounds the following warning:

> The approach adopted by the Operational Programme will result in increased pressures on the fragile environment. Due to the rapid expansion of the industry, projects which include new ideas or which aim to develop facilities on a scale not hitherto experienced in this country, are now being proposed, but no guidelines have been drawn up for such developments.

While implicit in what Meldon says is that the regulatory framework is failing in the face of tourism development, from the perspective of the current discussion the concern should be that activities which generate negative externalities should not be subsidised, as the theory above would advise. Specifically, Meldon identifies the subsidies to golf courses, integrated leisure developments in heritage landscapes and marina developments as posing problems for the environment. In addition she points out that under the programme there is a direct incentive to erect new buildings as visitor centres as opposed to using existing structures. Her general view is that the approach in the programme puts conservation in a secondary position and that grants should have been 'directed towards investment which would lead to the conservation and enhancement of the tourism attractions which make up the cultural and physical environment'.

Under the 1994-99 Operational Programme, subsidies to the private sector are available under two main sub-programmes, product development and marketing.[6] If Meldon's concerns regarding the 1989-93 programme were well founded then we would have to be concerned about the type of projects funded under the product development sub-programme. The largest category under the sub-programme is 'large tourism projects', accounting for IR£116m out of an anticipated spending total of IR£287m. It is proposed to subsidise a National Conference Centre under this category, providing 50 per cent assistance to the private sector to undertake the project. The other types of large tourism projects proposed include an integrated, dedicated holiday park for family visitors and a large-scale integrated holiday complex featuring high quality accommodation, conference and a mix of activity features. Whether such developments will have significant negative environmental impacts is unclear but they are more likely to have such effects than the type of conservation projects advocated by Meldon.

Subsidies to golf courses and marinas continue in the 1994-99 Operational Programme, with maximum grant rates of 25 and 50 per cent respectively so if negative externalities existed before they presumably continue. However, on a more positive note, grants of 50 per cent are also made available for the restoration of 'great gardens'. Grants of 50 per cent are also made available for the improvement and presentation of tourist facilities at historical buildings and stately homes but such grants could have a negative effect. If too many visitors are attracted by the improved facilities, the type of consumption externalities discussed above might result. Hence, there may be a need to charge admission or to restrict numbers in another way.

Under the marketing sub-programme, we see a grant and incentive structure that is more in line with the concerns about greater tourism numbers and environmental pressures. Under the section of the sub-programme which is labelled 'access/product/niche/high-yield' different maximum aid rates are applied depending on the time of year that the marketing is aimed at. The highest maximum rate applies to the off peak period (50 per cent), with the lower rates of 30 and 20 per cent applying to the shoulder and peak respectively. This structure addresses itself to the seasonality and congestion concerns quite directly and can be considered a good example of an economic instrument for environmental protection in tourism.

One additional point of note on the environmental impact of the 1989-93 Operational Programme can be distilled from the report of Fitz Gerald et al. (1993).

When questioning the value of the regional spread of expenditure, they mention that an objective of the strategy may have been 'to redistribute the pattern of visitor patronage around the country'. They go on to point out, however, that if this was the objective, the strategy failed. As was seen in Table 8.2 above, the regional concentration of visitors remained pretty constant over the period. It will be interesting to see if the 1994-99 Operational Programme is any more successful in spreading visitors over the country.

### 8.3.2 Tax relief scheme for certain resort areas

In addition to the grants under the Operational Programmes, in 1995 the Government introduced a range of tax incentives which are aimed at improving facilities in 15 seaside resorts such as Tramore, Lahinch and Bundoran. The design of the incentives is similar to those that are in operation in the urban renewal areas.[7] The costs of construction and refurbishment of facilities such as hotels, guesthouses, bars and restaurants can be written off against tax liabilities. The refurbishment, however, in order to qualify must add at least 20 per cent to the value of the existing building so to an extent the allowance favours new construction over refurbishment. It is not possible at this point to say what the environmental impact of these schemes is.

### 8.3.3 Capital allowances

Capital allowances of 4 per cent per annum are allowed for the construction of holiday camps and cottages registered with Bord Failte. This allowance is 15 per cent for hotels. This again creates an incentive for possibly intrusive building.

### 8.4 Suggested economic instruments

While we may not be able to say, given our existing level of knowledge, whether carrying capacity is being approached or breached, let us proceed on the basis that a problem does exist and that the environmental pressures described in Section 8.1 are leading to environmental damage. In that section, we framed the pressures in such a way that they could be thought of as peak-load problems (temporary high level usage of environmental services), production externalities (tourism related construction) and consumption externalities (degradation and congestion caused by tourists). We will now outline the standard proposed solutions to these problems and ask whether these proposals are implementable in the tourism context.

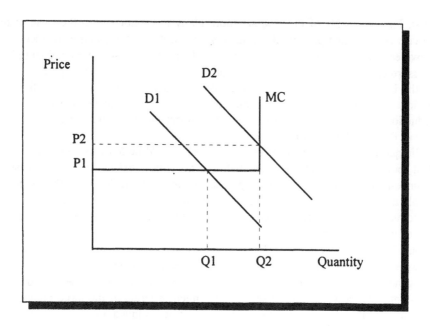

**Figure 8.2   The peak-load problem**

*8.4.1 Peak-load problem[8]*

We will outline the peak-load problem using Figure 8.2. The problem is typically motivated by presenting the example of a power station for whose output demand is higher during the day than the night-time. In terms of the diagram, D1 and D2 represent demand during the night and day respectively; MC represents the marginal cost of providing the service. It can be seen from the diagram that the capacity of the power station is Q2. During night-time hours, charging a price of P1 brings about a level of demand Q1; from standard economic theory we know this is economically efficient because price is equal to marginal cost. However, by charging a price of P1 during the day, demand will be greater than capacity. The power could be rationed but the economically efficient approach would be to charge a higher price during the day. In this way, the service is provided to those who value it most highly.[9]

The relevance of this example to the environmental pressure caused by tourists when they put demands on environmental services should be clear. Although the peak-load problem is not seen over a twenty-four hour period, it is clear that over the twelve months of the year, such a problem arises. What is more, the textbook solution of the differential pricing strategy is also of relevance. By charging a higher price for services during the peak-load times, two effects are generated, in theory at least. First, residents of the area are more likely to economise on their use of the service so, for example, by charging more for water in the summer residents are provided with an incentive to economise on their water consumption and so reduce pressure on the service. In addition, assuming hotels and guesthouses pass on some of the increase of their costs to guests, the rise in the cost of staying in the area during the peak period should reduce demand to stay. With compensating price reductions in the off-peak period, tourist numbers can be smoothed over the year and so the peak-load problem is avoided.

The question of how practical such a proposal would be must be addressed.[10] The first point to be made is that without the prior existence of meter-based volume-related charging, the strategy cannot be implemented. Clearly for many local authorities, this represents a constraint. A second constraint on the effectiveness of the strategy concerns the ability of residents to alter their level of use of the service over the course of the year. Whatever the potential difficulties, it should be pointed out that the city of Athens in Greece has used a system of varying charges for water as drought conditions have eased or worsened.[11]

A general point should be made at this point. The fundamental cause of a strain on environmental services can be seen not so much in terms of the large numbers of tourists but rather in the provision of the services at too low a price. As long as price reflects the tension between supply and demand, no excess demand will emerge. If the price of environmental services are adjusted to reflect large increases in demand at particular times, no excess demand will emerge and there will be no environmental strain.

### 8.4.2 Production externalities[12]

The production externality problem is typically framed in terms of an industrial firm whose emissions are the cause of pollution so we will develop this line of reasoning using Figure 8.3. The MR line represents marginal revenue, that is the extra revenue that the firm can generate through producing additional units of output. The PMC line represents private marginal cost. The firm, in the absence of any government intervention, will produce up to the point where the marginal revenue exceeds private marginal cost, i.e., output level Q1. The pollution caused by the firm is illustrated in the SMC line, the social marginal cost. Note that initially there is no pollution; this is because the assimilative capacity of the environment is not breached. However, after a certain level of output, social cost diverges from private by the amount of the external damage. At output Q1, the marginal benefit of output (as represented by revenue) is below social marginal cost and so output is above the

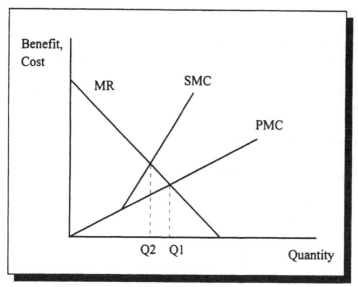

**Figure 8.3    Production (or consumption) externalities**

social optimum. The solution is to tax output at a rate equal to the value of the externality at output level Q2, i.e., the standard Pigovian tax.

We again have to ask how relevant this example is to the type of production externality that arises in tourism. In principle, we can say that the construction of hotels, guesthouses or some such tourist facilities that intrude upon the landscape are equivalent in nature to the polluting industry just described. Developers, if allowed, will build as long as marginal revenue exceeds private marginal cost, even though social marginal cost may exceed marginal revenue because of the intrusion of the additional buildings into the landscape. As such, the economic instrument which arises from the theory is a tax on construction equal to the marginal social damage done by the construction.

In this case, however, there are characteristics of construction that may make the traditional regulatory approach more appropriate.[13] Whereas the polluting industry is thought of as producing a continuous stream of emissions which can be scaled back or increased as the tax is altered, construction is more discrete in nature. Given that the estimation of the correct Pigouvian tax is a complicated task, it is likely that such a tax would be changed from time to time so that the optimal level of emissions is arrived at. In the case of construction, however, there is less room for altering the tax and production outcomes. Once something is built, it is expensive to remove it and so the cost of setting a wrong Pigovian tax may be great. While buildings may not belong entirely in that category of events that are irreversible, their semi-permanent characteristic means that direct regulation through planning laws may be more effective in environmental protection.

195

Having played down the possible use of economic instruments in this regard, one important additional point can be made. While it may not make sense to tax developments of an environmentally damaging nature, it certainly does not make sense to subsidise them unless the economic benefits that accrue outweigh those costs. As ever, the difficulty in implementing this strategy lies in estimating the environmental costs and economic benefits but the general principle should at least be explicit.

### 8.4.3 Consumption externalities

We have grouped two environmental effects of tourism into this one category because of their analytical similarity. Whether we are talking about the damage done to an area or a facility by tourists or the congestion generated by them, the problem in both cases is that the cost to the tourists of visiting does not reflect the full cost of their presence. This can be demonstrated using Figure 8.3 again. The MR line can now be viewed as the tourists' demand curve. If a price of zero is charged, the quantity demanded will be at the intersection of the demand curve and the quantity axis and clearly social marginal cost exceeds the marginal benefit. Even if tourists are charged the internal cost as represented by the PMC line, demand will be above the optimum. As before, to achieve the optimal level of demand, a Pigovian tax must be imposed. Without the tax, there is likely to be a continued excessive use of the tourist services of an area. Over time, continued overuse will result in a decline in the quality of the tourism resource, possibly to the point that the original attraction is lost.

In order to get a fuller understanding of the nature of the consumption externality problem, one can think of the general problem of the exploitation of commonly held resources. Dales (1968) provides some good examples of how commonly owned resources can become depleted and how the threat of depletion leads to restrictions on use; in particular he mentions the problems of the over-exploitation in medieval agriculture and animal species that are now extinct. The general feature of commonly held property is that no one individual has an incentive to conserve on use but rather all have an incentive to exploit.

The relevance of this to tourism is that many tourist resources have common-property characteristics such as scenery, coastlines and mountains. Like other common properties, such as land in the American West in the last century, when the supply of these properties far outweighs demand, the common property characteristic is not a problem. But as demand rises, the potential for over-exploitation arises and so the need to restrict access also arises. By the over-exploitation of tourist resources, what is meant is the destruction of the peace and beauty of an area through the influx of too many tourists, where too many would be defined relative to the carrying capacity. Hardin, also writing in 1968, illustrates the point as follows:

The National Parks present another instance of the working out of the tragedy of the commons. At present, they are open to all, without limit. The parks themselves are limited in extent - there is only one Yosemite Valley - whereas population seems to grow without limit. The values that visitors seek in the parks are steadily eroding. Plainly, we must cease soon to treat the parks as commons or they shall be of no value to anyone.

The next question, of course, is what is to be done. Hardin makes some suggestions, all of which would lead to restrictions being placed on entry. As far as economic instruments are concerned, the general principle is that visitors should be charged and specifically, they should be charged the full cost of their visit, i.e., account should be taken of the external effects. This can be achieved by either the government levying the charge or the common property becoming private property whereby the owner will have the incentive to charge admission and to ensure the conservation of the facility.

Again, we have to ask what the relevance of this is to aspects of Irish tourism. There are two main constraints on charging for access to environmentally sensitive areas. One is the simple matter that charging may be completely infeasible if exclusion is impossible. Fencing off the Burren would clearly be an enormous task and would itself be an environmental intrusion. In the case of facilities such as art galleries, however, exclusion is possible and so restrictions could be implementable. This leads to a second constraint, i.e., the political and social sensitivities which arise because of the distributional implications of restricting access to some of the nation's greatest resources on the basis of payment. In addition to this distributional concern, there is also the possibility that visiting, for example, art galleries produces a positive externality which is similar to that produced by education. In this case restriction may be sub-optimal. One possible solution to this would be to charge at most times but to provide free admission at some times or on certain days. Referring to the peak-load discussion above, free access could be given when demand is lowest. In this way, access is not denied because of ability to pay but merely restricted to certain times.

Just as we do not actually tax car pollution but rather we tax the input, fuel, we have to ask if it is possible to apply economic instruments to some dimension of the tourism inputs. One possible approach which would mirror the approach taken to pollution from cars would be to apply differential rates of tax to hotel rooms according to how restrictions on numbers might be desirable. Just as different tax rates are applied to leaded and unleaded petrol, it could be that different VAT or excise rates would apply to hotels at different times of the year and in different locations. This would go some way to capturing the different environmental impact of those arriving when and where there are few tourists around, relative to the impact of those who arrive along with very many others.

It may be argued that if the hotel rooms exist then it does not make sense to restrict numbers below capacity. Such an argument does not take account of the fact the an area may have sufficient hotel capacity for a given number of guests, but that this number may exceed carrying capacity along other dimensions such as congestion of other facilities. In addition, revenue generated through the higher peak-time tax allows tax reductions at other times and so a boost to tourism at off-peak times is created.

## 8.5 Conclusion

The primary goal of this chapter has been to consider the environmental pressures associated with tourism in a framework of public-economics theory and to derive from this framework suggestions for the application of economic instruments for the control of these environmental pressures. This approach leads to the following conclusions.

1   In the case of environmental services and tourist facilities for which charging is feasible, the standard textbook approaches of peak-load pricing and Pigovian taxing can be implemented.

2   The environmental pressures associated with tourism construction may best be controlled by planning laws rather than economic instruments. This is because of the semi-irreversible nature of construction.

3   Finally, for tourism facilities that allow for the possibility of admission charges, applying such charges at peak-times reduces congestion without denying access to those unable to pay. Where admission charges cannot be applied, such as mountainous regions, the use of economic instruments requires the taxation of a related product or service if numbers are to be controlled. In this regard, differential tax rates on accommodation over time and space in Ireland may go some way to alleviating the problems associated with the concentrations of our tourists.

While the above may be the ideal, we have seen evidence that the fiscal system in Ireland may be contributing to tourism pressures through the subsidising of activities that may generate negative externalities. In many ways this merely reflects the usual tension between the desire to achieve economic growth and the need to protect the environment but there are aspects of tourism that make this tension that bit stronger. Tourism is a large component of our economy but more importantly, it is a sector which holds the potential to contribute to employment growth, due to its relative labour intensity, and to regional development, due to its dispersed nature. With such potential, it is little wonder that the focus would be on expansion as opposed to restriction. However, it is important to be mindful of the environmental consequences of tourism expansion, both in terms of the quality of life impacts and the impacts on the tourist resource itself, and to have the policy tools to deal with the impacts.

## Notes

1. Some of the discussion is taken from Bord Failte (1994), Convery and Flanagan (1992) and Hartley and Hooper (1992).
2. See Bord Failte (1994), page 90.
3. Report on Morning Ireland, RTE Radio, Wednesday 5 June 1996.
4. See, for example, Pearce and Turner (1990).
5. We are grateful to Brian O'Reilly of Mayo Co. Co. for providing us with the details of these cases.
6. The details of the Operational Programme 1994-99 are taken from Government of Ireland (1994) *Operational Programme for Tourism, 1994/1999*.
7. The urban renewal areas are discussed in Chapter 9.
8. For a standard textbook discussion of peak-load pricing see Musgrave and Musgrave (1976), page 698.
9. If additional capacity is to be built, the peak-load price should be related to long-run marginal cost to ensure efficiency. In this case, however, we are assuming that no additional capacity will be built.
10. Chapter 5 contains a fuller discussion of charging for environmental services.
11. See the Environmental Institute (1996).
12. For a general discussion of externalities and optimal pricing in their presence, see Baumol and Oates (1988), Chapter 3.
13. The points made in this paragraph are dealt with more fully in Chapter 9.

# References

Baumol, W. and Oates, W. (1988), *The Theory of Environmental Policy* (2nd edition), Cambridge University Press, Cambridge.

Bord Failte (1994), *Developing Sustainable Tourism*, Bord Failte, Dublin.

Coccossis, H. and Parpairis, A. (1992), 'Tourism and the Environment: Some Observations on the Concept of Carrying Capacity', in Briassoulis, van der Straaten, H. and J. (eds.) *Tourism and the Environment: Regional, Economic and Policy Issues*, Kluwer Academic Publishers, Dordrecht.

Convery, F.J. and Flanagan, S. (1992), 'Tourism and the Environment - Impacts and Strategies', in Briassoulis, H. and J van der Straaten (eds.) *Tourism and the Environment: Regional, Economic and Policy Issues*, Kluwer Academic Publishers, Dordrecht.

Dales, J.H. (1968), *Pollution, Property and Prices*, University of Toronto Press, Toronto; reprinted in Markandya, A. and J. Richardson (eds.) *Environmental Economics: A Reader*, St. Martin's Press, New York (1992).

Environmental Institute (1996), The Potential Benefits of Integration of Environmental and Economic Policies in the European Periphery (Cohesion Countries), report prepared for the Commission of the European Community, DG XI.

Fitz Gerald, J. et al. (1993), *The Community Support Framework 1989-1993: Evaluation and Recommendations fro the 1994-1997 Framework*. Report to the Department of Finance.

Gill, P. and Cullen, C. (1996), *Interim Report on an Estimation of Infra-Structural Pressure for Ireland's Offshore Islands*, Centre for Island Studies, Westport, Co. Mayo.

Government of Ireland (1994), *Operational Programme for Tourism, 1994/1999*, Stationery Office, Dublin.

Hardin, G. (1968), 'The Tragedy of the Commons', *Science* Vol. 162; reprinted in Markandya, A. and J. Richardson (eds.) *Environmental Economics: A Reader*, St. Martin's Press, New York (1992).

Hartley, K. and Hooper, N. (1992), 'Tourism Policy: Market Failure and Public Choice' in Johnson, P. and Thomas, B. (ed.) *Perspectives on Tourism Policy*, Mansell, London.

Meldon, J. (1992), *Structural Funds and the Environment: Problems and Prospects*, An Taisce, Dublin.

Musgrave, R. and Musgrave, P. (1976), *Public Finance in Theory and Practice* (2nd edition), McGraw-Hill, New York.

Pearce, D. and Turner, R.K. (1990), *Economic of Natural Resources and the Environment*, Harvester Wheatsheaf, London.

# 9 Construction

*A. Barrett*

## 9.1 Introduction

In this chapter we will consider the construction sector. As with the other sectors being considered, we will look at its environmental impact. We will then look at how the fiscal structure currently impacts upon construction and how this in turn impacts upon the environment. We will also set out what fiscal measures might be taken if economic instruments are to be used for environmental protection in this sector.

Before proceeding to the main discussion, one point of interest can be made. In looking at publications on economic instruments for environmental protection such as those of the OECD (1994, 1996), one finds no mention of such instruments being used in construction. We will see below, in the discussion of urban renewal schemes, that economic instruments are used in this area but it is true to say that the theory and practice of their use has been more clearly elaborated in areas such as transport and energy. In the discussion, we will ask if this lack of elaboration is related to a difficulty with applying economic instruments in construction.

It is important to specify what aspects of construction we will be considering in this chapter so we shall do that here. Our focus will be on buildings and in particular on the environmental implications of new buildings and the refurbishment of existing structures. Clearly this sector interacts with the environment in other ways. For example, the integration of energy saving measures in the design and construction of buildings can reduce fuel consumption. Also, the construction of roads brings the possibility of intrusion into both the natural and built environments. As issues relating to both energy and transport have been discussed at length in earlier chapters, we adapt our particular focus here.

## 9.2 Environmental impact

The construction of buildings can have either a positive or a negative effect on the environment which makes it somewhat different from other sectors. The negative effects arise when new buildings intrude upon a natural landscape, or when they intrude upon the built environment because their size or style is not in keeping with other buildings in the area. In the case of intrusion upon the existing built environment, the demolition of an existing structure which has appealing architectural or historical features and its replacement with a less appealing structure represents a double intrusion. The case of Georgian houses in Dublin making way for modern office buildings is an example of this.

Having said that, we must bring up another issue which makes construction different to some of the other sectors at which we are looking. In the case of, for example, carbon emissions from the burning of fossil fuels there is very broad agreement that these emissions, at least above a certain threshold, create pollution in the sense that the environment is damaged in some way.[1] In the case of many buildings, however, there is likely to be much less agreement on what constitutes environmental damage. In the extreme there will probably be broad agreement that a particular building is intrusive but in many cases one person's view of environmental damage could be seen by others as being an environmental improvement.[2]

The reason for the greater certainty regarding environmental damage in the case of carbon emissions is that most of us can agree that emissions which generate adverse health effects or which lead to global warming with all of its harmful effects are undesirable. There are clear objective criteria by which we can say that carbon emissions are polluting. In the case of construction, however, we are dealing, in part, with aesthetic qualities and so the application of objective criteria to determine what is and what is not polluting is more difficult than in the case of carbon emissions. In the case of the historical or cultural attributes of a building, it may be that some would prefer to see the old being replaced by the new.

Putting the aesthetic and cultural issues aside for the moment, we can say that in a free market[3] the type of environmental damage associated with construction is likely to be above the social optimum. As is the case with other forms of environmental damage, in a free market the generators of such damage (in this case developers) are not charged for the external costs of their production (in this case the loss of visual appeal resulting from building an unwelcome structure). As such, building activity will be above the social optimum and there is a need for the government to intervene. Typically, the command-and-control approach to environmental protection has been used in this area, via the use of planning laws. Below, we will consider if economic instruments can be used in addition to or in place of the command-and-control approach and ask if the benefits of economic instruments as set out in Chapter 3 hold in this sector.

As already mentioned, construction can also have positive environmental effects and it can do so in two ways. First, the construction of an aesthetically pleasing building which fits in well with its surroundings can enhance the environment. Again, however, one person's view of a positive environmental effect is another's view of an environmental mistake. Second, efforts to rebuild and refurbish in areas which are rundown and derelict can transform an aesthetically unpleasant area into a pleasing one. In addition, such 'renewal' of an area can have social, cultural and economic effects if it brings life back to a previously deserted area. The Temple Bar area of Dublin is a possible example of this effect but again, there is disagreement as to the actual environmental benefits.[4]

Leaving aside the aesthetic disputes again, we can ask whether environmentally positive construction will be provided at its optimum level by the free market and as before the answer is no. In this case there is a positive effect that is not captured by developers in the form of revenue accruing to them. As such, there is a need for the government to intervene to encourage the activity. This can be done by offering subsidies or by imposing taxes on owners of property that is judged to be imposing negative externalities.

As mentioned in Chapter 3, it is possible to use taxes in a way that is more targeted than simply discouraging an activity relative to all other. By applying differential tax rates to activities that are close substitutes, it is possible to generate a substitution effect between the two. For refurbishment that is more environmentally desirable than new construction, a favourable tax treatment of such refurbishment relative to the alternative should be encouraged.

While clearly there will be disagreement about whether or not specific building projects are environmentally damaging or intrusive, we shall proceed on the basis that the refurbishment of existing structures is generally less likely to cause such a problem. As such, if there is to be a bias in the tax code, it should not be in favour of new building, unless the new building is shown to be environmentally beneficial.

## 9.3 Fiscal treatment

We will begin our consideration of the fiscal treatment of construction by reviewing two pieces which, although written on this topic a number of years ago, address many of the issues still of relevance today. We will then outline the current fiscal treatment and ask what its environmental implications might be.

The first piece we will refer to is that of Dowling (1988). Given the point made above that in general, from an environmental perspective, refurbishment should be encouraged relative to new construction, the following quote is very telling of the structure of the fiscal system as he was writing: 'Most tax incentives directed towards building are oriented towards new building. In certain instances, there are positive disincentives towards renewal of buildings relative to new construction'.

Dowling then goes on to illustrate this point and mentions some of the tax provisions generating this bias. Referring to industrial buildings, he notes that investors in factory space let to a qualifying manufacturing industry could write up to 50 per cent of the cost off their current income and the balance could be written off against the rental income. This did not apply to the refurbishment of existing property but only to newly constructed plants so the bias is clear.

He also maintains that Section 23 of the Finance Act 1981 and Section 29 of the Finance Act 1984 were biased towards new construction. Section 23 allowed for depreciation of the capital cost to be written off against the rental income from both the newly constructed properties and the existing rental income; Section 29 confined relief to rental income from the relevant property. Finally, he identifies stamp duties which apply to existing houses but not to new houses as another source of the tax bias in favour new building.

Dowling makes two additional points in his article which are worthy of note here. First, it was argued that the structure of tax incentives was designed to achieve certain objectives; for example in the case of Section 23 and 29 tax breaks the objective was to provide low cost rental accommodation. However, he maintains that the incentives failed to achieve their objectives and so cannot be effectively defended on those grounds. Second, he also details how government expenditure was also biased towards new construction. One example he uses to illustrate this is the provision of public housing which appeared to be dominated by building new dwellings as opposed to acquiring and renovating existing ones.

Writing in the same volume, Convery concurs broadly with Dowling's argument but does also point out some aspects of the tax code which had more positive environmental impacts. He mentions Section 19 of the 1982 Finance Act which allowed owners of certain buildings to treat expenditure on renovations as if they were losses for tax purposes. The buildings involved had to be of cultural or historic interest and an amount of public access was required. In addition he describes how the 1988 Finance Act allowed the expenditure involved in the conversion of an existing single dwelling into two or more residential units to be written off against rental income. In these two provisions we see clear biases in favour of renovation as opposed to new construction and, as such, early examples of the use of economic instruments supporting environmental protection. From this we can see that the principle of the use of economic instruments in this regard clearly existed in the early 1980s.

Another form of fiscal intervention mentioned by Convery were the home improvements grants which existed at different times, most recently between 1985 and 1987. He also notes, however, that in general the grants involved were small relative to grants for new houses and so the overall system was mis-directing the grant money, even though the specific provision was aimed in the right direction.

One final interesting note should be taken from Convery's piece. He says the following: 'It is very encouraging to be able to say that, while the existing building stock still suffers some discrimination relative to new building, the situation has improved very much over the past four years'. He notes that grants for new buildings had declined and that VAT had been imposed on new buildings. Given this perceived environmental improvement in the fiscal system between 1984 and 1988, it is now of interest to look at the fiscal system today and its environmental implications.

We want now to outline the elements of the present tax code that relate to construction.[5] Looking firstly at residential property we find the following provisions regarding owner-occupiers:

1   First time buyer's grant: The grant is available in respect of individuals acquiring their first property. The property must be new and under 125 sq. metres. The grant is currently £3000.

2   Stamp duty exemption: The exemption is available on the purchase of new houses under 125 sq. metres. When the new house exceeds 125 sq. metres the stamp duty is chargeable on the site cost or 25 per cent of the house price, whichever is higher.

3   Mortgage interest relief: Interest relief is available on monies borrowed for the purchase, improvement or repair of an individual's principal private residence. There are restrictions on the amount of qualifying interest with increased relief for first time buyers. This applies equally to new and old houses.

4   Capital gains tax exemption: There is an exemption from capital gains tax on disposal of an individual's principal private residence.

5   Significant buildings: In the case of certain buildings which are of significant scientific, historical, architectural or aesthetic interest and reasonable access is granted to the public, the following reliefs are available: tax relief is available on expenditure to maintain, repair and reconstruct the building and garden; exemption from residential property tax; possible exemption from capital acquisition tax.

Provisions 1 and 2 create a bias towards new construction and so may be questionable on environmental grounds, should the new construction have negative externalities associated. Items 3 and 4 appear environmentally neutral, but item 5 is clearly an environmentally positive measure. Having said that, the requirement that reasonable access be allowed may act as a disincentive to avail of the relief. It could be that a restored property has an existence value, whereby it is valued not because it can be visited but simply as an end in itself. In this case, the reasonable access requirement may be misplaced.

We can look now at the tax measures in residential property as they apply to landlords.

1    Capital allowances: Capital allowances are available on furniture and fittings purchased in connection with the rented property.

2    Interest relief: Full interest relief is available on loans used to purchase, improve or repair the residential property.

3    Repairs: Repairs to property will normally qualify for deduction against taxable rents provided no element of improvement is involved.

There appears to be an environmentally positive bias here in that expenditure on repairs are deductible (see item 3) but expenditure on new construction is not, assuming that repairs are considered more environmentally friendly than construction. At a minimum, it is positive that the bias is not towards new construction.

As a final element in the residential property area, we can note the provisions that relate to tenants. Rent allowances are available for all tenants against taxable income, with increased allowances applying to individuals over 55 years.

Commercial and industrial premises are treated quite differently in the tax code but here we will mention the most important provisions that apply to them. These are as follows.

1    Capital allowances: For industrial buildings, capital allowances are available on expenditure incurred in their construction. The allowances generally available are 4 per cent per annum and are 15 per cent per annum in the case of hotels and farm buildings. Capital allowances of 15 per cent per annum are also available in respect of expenditure on plant and machinery, which can include refurbishment expenditure. In addition, there are an accelerated allowances for industry in urban renewal areas.[6]

2    Business Expansion Scheme: Funds can be raised under this scheme for the construction and refurbishment of hotels and holiday camps.

Under the capital allowances, the higher write-off rate for refurbishment would appear to be a positive feature, although there is an amount of ambiguity over what type of work qualifies. The installation of lifts, heating and ventilation systems and sprinkler systems are among the items that do qualify, but there have been numerous legal challenges regarding other types of work.

We noted earlier that renovation and reconstruction in derelict areas can have a positive environmental and economic effect and it was in pursuit of those benefits that the urban renewal incentives were introduced in 1985. Before discussing those schemes, however, we should mention another measure that is designed to counter the negative externalities associated with dereliction, that is the derelict sites levy. Introduced in 1990, this is a tax of 3 per cent per annum of the value of an urban property's market value, where the property is deemed by the local authority to detract from the amenity character or appearance of land or property in the neighbourhood. The tax applies in cities, boroughs, urban districts and towns. While the intention behind the tax is laudable, there is a problem in enforcement. For the year ended 1994, only £21,000 was collected and this was down from £47,000 in 1993. The figure for 1994 represents only 5 per cent of the total amount due. Difficulties arise in locating the owners of the property and sometimes they may be abroad. The tax, however, stands as a charge on the property at the time of sale. In addition, if a site is deemed to be derelict, the local authority can be granted a compulsory purchase order and the provision exists for the taxes outstanding to be deducted from the purchase price.[7]

Before leaving the issue of dereliction, it is interesting to note that the legislative controlling of rent created part of the dereliction problem in the country, although the particular provision has been repealed. Given that landlords were prevented from increasing rents the incentive to maintain properties was reduced and so many properties fell into disrepair. Like many of the tax provisions we have been discussing, this is an example of a policy having an environmental side-effect that was totally unintended.

We turn now to the Urban Renewal Schemes. Having introduced the schemes in 1985, the range of areas qualifying for the incentives was extended in 1988 and in 1990 and a revised package of incentives was introduced in 1994. The original set of incentives were as follows (we will quote directly from Blackwell and Convery, 1991):

> First, full rates remission is allowed on commercial development for 10 years, for the full value for new buildings and for the value added in the case of refurbished buildings. (note: under the 1994 package, the rates remission is based on a sliding scale with 100 per cent remission in 1994, and 10 percentage point falls in the following nine years.)
>
> Second, a tax allowance of 100 per cent of expenditure (50 per cent in the Dublin designated areas outside the Custom House Docks area) of a capital nature is allowed on the construction or reconstruction of commercial buildings. This allowance is available is respect of income tax or corporation tax.
>
> Third, double the rent is allowed against trading income for tax purposes for 10 years.
>
> Fourth, for residential development, 5 per cent of net construction (or reconstruction) cost per annum is allowed as a tax deduction to the first

owner occupier for a period of ten years, amounting to a maximum of 50 per cent of qualifying expenditure.

In addition, Blackwell and Convery mention a provision in the Finance Act 1989 which allowed tax deductions in respect of expenditure on refurbishment to buildings in designated areas which were deemed to be of historical or architectural significance. The deduction allowed was 25 per cent of the expenditure in the initial year, with 5 per cent allowed in each of the following five years.

While the package of incentives introduced specifically for Temple Bar in 1991 and the revised urban renewal package of 1994 are similar to the original package, they include a move to give greater incentives to refurbishment relative to new building. This would indicate that policy-makers have accepted the greater desirability of the former in these areas. In the case of Temple Bar, a capital allowance of 100 per cent in respect of refurbishment was introduced for commercial properties; the allowance is 50 per cent in respect of new building. For owner-occupied housing, the 5 per cent relief that applied in the designated areas was applied to Temple Bar also, but in addition a 10 per cent allowance for refurbishment was put in place. The acquisition costs of commercial buildings can also be written off which is probably an environmental plus, given that such buildings are more likely to fall into disrepair if left unsold.

The move towards incentives to refurbish are seen in the 1994 package in the extension of capital allowances in the case of commercial and industrial properties to include expenditure on refurbishment. For owner-occupied housing, the 5 per cent/10 per cent structure that applies in Temple Bar now applies to all designated areas. In addition, the 1994 package included an incentive to encourage the use for residential purposes of the space over businesses. Relief is available on 100 per cent of expenditure incurred on the refurbishment or conversion of certain buildings for rented residential accommodation.[8] As part of this scheme, 100 per cent of the cost of refurbishing the commercial part of the property can also be written off, once this element of the spending is less than that on the residential element.

The evidence to date on the effects of the urban renewal schemes is patchy but we can refer to what has been written.[9] Blackwell and Convery (1991) used a survey of developers to estimate that 85 per cent of investment in designated areas was related to the incentives. While clearly this was good for the designated areas, it is surely the case that some of this investment is being diverted from others areas. This is not a concern if the externalities associated with investment in the designated areas are such that this diversion is worthwhile. However, the diversion should be seen as a cost of urban renewal programmes and should be factored into evaluations.

Dowling and Keegan (1992) introduce a note of caution regarding the urban renewal programmes, not from the perspectives of effects but from the perspective of costs. They refer to a seminar at which it was suggested that the potential cost to the Exchequer in present value terms per £100 of private funds invested in commercial property in the designated areas is £84. Given that an amount of investment would take place in the designated areas in the absence of the incentives, this means that the government is close to building the property and giving it away. The figures used by Dowling and Keegan are very tentative but the general point made is important. It is possible that whatever effect is being generated by the urban renewal schemes is being achieved at a high cost. As always, it is important that the costs of the schemes be weighed against the benefits.

Whatever the value of the direct environmental benefits of the urban renewal schemes, it should be pointed out that they also generate an indirect benefit in terms of reducing the need to build in greenfield suburban areas. This benefit has often been omitted in discussions of the schemes but it could be significant and should be measured as part of any overall evaluation.

The final piece we will refer to is the report for An Taisce (an Irish non-governmental organisation which campaigns for environmental protection) written specifically about the Temple Bar scheme (Smith and Convery, 1996). Although elements of this report has been criticised,[10] we will distil some of the concerns that have been expressed in the report as examples of possible concerns, without necessarily saying that the concerns are valid in this particular case. One general theme to emerge from the report is that the Temple Bar project has not been a success in terms of conservation. The authors feel that many buildings of distinction have been either demolished or significantly diminished and list 26 examples. They suggest a number of reasons as to why this has happened, but one seems particularly interesting in the current context. Although there was a differential incentive which favoured refurbishment relative to new construction (as described above), the authors say that 'it was clear that the advantages of having a 'tabula rasa' to work from were sufficiently attractive in many cases that the demolition and new build was preferred to refurbishment'. Hence, the tax differential did not achieve the substitution effect to the degree that Smith and Convery would have liked. We will return to this point below when we discuss the general suitability of economic instruments in the construction context.

In addition to the inadequate incentives for refurbishment, Smith and Convery see the lack of a proper inventory of the buildings in designated areas as posing a problem for conservation. They also point out that structural and safety regulations often render the refurbishment of older buildings impractical.


## 9.3 A possible approach

In Section 9.2 of this chapter we described how there can be either positive or negative externalities associated with construction. Following the general principles of public economics, this implies that some forms of construction should be subsidised while others should be taxed. Alternatively, differential rates of tax (or subsidy) should apply to different types of construction, depending on the nature of the associated externalities. Finally, we should be cautious regarding the subsidising of construction which imposes negative externalities.

Looking firstly at the requirement to subsidise where positive externalities exist, we can say that the urban renewal incentives represent an environmentally friendly aspect of the tax code. This does not mean, however, that their retention or expansion should be recommended. As Dowling and Keegan pointed out, it could be that the schemes are extremely costly and as with all programmes it is necessary to ensure that the benefits exceed the costs. Towards this end, it would be an interesting exercise to attempt to quantify the benefits of, for example, the Temple Bar project and to compare the estimated benefits with the costs. Indeed, it would have been advisable to undertake such an exercise before the expansion of the urban renewal schemes in 1994. And in addition to the cost/benefit calculation, it will also be of interest to monitor the sustainability or otherwise of the designated areas once the reliefs run out. Part of the thinking behind urban renewal is that the activity generated should ultimately sustain itself on a commercial footing.

In the spirit of the urban renewal schemes, it would be desirable to provide incentives for the re-utilisation of sites which are no longer needed for industrial or commercial uses. Even if demolition and rebuild is required, the re-use of these areas would reduce the need for intrusion into greenfield areas.

As part of the effort to subsidise environmentally positive construction, it would be desirable to extend the provision of the Finance Act 1989 that allows refurbishment expenditure on buildings of historical or architectural significance in designated areas to all areas. This could be done on the basis of a proper listing of buildings throughout the nation, which in and of itself might contribute to the conservation effort. What is more, the re-introduction of home improvement grants would help to maintain the existing housing stock and reduce the chances of neighbourhoods falling into disrepair. This re-introduction should, however, learn from the lessons of previous schemes of a similar nature, such as the home improvement grants of 1985 to 1987. Some have expressed the view that much of the work financed under this scheme was possibly unnecessary and probably of limited or no environmental merit (Lumley 1996). It would be preferable to target such grants so that work which truly incorporates environmental externalities is being subsidised.[11]

The extension of refurbishment allowances and the re-introduction of home improvement grants will clearly impose some cost on the Exchequer. We can, however, suggest how the removal of two incentives to build as opposed to conserve might be scaled back thereby achieving savings for the Exchequer. First, as mentioned above the imposition of stamp duty on existing houses but not on new creates the type of bias which is counter to environmental considerations. The imposition of stamp duty on new houses would eliminate this bias and would generate revenue to fund the grants and reliefs suggested above.[12] To get some idea of what the revenue might be, consider the following. The value of new private residential construction in 1995 is forecast to be £1354.7m (Department of the Environment, 1995). Applying a tax of 3 per cent would yield £40.6m, assuming no response in demand.[13]

Second, the grant of £3000 given to first-time home-buyers is only given if a new house is being bought so again, the bias is clear. In 1995, around £30m was paid out under this scheme. This grant could be removed or targeted along some environmental criteria, for example, not given if a clear negative externality is associated. In the case of this suggestion and the previous one, the fear could be expressed that both stimulate employment in the construction industry and so their social benefit is employment related. Two points can be made in response. First, in either case, the revenue raised or saved can be recycled into construction but into the more environmentally friendly activity of refurbishment. Second, in the case of the first time buyer's grant, it is likely that a proportion of the £3000, through its effect on demand, raises the price of new houses in combination with a possible supply effect. Hence, it is not the case that all the benefit is going to either first time buyers or construction workers. Rather, a portion of the £3000 is merely a transfer to the building industry. If such transfers are to be made, it would be preferable if they were made without negative environmental consequences.

Although mortgage interest relief does not create a bias between refurbishment and new construction, it could be used for such a purpose by altering rates of relief according to the environmental characteristics of the relevant property. Given the recent reductions in the generosity of this provision, however, further tampering might be considered politically infeasible and so we will not recommend such a use.

While the principle of removing the incentive towards new building is supported by economic theory, we have to ask what the effect might be. In the case of housing, we would have to say that the effect would be marginal. The demand for housing is partly a function of demographics and household composition. In Ireland, these factors are contributing to a sizeable increase in the demand for housing and so the pressure for new building would be considerable, even in the absence of any favourable tax provisions.

In addition to these demand issues, there is also the issue of builders' preferences for working on cleared sites rather than refurbishing. New build is often cheaper and costs can be estimated more reliably. When combined with the desire of many house buyers to buy a new house, it is clear that refurbishment will not be able to meet housing needs. However, we still believe it is preferable not to aggravate the situation, even if the effect is marginal.

We want to turn now to consider the issue of taxing construction which gives rise to negative externalities, as opposed to merely removing current incentives towards new building. The cornerstone of all that we are exploring in this report is that economic instruments offer advantages over the regulatory approach to environmental protection and in Chapter 3 we demonstrated what these advantages are. But we also mentioned at the outset of this chapter that the use of economic instruments in the construction context has not been as well documented in other sectors. We want now to suggest why the prevention of environmental damage related to construction may be dealt with best by the regulatory approach, specifically planning laws.

If we think back to the discussion in Chapter 3 of a firm or farm whose output gave rise to pollution, we imposed a dynamic element into an otherwise static analysis which, while appropriate in many cases, may not be appropriate in construction. The dynamic element concerned the idea that by imposing a tax on a firm or farm, the output would be reduced (or a cleaner technology used) in such a way that they would no longer be polluting. We assumed (as do most writers) that the pollution was then solved, thereby neglecting the possibility that a stock of pollution would have built up and, while no longer being added to, this stock meant that a pollution problem still existed. While rarely explicitly stated, the underlying assumption is that over time the re-generative capacity of the environment is such that the stock of pollution will eventually be absorbed and will cease to constitute pollution.

In the case of something like emissions into the air or water, it is reasonable to think of the environment acting in this assimilative way and so our neglect of the stock of pollution does not render our analysis redundant. However, in the case of construction the story is quite different. Once a building which amounts to an environmental intrusion is erected, it will not be assimilated into the environment in the way that gaseous emissions are. While it can be demolished, the cost will be large. Similarly, the demolition of a building, particularly one of historical or architectural significance is akin to the extinction of a species. Its loss is irreversible.

Given these characteristics of built environments, the use of economic instruments for environmental protection in isolation would be unwise. As discussed in Chapter 3, given our current state of knowledge regarding the valuation of the environment, be it natural or built, it is unlikely that the correct Pigovian tax can be set and an iterative approach might be required whereby the optimum level of emissions is arrived at by varying the environmental tax. In the case of certain emissions, the cost of getting the tax 'wrong' may not be too great; in the case of construction, however, the cost of a mistake may be great due to the irreversibilities just discussed.

It is appropriate to impose taxes on construction that is environmentally damaging. If a developer is spoiling a view, he is imposing a cost on society and, in keeping with the Polluters Pays Principle, it is right that this cost be internalised. Similarly, demolitions which impose a cost on society should be taxed. In this way, intrusive development and unfortunate demolition could be reduced. However, these taxes should be supported by good planning laws so that no irreversible damage is done.

We can refer to the Smith and Convery report on Temple Bar to see an example of how a mistake in the application of an economic instrument can have damaging effects. As we noted in discussing this report earlier, the authors believe that an excessive amount of demolition occurred in Temple Bar even with the tax bias towards renovation. They call for the widening in the tax differential but they also note that more demolition would have occurred had it not been for the Dublin Corporation Planning Department. As we noted before, it has been argued that Smith and Convery overstate the problem (Temple Bar Properties, 1996) but the principle they point out is important.

## 9.4 Conclusion

From an environmental point of view construction which has a positive environmental impact should be treated more favourably in the fiscal system relative to environmentally damaging construction. While this might appear to be an obvious statement, we have shown that the Irish tax system has not always followed this approach, at least as far as ensuring that new build is not favoured relative to refurbishment. In recent years, the system has become more environmentally friendly with regard to construction but we would suggest the following:

1    In general, the tax system should at least attempt not to be biased in favour of new construction.

2    Tax reliefs and grants for renovation be extended.

3    Stamp duty be imposed on new houses so as to eliminate the current bias in favour of new building. At a tax rate of 3 per cent and assuming no reduction in demand this would yield around £40m.

4    The first-time house buyers grant should be eliminated or restricted.

5    With regard to environmentally damaging construction, taxes should be imposed so that the polluter pays principle is in force in this sector; a tax related to the value of the development could be applied if the planning authority determined that the construction, while not damaging enough to be prevented, was an intrusion. However, the role of environmental protector should ultimately be left with the planning authorities through planning regulations.

6    In the case of the dereliction tax, the current low proportion of revenue being collected points to a low incentive to comply. The possibility of seizure as opposed to the worst case scenario of compulsory purchase would strengthen this measure.

## Notes

1     In saying that, however, we do recognise that there may be significant dispute over what the threshold might be.
2     Although individual disagreements as to the aesthetic value of certain buildings exist, contingent valuation methods can be used to estimate average, or societal, valuations. One such example is the study of Willis (1994).
3     By free market we mean no government intervention of either a regulatory or fiscal nature.
4     See Smith and Convery (1996).
5     We are very grateful to Roger Murphy of Price Waterhouse for providing the information on the current fiscal arrangements.
6     The Urban Renewal Areas are discussed below.
7     The Department of the Environment provided the details in this section.
8     Also relevant here are the reliefs available under the Pilot Tax Relief Scheme for Certain Resort Areas which are discussed in Chapter 8.
9     The Department of the Environment has commissioned a study of the urban renewal schemes which will hopefully identify and quantify the effects in a more comprehensive manner than hitherto.
10    The criticisms can be found in Temple Bar Properties (1996).
11    We should point out that the government is currently inclined against the re-introduction of home improvement grants. As the previous scheme was relatively costly, the Government's priorities in the housing area are the expansion of the local authority and other social housing programmes and the upgrading of deficient local authority dwellings.
12    Of course, this revenue could be raised for any other purposes and should be used in the most valuable ones.
13    While this proposal makes sense from an environmental point of view, we should point out the disadvantages. First, stamp duty is an inequitable tax in that those who have to move often for employment purposes pay more than others. Also, stamp duty may discourage movement for employment purposes, even though such movement may improve economic efficiency. Second, the extension of stamp duty may make housing more expensive and so increase the demand for social housing.

# References

Convery, F. (1988), 'Replace or Retain: An Overview' in *Replace or Retain? Irish Policies for Buildings Analysed*, Resource and Environmental Policy Centre, UCD.

Blackwell, J. and Convery, F. (1991), 'The Impact of the Urban Incentives in Ireland' in *Proceedings of the Sixth Annual Conference of the Foundation of Fiscal Studies*.

Department of the Environment (1995), *Construction Industry Review '94 Outlook '95*, Government of Ireland, Dublin.

Dowling, B. (1988), 'Fiscal Instruments' in *Replace or Retain? Irish Policies for Buildings Analysed*, Resource and Environmental Policy Centre, UCD.

Dowling, B. and Keegan, O. (1992), 'Fiscal Policies and the Built Environment' in *Environment and Development in Ireland*, Environmental Institute, UCD.

Lumley, Ian, Dublin Civic Trust (1996), personal communication.

OECD (1994), *Managing the Environment: The Role of Economic Instruments*, OECD, Paris.

OECD (1996), *Implementation Strategies for Environmental Taxes*, OECD, Paris.

Smith, M. and Convery, F.J. (1996), Ireland's Designated Areas - Lessons from Temple Bar, An Taisce Discussion Paper.

Temple Bar Properties (1996), Temple Bar Properties' Response to An Taisce's Publication: Ireland's Designated Areas: Lessons from Temple Bar, Temple Bar Properties, Dublin.

Willis, K. (1994), 'Paying for Heritage: What Price for Durham Cathedral?', *Journal of Environmental Planning and Management*, Vol. 37 No. 3.

# 10 Conclusions

*A. Barrett, J. Lawlor and S. Scott*

We have now completed our sector by sector examination of the fiscal system in Ireland and how it impacts upon the environment through the incentives it creates. We have also made a range of recommendations as to how the system can be altered so that the Polluter Pays Principle is applied more intensively and extensively, thus providing incentives for environmental protection. In Chapter 3 we outlined why we are promoting this approach to environmental policy, in contrast to the more traditional regulatory approach.

In this concluding chapter, we will bring our recommendations together, in two main groups. First, we will present those recommendations which we believe (a) to be the most readily implementable and (b) to have the greatest potential for a significant environmental impact. Second, we will present those recommendations which should form the basis of additional reforms in this area, once the initial steps have been taken. In the case of each proposal, our concern is that households and enterprises will face the environmental costs of their actions and so will take these costs into account in making consumption and production decisions.

## 10.1 The primary recommendations

### 10.1.1 Agriculture

In order to tackle the serious problem of the eutrophication of surface waters from over-application of nutrients (such as fertilisers) and insensitive management of manure, the main recommendation in agriculture is that VAT, or a similar tax, be imposed on fertiliser and feed. This would have neutral revenue effects, in so far as VAT paid is rebated, one way or another. Small farmers would be compensated through higher flat-rate rebates, such that only relatively fertiliser-intensive farmers would be worse off. Large farmers who are registered for VAT (and number about 2000) would receive the rebate. In order to increase the effectiveness of this measure, it would be ideal if the rebate could be made subject to a nutrient management balance being provided and be made payable in relation to good nutrient management. The VAT system already requires information on inputs and outputs, so that little extra documentation would be required. In this way excess nutrients can be taxed. Some alteration to the VAT rebating procedure would be required, but this may be a less serious obstacle than those confronting every other proposal made to date to alleviate this pressing problem. Failing such an alteration, an additional charge could be raised on fertilisers, which would be refunded on the evidence of good nutrient management. The procedures could vary according to the sensitivity of the region.

### 10.1.2 Environmental services

We considered environmental services (i.e. water supply, waste water, and solid waste) provided by local authorities and used by households, commerce and industry. In general, these services are being under-priced, leading to over-use and wastage, and consequent excess pollution damage to the environment. Present levels of cost recovery (capital and current costs combined) are roughly 54 per cent for water supply, 8 per cent for waste water, and 23 per cent for solid waste. While at present the EU is paying a large share of the capital costs of water supply and waste water services, and will continue to do so until the end of this decade, capital costs will have to be funded domestically beyond that date.

It is recommended that full cost recovery be gradually implemented, where feasible by means of volume-related charges, to recover both operating and capital costs of the three services. Charges that might cover some of the external (environmental) costs relating to these services could also be considered.

The effect of volume-charging could be considerable in that households and enterprises would have an incentive to reduce their generation of solid waste and waste-water and to economise on their use of water. We would foresee the effect as being particularly strong in the long run. We recommend that full cost recovery would be phased in over about 10 years, and that this should be announced and implemented immediately.

The evidence suggests that the incentive effects of use-related charges on quantities of the services demanded would bring environmental benefits. There will also be implications for government finances, at both local and central level. It is proposed that we move from a system of paying for services through general taxes, to one of paying for them by user charges. Tax revenue which would have been used to provide environmental services would be released for other purposes, such as reducing other taxes. Full cost recovery will save local and central government some £271 million per annum, at future cost levels (after allowing for increases in social welfare to compensate low-income households, this might become £214 million). A landfill levy in addition could bring in an extra £15 million annually. Finally, surveys referred to in Chapter 2 indicate that the public prefers to pay for improved services this way, rather than through increased general taxes.

*10.1.3 Energy*

In the energy sector, we recommend the following as priority measures.

1    VAT on heating fuels and power should be raised from the reduced rate of 12.5 per cent to the standard rate of 21 per cent, with compensating social welfare payments. The net revenue yield could be £45 million, after the expected 2½ to 4½ per cent decline in consumption compared to what it would have been.

2    An energy tax along the lines of the EU's proposed carbon tax should be introduced unilaterally and gradually adopted in Ireland, as the rate of tax appears to be of the right order of magnitude by reference to estimates of damage costs of energy use, even though these estimates relate to other countries. The introduction should be simultaneous with an enhanced programme for aiding efficient energy use on the part of those who cannot afford to undertake energy saving investment. A decline in energy use of some 3 per cent is forecast, but the on-going and predictable encouragement to technological development should bring further savings. Total revenue from the carbon tax of nearly £700 million is foreseen, after diverting a part of the funds to aid low-income households. According to the results of the ESRI's Medium Term Model, if the revenue from the carbon tax is used to reduce PRSI contributions, there is a net gain to the economy and to industry in particular.

*10.1.4 Transport*

Our primary recommendations with respect to transport relate specifically to the air pollution associated with road transport. We recommend the following.

1    Increase the tax advantage of less polluting fuels, especially cleaner forms of diesel and possibly natural gas (e.g. for fleets); this would be paid for by increasing the tax on regular fuels.

2    Give grants for the retro-fitting of catalytic converters, for LPG conversion, and possibly for conversion to natural gas; this would be paid for by increases in car tax on cars without catalytic converters, and increases in the price of fuel.

*10.1.5 Revenue implications*

Although we are not primarily concerned with raising revenue but rather with environmental protection, it is of interest to consider the revenue implications of the proposals. Looking only at our proposals with respect to environmental services and energy, we can see that the revenue implications are considerable. Under environmental services we foresee eventual revenue of around £200 million added to the present revenue from charges; increased VAT on heating fuels and power could yield £45 million; a carbon tax could yield around £700 million. In total, these three measures could yield over £900 million in the long run.

## 10.2 Secondary recommendations

### 10.2.1 Agriculture

The use of pesticides in agriculture can impose social costs not recognised by the farmer. This puts an obligation on the authorities to monitor behaviour and inform farmers about best practice. Inasmuch as there is a built-in tendency to over-apply agri-chemicals, their sale should be subject to a charge, the proceeds of which should be applied to cover the costs of monitoring and education. There are no net revenue implications.

There is also scope for using a tendering process for bio-diversity conservation in some instances. Where a species, habitat or eco-system is under threat, farmers could be invited to tender to preserve them. In this way, more protection for a given cost will be achieved.

### 10.2.2 Forestry

The potential for bestowing external benefits lies in the carbon sequestration of trees, provided that they are not planted on peat soil where net sequestration may be zero or negative. If the EU's proposed rate of carbon tax (the part relating to carbon only) were applied in reverse manner as a grant for carbon sequestration, the amount payable might be some £38 million per year. Another external benefit which could be subsidised is the provision of habitats for wildlife by mature forests, and broadleaved forests in particular. These two annual subsidies would sum over five years to over £200 million, which is roughly the intended expenditure under the present afforestation subsidy programme for 1994-1999. As the afforestation expenditure appears set to continue in some form beyond the five years, these two subsidies to carbon sequestration and to habitats, should be substituted for the existing programme.

### 10.2.3 Energy

1    The $SO_2$ and $NO_x$ quotas allocated to Northern Ireland and the Republic should become tradeable between establishments. In addition to encouraging the search for least-cost methods of abatement, this would achieve the specified targets at minimum cost.

2      Subsidies and grants to households and enterprises for energy conservation
will not be so necessary with the carbon tax in place, as the tax will generate
the incentive for the installation of conservation measures. However, in order
to encourage economies of scale and to combat lack of information and
inertia which may prevent the realisation of the external benefits associated
with energy conservation, some state aid may be justified.

### 10.2.4 Transport

Returning to air pollution related to road transport, consideration might be given to
moving from a cubic capacity-based road tax to one based directly on fuel
efficiency.
  In addition to air pollution, we identified other problems related to road transport
and made the following recommendations:

1      While more research is needed to ascertain the viability of anti-congestion
measures (such as road pricing) in an Irish context, in the meantime, the costs
of urban parking should be increased, through increased on-road metering,
perhaps (partially) basing local authority rates on the number of parking
spaces on a premises, and removing the tax benefits for building multi-storey
car parks.

2      With respect to damage done to the road transport infrastructure, the most
important step here would be to change the tax on heavy goods vehicles to
one based on laden weight per axle and distance travelled. This may require
an EU-wide approach however.

3      If it is not possible to internalise all the costs of other modes of transport,
there is a justification for measures to encourage the use of public transport.
One possibility is to make commuting by public transport a tax deduction;
this could be paid for by increasing the road tax on cars. In addition, we
would recommend that the current rebate on fuel tax for public transport be
replaced by some other form of subsidy, since the present arrangement
discourages fuel efficiency.

4      If it is possible under EU regulations, it is desirable that all costs related to
vehicle maintenance be subject to a uniform low rate of VAT. At present
most maintenance services are subject to the low rate of VAT, while car parts
purchased separately are subject to the standard rate. This anomaly may
disadvantage low-income car owners, who might be more likely to do their
own maintenance. The change of itself would encourage more maintenance,
which would in part pay for the measure. The introduction of mandatory
vehicle testing for private cars, due at the start of 1998, will generate more of
a market for maintenance services, which will also generate more tax

revenue. Any shortfall in revenue could be made up by increased road tax, petrol tax or vehicle registration tax.

As for the air transport sector, there are many uncertainties about the external damage caused by air travel, and these would need to be resolved before strong recommendations could be made about fiscal measures. The main areas of concern, both in an international and Irish context are air pollution and noise. In the meantime, it would seem appropriate to introduce increased fees on noisy aircraft in advance of research, since we know that some damage is being caused. For the same reason a tax on air transport fuel is also justified. International action is required before this could be implemented, but the Irish government could lend its support to EU moves in this direction.

### 10.2.5 Tourism

Tourism pressures on the environment arise from the need to build additional facilities to cater for tourists and from the tourists themselves in terms of the congestion they create and the damage they do. They also put pressure on environmental services at certain times and so generate a standard peak load problem. In the case of tourist facilities for which charging for admission is possible, we recommend imposing charges at least at peak times. This will alleviate congestion problems. Similarly, a higher charge for environmental services should be imposed where tourist pressures are intense. If this higher charge is passed onto tourists in the form of higher accommodation charges, it will provide an incentive for visits to be spread away from the peak time. Finally, in areas where environmental damage occurs because of large tourist numbers arriving at a certain time, a higher tax on accommodation in the high season, balanced by a lower tax in the low season, might help to spread tourists over time and thus relieve congestion and the damage associated with large numbers.

### 10.2.6 Construction

In the construction sector, environmental damage can occur when new buildings intrude on either a scenic landscape, or when new buildings do not fit in with existing structures. The demolition of existing buildings is also environmentally damaging if those buildings were of some merit, be it historical, cultural or whatever. Renovation on the other hand can improve the appearance of a building, and hence an area, and also reduces the need for new construction. In general then, the tax code should not create incentives to build as opposed to renovate and, if a bias is to exist, it should be towards renovation. As such, we recommend that stamp duty apply to all houses and that the exemption for new houses be abolished. We also think that the first-time buyers grant should be abolished or that it should apply to all and not just new houses. Grants and reliefs for renovation should be extended, especially in the case of listed buildings. Given the nature of construction, however, and in particular its somewhat irreversible nature, the task of environmental protection should fall primarily on planning laws, supported rather than thwarted by economic instruments.


## 10.3 Additional issues

A number of points should be made in closing which are relevant to most of the issues raised and recommendations made. The first of these points is that much more information is needed in this area if economic instruments for environmental protection are to be used to greatest effect. This information requirement exists along a range of dimensions so we will outline them in turn.

1     As discussed in Chapter 3, the ideal environmental tax requires a knowledge of the value of the damage that is the focus of the tax. Without valuation of the damage, the extent to which the damage should be reduced and hence the optimal level of the associated tax are simply guesses.

2     Even if we know the level to which emissions and pollution should be reduced, we need to know the extent to which agents will respond to taxes and charges before we know what level of tax will achieve the required reduction. Putting this in more economic terms, we need to know the elasticity of emissions with respect to the tax.

3     In order to estimate properly the revenue implications of the reforms we propose, more precise information on the levels of the activities is required. It is only when we know precisely what the tax base is that we can know what the revenue from a given level of tax might be.

These three dimensions of the information issue all call for more research in this area. Another dimension to the information issue is somewhat different, but it is still important. All the proposals we have made assume to a degree that people have the required information that will allow them to respond to environmental taxes and charges; we assume that people know what the 'green' products and processes are towards which they can substitute. Clearly, this may not always be the case and so there is an important role for government in providing information, given the scale economies involved and the fact that information, once discovered, can be provided cheaply to all.

In addition to information, there are other conditions which need to be met if markets for 'green' products and services are to function efficiently. Industries of a more innovative nature may experience difficulties in raising capital due to the uncertainties surrounding their potential for commercial success. Also, the existence of monopolies and cartels leads to the restricted provision of goods and services. In either case, there may be a role for government in ensuring that a market for alternatives operates freely, again so that substitution towards them is possible.

As a final point, many actions which seek to bring about environmental improvements are best pursued at an international level, given the transboundary nature of much pollution. The proposals which we made with respect to, for example, air pollution should be implemented nationally but efforts should also be made to promote similar policies at an international level. Unilateral action related to taxes and charges will always be hampered by national concerns that competitiveness will suffer if additional costs are imposed on domestic industry while industry elsewhere is left free of the same taxes. As we discussed in Chapter 3, cost disadvantages resulting from environmental taxes can be offset through other types of subsidies. However, it would be preferable if the competitiveness concern could be dealt with through international implementation of the Polluter Pays Principle so that a level playing field in international trade is maintained alongside increased environmental protection.

For Product Safety Concerns and Information please contact our EU
representative GPSR@taylorandfrancis.com Taylor & Francis Verlag GmbH,
Kaufingerstraße 24, 80331 München, Germany


Printed and bound by CPI Group (UK) Ltd, Croydon, CR0 4YY
08/05/2025
01864371-0001